Theology for
a Troubled Believer

Other books by Diogenes Allen

Christian Belief in a Postmodern World
Steps along the Way: A Spiritual Autobiography
Spiritual Theology
Love: Friendship, Christian Romance, and Marriage
Quest: The Search for Meaning through Christ
Nature, Spirit, and Community: Issues in the Thought of Simone Weil
    (with Eric O. Springsted)
The Reasonableness of Faith
The Path of Perfect Love
Temptation
Traces of God in a Frequently Hostile World
Three Outsiders: Pascal, Kierkegaard, and Simone Weil
Mechanical Explanations and the Ultimate Origin of the Universe according
    to Leibniz
Leibniz's Theodicy (edited and abridged)
"Philosophy," in *The Oxford Companion to Christian Thought*
Philosophy for Understanding Theology, second edition
    (with Eric O. Springsted)

Theology for a Troubled Believer

An Introduction to the Christian Faith

Diogenes Allen

WESTMINSTER
JOHN KNOX PRESS
LOUISVILLE • KENTUCKY

First edition
Published by Westminster John Knox Press
Louisville, Kentucky

10 11 12 13 14 15 16 17 18 19—10 9 8 7 6 5 4 3 2 1

Book design by Sharon Adams
Cover design by Lisa Buckley
Cover art: Corbis, © Dan Lepp/Esta/Corbis

Library of Congress Cataloging-in-Publication Data

Allen, Diogenes.
　　Theology for a troubled believer : an introduction to the Christian faith / Diogenes Allen.—
1st ed.
　　　　p. cm.
　　Includes index.
　　ISBN 978-0-664-22322-9 (alk. paper)
　　1. Theology, Doctrinal—Popular works.　I. Title.
　　BT77.A37　2010
　　230—c22

　　　　　　　　　　　　　　　　　　　　　　　　　　　　　　　　　　　2009033741

PRINTED IN THE UNITED STATES OF AMERICA

♾ The paper used in this publication meets the minimum requirements
of the American National Standard for Information Sciences—Permanence
of Paper for Printed Library Materials, ANSI Z39.48-1992.

Westminster John Knox Press advocates the responsible use of our natural resources.
The text paper of this book is made from 30% postconsumer waste.

In Gratitude
to the group from All Saints' Church,
Princeton, New Jersey, who met weekly
to discuss this work as it was developing

Contents

Preface

A Different Approach to Introducing Theology

Writers often begin by explaining why they are writing their book, and I will do the same. It was prompted by a letter I received from a very accomplished and intelligent man, who had been a churchgoer all his life. He had heard me speak several times at his church, and those talks had prompted him to ask himself, Do I believe in God? He wrote, "If you were born in the United States during the twentieth century, you grew up being taught that there is a God who is infinitely good, omniscient, and omnipotent. And who taught you? The church. And what was its authority? The Bible. (*Written back when the earth was still flat.*) But when what you were taught is contradicted by reality, you have what we nowadays call a 'conflict.'"

Then he went on to describe his attempt to deal with this conflict:

> Recently Norman Mailer, the author of *The Naked and the Dead*, was asked if he believed in God. Norman said, "Yes, God was a Jewish invention." Then they asked, "So how do you explain the Holocaust?" Norman said, "There was so much going on at the time that God was distracted." That gives you a God who exists but is not omniscient.
>
> When I was six years old, a little girl in my Sunday school class died. I remember looking over the edge of the casket, lined with white satin and

fresh flowers, and with a white lace coverlet. The sun came down through the gothic filigree of the stained-glass windows, illuminating her profile, and she was the most beautiful little girl I had ever seen, and she was on her way to the grave.

There was an enormous silence in the sanctuary; and her mother's shoulders were heaving, and her father had an arm around her mother, holding her together. At the pulpit the minister in his pale grey robe and white lace-edged shawl told us not to despair because this little girl was escaping this vale of tears to a land of eternal peace and happiness. And I thought, "If it's that great, why don't we all go? And why is everybody crying?" And when I got home, I asked my mother, "If God does everything, why did he do this?" And she said, "God works in mysterious ways, His wonders to perform." That gives you a God who exists but is incomprehensible.

Do I believe in God? I think it was René Descartes who said: "I think, therefore I exist." Whoever said it, it makes sense and I understand it. I would like to add: "I pray, therefore I believe, whether I understand it or not."

I think this sort of troubled reflection is quite typical of any thinking person, *given the data* we usually have to work with in our culture today. It takes a lot of effort for a reflective person to make sense of the Christian faith, but it is impossible to do so when a person lacks enough knowledge to think it through. The man who wrote this letter, who was a successful advertising executive and author of many novels, is like a person who has only a few pieces of a jigsaw puzzle and is trying to fit them together to make a coherent picture that more or less matches the picture on the top of the box that holds the pieces of the puzzle. His heart is in the right place, and he has been moved by God's Spirit to respond in prayer, yet he cannot put together what he knows as a modern person and what he hears said in churches. He needs many more puzzle pieces. He also needs to develop some skill in how to put them together if the Christian religion is to make sense to him.

This is why I am writing this book. I hope to supply more of the information (pieces of the puzzle) that are needed if a person is to make more sense of the Christian understanding of God and our life in the universe. Following the analogy of a puzzle, I do not mean that I will supply all the pieces needed to complete the entire puzzle—that is beyond anyone, since there is so much that is not known about God and the world under God. In addition, not all the pieces that I do supply have a nice, tight perfect fit as do pieces of a puzzle, and the parts of the picture that do emerge are not all equally clear in their significance. For we are dealing with God, who is not fully knowable by us.

We may compare God to the sun. God wants to share God's life with us, to elevate us into God's realm or kingdom. God's presence is like the rays of the sun: only a few rays are needed for the earth to be brilliantly illumined and for crops to grow. The rest of the sun's immense energy falls elsewhere. The entire energy of the sun would utterly destroy us. So God has lowered God's intensity. This is apparent in the two great experiences of God's holiness that we will examine in the Old Testament, and above all in the way God has come to us in great humility in the person of God the Son, through whom God calls us into the kingdom. God treats us gently in Jesus as God calls us to share in the divine life, to share in it now and always. We are to respond to this overwhelmingly great invitation, an invitation gently toned down to the person of Jesus, so that we are not overwhelmed, as we would be, by God's full intensity. This reduction of God's intensity means that most of God's greatness is not apparent to us. But though only a small part of God reaches us, as does only a small part of the sun's rays, we can recognize in what we do receive that there is much, much more and feel ourselves drawn into it. Though toned down in intensity, what does reach us in Christ is of the same *quality* of goodness, mercy, power, and wisdom as is in the Father. We will have much more to say of this. But here we mention it only as a caution that in our account of Christian doctrine, there is no presumption that we can ever fully explain God and God's relation to us.

Although this book is meant to supply the information that readers need to help them in their own thought and life, it is more personal than most books introducing theology. This is not because I will supply mere personal and idio-syncratic opinions in contrast to the material that is broadly accepted as orthodox Christian teaching as I understand it, but because I want to help readers develop some of the skills needed to put the pieces together by going through some of the steps that I myself have gone through in trying to help this man (with whose let-ter we began) to gain a coherent understanding of what to believe. This is a more personal approach than found in the usual introduction to theology—presenting what makes sense to me, and why it is defensible—and should make it easier for readers to succeed for themselves. Often theology is taught like chess. The teacher gives the names of the pieces and the moves each piece is permitted to make. But no actual game of chess is played. So one can recite what one has learned, but one has no skill in using the information to understand life under God.

What I like about the writer of the letter I quoted a few moments ago is that at least he has tried hard to make sense of life with the doctrines he had—that God is all good, omniscient, omnipotent—even if he did not have enough informa-tion to do the job well enough to satisfy his own mind. But even so, he shows that he is on a journey with a critical mind, seeking to understand life under God—unlike a skeptic who is not seeking and who resists accepting anything, no matter how well attested. The effort he made is what I hope readers will also make, but hopefully with more success because they have the information provided here. Although I am more personal in approach, I seek to give an introduction to orthodox Christian teaching without being patronizing, and I assume my audi-ence to be intelligent readers who want to understand Christian theology well enough to conceive of the world we live in today under God, people who want to direct their lives better. I hope that readers will find enough information and gain enough skill themselves to make more sense of a world as seen from a Christian perspective, more sense than they have hitherto been able to achieve.

The task of supplying readers with a workable amount of material for them to use in directing their lives is rather daunting, not only because of the large scope of resources and the difficulty of the subject, but also because of the ease of misunderstanding. A person who teaches communication theory once put it this way: The speaker says, "Blue, blue, blue." The audience is thinking, "Yellow, yellow, yellow." What they hear is "Green, green, green." Even this is oversimplified since people in an audience are not all thinking "yellow," so to speak, but in many different colors. So readers who approach this book with different experiences of Christianity and previous understandings of Christian faith may easily misunderstand what is being presented. People have been exposed to different church traditions, or to no particular tradition; some have had positive experiences with Christianity; others have had negative encounters. They have different attitudes: some are skeptical, others are critical but open-minded, still others may suspend their critical attitude too readily. People also differ in degrees of imagination, conceptual habits, and intuitive reasoning. Many have been trained to have quite different mental habits: Engineers, lawyers, doctors, stock analysts, dancers, mechanics, civil servants, reporters, and artists do not all approach matters the same way, and probably none of them think like a theologian or a philosopher.

There is one possible misunderstanding about how to use the Bible that we need to tackle immediately. The letter writer rightly pointed out that the Bible is the church's authority, but he seems to signal his reservations about its reliability by stressing that it was written back when the earth was considered to be flat. But this does not bother scholars, most theologians, and many believers because they do not consider the Bible to have been dictated word by word by God. The Bible is called "the Word of God" because through the Bible, God can communicate God's presence and purposes to us. Yet the Bible is understood to be the result of interaction between God and the people who responded to God's initiative and those who formed and passed on oral traditions. Theologians consider the Bible to be a witness to that interaction, a written witness that includes many edits and reedits over the centuries until an authoritative text was agreed upon. Under God's inspiration, the Bible is a result of human beings' understanding of God and God's purposes. Since God seeks to make God's nature and purposes known, the Bible is not a merely human product. A flat earth is assumed by the writers of the Bible is because that was the human understanding of the earth's shape during the time the Bible was formed; but that understanding does not affect the profundity of the understanding of God and God's purposes by those who responded to God.

Like many other theologians, I rely on the critical study of the Bible by professional scholars, and I find the so-called historical-critical method invaluable for understanding the Bible. Such scholarly study is not infallible nor, as sometimes misleadingly put, scientific. It is a historical and literary approach and, like all historical and literary study, it belongs to the arts, not to the sciences. Even though we do not obtain infallible judgments in biblical studies any more than we do elsewhere, we do gain carefully warranted views on the interpretation of the Bible. So although the Bible was written when the world was still considered flat, we do not need to read it today as if we too believe it is flat in order to determine what it teaches us of God and of God's purposes.

In my interpretation, I follow a principle used by the church from the very beginning: the Old Testament is to be interpreted in the light of Christ. So, for example, a psalm that rejoices in the killing of the Israelites' enemies ("Happy shall they be who pay you back what you have done to us! Happy shall they be who take your little ones and dash them against the rock!" Ps. 137:8b–9) is not one we are to take as authoritative. With Christ's coming, we know that we are not to seek revenge. When I read such a passage, I find it quite helpful to interpret my evil impulses as my enemies, which I would be happy to destroy, even though that was not the intent of the original author. Since Christ is the Word of God, we use Christ as the standard for a new understanding of the ancient text.

Even though the Bible was written a long time ago, the majority of biblical scholars now agree that what the New Testament church tells us that Jesus was, did, and taught is in essential continuity with the historical Jesus. This may not be what is highlighted by the media today, which give great publicity to those who differ from this consensus. Nevertheless, the nineteenth-century claim that there is an essential difference between what the New Testament church taught about Jesus and the historical Jesus is no longer credible on the basis of historical-critical scholarship.

It takes a lot of time and practice to learn how to read the Bible well because it is so deeply rooted in the history of the times in which the events took place and in which it was written, a period of time so different from our own. It is additionally difficult with the Bible because God's nature is unique and beyond our powers to fully conceive it. God must be described in terms of likenesses and comparisons, which leads to quite a lot of anthropomorphism (interpreting what is not human as having human characteristics). We need a lot of instruction and also the power to use our imagination.

There is more that could be said, but at this stage I hope that enough has been shared to prevent a person from immediately being put off by my first chapter. There we consider Moses being called by God. Moses is caring for a flock of sheep when he notices a burning bush that is not consumed by the flames, and he turns aside to examine it. Then he hears the voice of God. It looks rather like a fable for children, but the reader must not therefore dismiss it. Rather, one must suspend the issue of the literal accuracy of the story to consider the *content* of the story of Moses' encounter with God. *What* the story reveals, *and its significance*, is what should determine how one responds to the story.

One of the stumbling blocks in learning how to read the Bible is that so much of its contents reads just like history. Yet it is not history as we understand it today. Rather, it is often presented in a history-like form, seeking to tell us how significant the existence of the Israelite people is for themselves and for the world. In many cases scholarly study can give us a rather sound idea of what is historical in *our* sense of history, but that of itself does not tell us the purposes of God. Rather than what we call "history," the materials of the Bible are shaped in various ways in order to convey the nature and purposes of God. That, rather than literal history as we seek to write it, is its intention.

Some other misunderstandings of this book can also be prevented if a person is self-conscious about what they are looking for from the Christian religion. People begin their journey and become Christians for *at least* six major reasons, all of which are combined in various degrees. First, some people's lives have become unworkable. This may be because of alcohol, major illness, a great loss, family breakup, and the like. They turn to Christianity seeking to have their broken lives healed. Many of them—when they find a significant degree of restoration to a more normal life and access to a life more significant than they had known before—may have little interest in learning more about Christian doctrines. They respond primarily to what they find helpful for dealing with their deep personal needs and problems. There may be little theoretical interest because their personal needs are so pressing. Understandably and rightly, they are primarily concerned with what can help them deal with their broken and ensnared lives.

The second reason people are attracted to Christianity is the beauty of its ideals. Love between people, service to others, the desire for a wholesome and noble life, and admirable aspirations for purity and goodness—all draw them to Christianity. Jesus and great Christian lives, both past and present, inspire and elevate their outlook and behavior. They respond mostly to inspirational stories, music, and pictures.

The third motive that draws people to Christianity is closely related to high and noble aspirations: failure and the guilt that accompanies failure. People with high standards and aspirations are particularly vulnerable to failure and severe remorse for failure, but many people of ordinary decency also often feel the discomfort of guilt over their failures. It is quite appealing to grasp the portrayal of God's love, mercy, and unconditional forgiveness for those who repent of their failures and who desire to lead a better life. The relief as the gospel lifts the burden of guilt for the past, and the promise of help, support, encouragement, and guidance for the future—all give such people spiritual nourishment.

A fourth reason to be attracted to religious faith is an awareness of a hunger and lack in all that is earthly to satisfy that hunger. This is typified in Augustine's famous remark, "Our hearts are restless until they find rest in thee [God]," on the opening page of his *Confessions*. Yet a sense of dissatisfaction is recognized by Plato seven hundred years before Augustine. In his *Gorgias* (493b), Plato likens a human being "to a leaky jar, because it can never be filled." Some people today refer to this lack we sense as "the God-hole" within us, as does Francis S. Collins, the director of the government's genome project, in his account of why he became a Christian.[1]

The fifth motive is an unusual, powerful spiritual experience or experiences. They vary greatly, as can be seen from the collection of religious experiences by William James in his classic *Varieties of Religious Experience*. This approach seems to be quite common today with the loss of confidence in the power of reason to settle ultimate questions, and a corresponding reliance on personal experience. For example, about 39 percent of Protestants today describe themselves as "born-again" Christians, and many Christians of all denominations are "Pentecostals," with various degrees of emphasis on the presence of the Spirit. Different types of mystical experience are far more widespread than often realized. For example, in a study of high school seniors and first-year college students in England, a country with only about 5 percent of the population as regular churchgoers, it was found that 55 percent said they had an experience similar to a mystical episode as described in a passage quoted on the questionnaire. Virtually none of them had told anyone about it before, and all of them felt that the moment or moments were extremely important. Half of them had no idea what to make of their experiences. The rest understood them as experiences of the presence of God.[2]

Sixth, and finally, some are attracted to Christianity primarily because they are looking for an understanding of their world and their life within that world. This is especially common among those who are highly educated, even if, like the author of the letter with which I began, they are unable to gain a sufficient understanding to satisfy themselves. The drive for understanding is well described by Austin Farrer, an Oxford theologian who wrote in the middle of the last century. He spoke of it as the need "to spread the area of recognition," so that whatever the mind examined, it would seek to relate to God all that it knew and experienced. He wrote:

> Think of my mother, now—you have known women like her—a more unphilosophical thinker it would be difficult to find. Now suppose that in the heyday of my adolescent intellectualism I had told her that she had no right to her fervent evangelical faith, not being able to put together half a dozen consistent sentences in justification of her mere belief in God. What would she have said? She would have told me that admired intellects had bothered themselves with such inquiries, and been able to satisfy their minds: for her part, God had given her faith, and God had never let her down except it was by her manifest fault. . . .
>
> The centre of your Christian conviction, whatever you may think, will be where my mother's was—in your exploration of grace, in your walking with God. But faith perishes if it is walled in, or confined. If it is anywhere, it must be everywhere, like God himself: if God is in your life, he is in all things, for he is God. You must be able to spread the area of your recognition of him, and the basis of your conviction about him, as widely as your thought will range.[3]

Farrer's mother typified one way of affirming or holding to Christian teachings, a devotional or pious mode. The way is to be faithful in prayer, Scripture reading, and conduct. This mode is always a part of a person's relation to the Christian faith, even when one goes beyond simple faith and one's mind is also engaged with such matters as the grounds for Christian belief, and seeking to understand how a Christian vision relates to new knowledge in various fields of inquiry. This kind of Christian has a critical mind: even though committed to the Christian faith, they are able at times to step back and consider objections to Christianity, and consider new or different interpretations of Christian teachings. Such persons are willing to develop a new understanding of Christianity from an engagement with various fields of inquiry, and they are aware of the incompleteness of our theological understanding and of unresolved difficulties in our Christian beliefs. A critical person is not a skeptical person, who raises or looks for difficulties *in order to undermine Christianity and to avoid personal commitment.* Critical persons have faith and are seeking better to understand what they believe. To one who lives only in a pious mode, a person who at times is in a critical mode of speaking may appear threatening and even a skeptic. Some skeptics, on the other hand, take all believers to be merely pious people, without critical faculties, and they mistakenly identify faith with irrationality.

Just as a person can be both pious and critical, so too several of the six motives for being a Christian can be operative in a person at the same time. They can also change in their degree of importance over time. At one time a person's struggle with guilt may be more important than gaining understanding, but at a later time the relative importance of the two motives may be reversed. People may also change as they grow older, beginning their journey because of a powerful religious experience, but then later becoming more concerned with service to others.

This book is intended to increase a critical but pious person's understanding of the Christian religion. Any or all of the six reasons for being attracted to religious faith, however, may go hand in hand with various degrees of the desire for greater understanding of the Christian faith; thus this book's usefulness is not limited to those whose primary attraction to the Christian religion is a desire for understanding. But it is not intended to be a substitute for the indispensable spiritual nourishment that comes from worship, from prayer, from fellowship with other believers, from serving others, from inspirational sermons, and from classic and contemporary works on spirituality. It is primarily directed toward giving us a better understanding of the Christian vision of reality.

Yet it must be stressed that if the study of Christian beliefs has no effect whatsoever on one's spiritual life, then something has gone wrong. Religion is not mere beliefs, but it involves being deeply moved by what is portrayed. The relation of doctrines to life is well captured by the distinction drawn by John Henry Newman, the nineteenth-century theologian, between "notional" and "real" apprehension. It is one thing to know that a tiger is a dangerous and powerful animal, and another to be awakened from sleep in a tent by the powerful roar of a prowling tiger. It is one thing to know that cancer is a terrible disease, and another to be told by your doctor that you have cancer. It is one thing to know that jumping from an airplane is exciting, and another actually to be in free fall for the first time for a minute or so before a chute opens. In each of these contrasting cases, we have notional apprehension in contrast to real apprehension. A person may gain only a notional understanding of Christian doctrines from this book, but our aim is to help a person move toward a real understanding of them. This I hope to accomplish to at least some degree by giving people enough of the "pieces" of the puzzle for them to start putting them together in a sufficiently coherent way as to illumine their minds and give them guidance in their lives.

Introduction

What Is Theology?

The main source of Christian theology is the Bible, but Christian theology as an *academic* discipline would not exist without the kind of intellectual curiosity that was unique to ancient Greece. The ancient Egyptians said that the Greeks were like children because they were always asking "Why?" It is not that other ancient peoples, including the ancient Jews, did not ask for the whys and wherefores of many things. It is rather that in ancient Greece the practice became a matter of principle. The Greeks did not think of every significant question that has ever been raised, but they asked questions persistently and systematically as a deliberate program until they developed the very idea of disciplines: areas of *theoretical* knowledge, defined by principles, and investigated by appropriate methods of inquiry. A practical question, such as the need to determine boundaries of a piece of property, may start an investigation, but the various rules of thumb concerning the relation of lines to angles were not allowed to remain just rules of thumb even though they were perfectly satisfactory for all practical purposes. They were pushed until the theoretical science of geometry was created, a discipline that continues to yield new knowledge today. As a result of this particular attitude, which led to the very notion of a "discipline," the ancient Greeks became the founders of many of our traditional disciplines of thought.

In the Old Testament we find many instances of persistent questioning and inquiry, such as "Why do the righteous suffer and the wicked prosper?" This question arose from the Israelites' practical concern for the justice of God, and their desire for deliverance from oppression. It did not lead to a theoretical discipline. In addition, the range of their questions is much more limited than that of the ancient Greek philosophers, who sometimes became tiresome to the average Greek because of their predilection for theoretical questions and disputes.

The systematic search for reasons, or for the *logos* for anything and everything, is something we today take for granted. It is part of our mental makeup. We do it automatically. We share with the ancient Greeks a desire to push back the domain of the unknown and to unveil all mysteries, and we share with them the concept of *disciplines*, which have their distinctive principles and methods of inquiry. Likewise, it was part of the mental makeup of the early church fathers who fashioned Christian doctrine in a decisive way in the first centuries. These early theologians sought to retain a biblical understanding of God, but they were persistent in asking of various parts of the biblical revelation, "Why is that so?"

One of the most transparent examples of this mental outlook (although by no means the earliest) is the book by Athanasius, bishop of Alexandria (d. 373), *The Incarnation of the Word of God*. In this early work, Athanasius is concerned with why the Word of God, with whom and by whom the Father created the universe, became incarnate, became a human being. It did not happen by accident nor by necessity. It was a free action of God. But even free acts occur for a reason. In the case of the incarnation, it is clear in the Gospels that God became incarnate in order to save us. But the Gospels do not tell us why God chose this particular way or means to save us, nor how it saves us. Here is a small sample of Athanasius's reasoning:

> Man, who was created in God's image and in his possession of reason reflected the very Word Himself, was disappearing, and the work of God was being undone. The law of death, which followed from the Transgression, prevailed upon us, and from it there was no escape. The thing that was happening was in truth both monstrous and unfitting. It would, of course, have been unthinkable that God should go back upon His word and that man, having transgressed, should not die; but it was equally monstrous that beings which once had shared the nature of the Word should perish and turn back again into non-existence through corruption. . . . As, then the creatures whom He had created reasonable, like the Word, were in fact perishing, and such noble works were on the road to ruin, what then was God, being Good, to do? Was He to let corruption and death have their way with them? In that case, what was the use of having made them in the beginning? . . . It was impossible, therefore, that God should leave man to be carried off by corruption, because it would be unfitting and unworthy of Himself. . . .
>
> Repentance would not guard the Divine consistency. . . . Had it been a case of a trespass only, and not of a subsequent corruption, repentance would have been well enough. . . . What—or rather *Who*—was it that was needed? . . . Who, save the Word of God Himself, Who also in the begin-

ning had made all things out of nothing? His part it was, and His alone, both to bring again the corruptible to incorruption and to maintain for the Father His consistency of character with all. For he alone, being Word of the Father and above all, was in consequence both able to re-create all, and worthy to suffer on behalf of all and to be an ambassador for all with the Father. . . .

Taking a body like our own, because all our bodies were liable to the corruption of death, He surrendered His body to death instead of all, and offered it to the Father. This He did out of sheer love for us, so that in His death all might die, and the law of death thereby be abolished because, having fulfilled in His body that for which it was appointed, it was thereafter voided of its power for men.[1]

In addition to the main issues of why there was an incarnation, and how the death of the incarnate Word of God saves us from sin and death, Athanasius seeks to understand every aspect of the Gospel story. For example, he asks why the crucified Jesus remained in the tomb three days and not just one, two, four, or more.[2] With his Hellenically formed mind, he assumes that there is an explanation for everything that happens, including everything that God does. Since all things are rational, one can ask of anything, Why is that so? even if one does not always have the ability or information needed to find the answer.

Not only does Athanasius illustrate the attempt to answer many of the questions that the biblical story raises; he also illustrates the fact that theology deals with a revelation that is in the form of an unfolding story, taking place over a vast stretch of time: from the creation of the universe to the end of this present world and the arrival of the kingdom of God. Theology itself is, however, not in story form. Rather, theology is an examination of various themes in biblical history, such as creation and the incarnation, where possible asking and answering questions about what they mean and imply, and in that exploration often seeking to relate these themes to what other fields of investigation are uncovering, such as history, archaeology, cosmology, psychology, or biology. In addition, theology is usually organized under topics often called "rubrics" (from the Latin for "red" because they were once written in red in textbooks) such as creation, providence, incarnation, Holy Spirit, Trinity—rather than as a chronological story. Theologians select here and there from various parts of the biblical narrative the parts of it that relate to the particular topic or doctrine with which they are dealing.

The nonnarrative form of theology tends to make it abstract: it seeks to find reasons for the doctrine and implications of the doctrine for our self-understanding and behavior, as we saw in Athanasius's reflections on the incarnation and death of Jesus. It also finds connections between various doctrines and various parts of the long biblical story. In the attempts to answer questions, theologians often roam quite far into other disciplines, not only into philosophy (which in premodern times included virtually all subjects except law and medicine), but also into developments in modern times in the physical and the social sciences. The nonnarrative form of theology and its wide-ranging inquiry sometimes leaves the biblical story so far behind that theology can appear to be merely a philosophical, human construction, to be evaluated as we evaluate philosophical constructions.

For all these reasons, theology often seems utterly remote to those for whom achieving such an understanding is not a primary concern. This can happen even to those for whom understanding is a primary concern because theological constructions are usually so technical as to be impenetrable even for highly educated people, including those who are biblically informed. Indeed, theology today is conducted in such a specialized language that scholars in biblical studies and other seminary subjects find it difficult to understand what theologians are writing. Even professional theologians, who follow quite different approaches in their theological investigations, find it difficult to understand each other. We may compare the situation to a hub and spokes. At the hub all theologians can understand each other, but as theologians move from the hub and along different spokes into more and more specialization, the distance between the spokes increases so that mutual communications becomes more and more difficult.

Yet it is the biblical story with which all Christians begin, and every Christian needs some theological understanding of the biblical story. We all know that it is possible for all of us to go astray in our behavior, failing to live up to the teachings of Christ. In a parallel way we can also go astray in our ideas about God and God's purposes. Indeed, some theological understanding of the biblical story is necessary to keep us from going astray even in our behavior. A sound understanding of Christian doctrines, such as this book seeks to give, provides essential guidance for both our thoughts and actions. This point is so important that an extended example is called for.

Consider the familiar story of the Prodigal Son (Luke 15:11–32). A father has two sons, who in different ways disappoint him. Neither lives with their father in a harmonious and joyful way. The younger one asks for his inheritance and then goes to a far land, where he wastes it in loose living. He is reduced to caring for pigs (unclean animals for Jews) and is so hungry that he would gladly eat the fodder fed to the pigs. In time he comes to his senses, repents of his treatment of his father, and returns home. He plans to confess his fault to his father and beg to be hired as a servant. Before he can even speak, his father runs out to welcome him and then restores him to a place of honor as a son. The elder son is furious at this reception of his younger brother, rebukes his father, and will not join in the celebration of the return of his brother, whom his father says has been lost, but now is found.

The story occurs in a chapter entirely devoted to the theme of being lost. Luke 15 gives us three parables about being lost: the parable of the Lost Sheep, the parable of the Lost Coin, and the parable of the Lost Son. Together they give an extraordinary account of God's concern for us. In the first parable Jesus asks his listeners, "Which one of you, having a hundred sheep and losing one, does not leave the ninety-nine in the wilderness and go after the one that is lost until he finds it?" A flock of a hundred sheep would make a large herd in Jesus' day, but even so, the loss of a single sheep would have been a serious matter.

And Jesus surely knows that his listeners would immediately agree that a shepherd would leave the rest of his flock in someone's care, go out searching, and continue to search until he found the stray. What is unusual about the parable is that Jesus applies it to God. Jesus teaches us that his Father seeks those who are lost and have no ability to return home, just like lost sheep. Each of us so matters to God that God will go to a lot of trouble to seek and to find those who are lost and bewildered. In the second parable our value is stressed even more. Not only is the loss of one silver coin out of ten a greater proportionate loss than one out of a hundred sheep; the silver coins probably also represent the life savings of a poor woman. Hence the diligence of her search for the lost coin and the greatness of her joy at finding it.

Although the virtues of repentance are gloriously praised in the ancient Jewish faith, the *direct search, this going out to seek* the sinner, that Jesus teaches is utterly new. It is Jesus, and only Jesus, who first taught us that God takes the initiative to find the lost, that his Father greatly puts himself out to search diligently, and that his Spirit is at work in people before they even realize it as they come to their senses and turn to him. Jesus stresses that instead of looking with disdain on those who have gone astray, God rejoices when he finds those who are lost. But perhaps we do not feel ourselves to be particularly involved in all of this; for we do not have the demands of the ancient Jewish law, which restricted the outlook of the Jewish religious leaders and people.

Yet all three parables do strongly impinge on us and indeed in our daily lives at every moment. Everything we do, think, and wish for takes us toward God or away from God and the destiny he has for each one of us. We are not mere products of biology, with a limited life span, followed by oblivion, as so much of the intellectual culture has taught us to think. The stories of the Lost Sheep, the Lost Coin, and the Lost Son stress that God takes each of us very seriously, far more seriously than we take ourselves. Each of us is so valuable to God that God seeks to find us and to welcome us into his glorious kingdom. The figure of the good shepherd who seeks and rejoices when he finds the lost sheep; the housewife who is frantic at the loss of a coin from her small collection of ten coins, which likely represents the entire family's savings, and who scours the house until she finds it; a deeply insulted father who rushes out to welcome his wastrel son—all introduced something that was utterly new to the entire world. No one had ever taught that every person is of imperishable value.

This understanding of the equal and inalienable value of people has steadily made its way into people's thinking wherever Christianity has spread, so much so that every ethical theory by Western philosophers, however much they differ from each other, assumes and is based upon the absolute value of every human being.[3] Since this teaching of Jesus took hold in Western civilization, our legal systems, our understanding of human rights, the slow and gradual rise of democracy, and the emancipation of women and slaves—all rest on and are inspired by such simple parables as that of a Lost Sheep, a Lost Coin, a Lost Son, because they teach us that every person must be taken with ultimate seriousness. These stories encapsulate the core of the gospel: each and every person so matters to God that God the Son became a human being to seek us.

Nothing can give us the value and worth that underlies our civilization's convictions concerning human rights, which is spreading to the rest of the world today—nothing except the love of God. To reject God, to ignore God, or to neglect God is at the same time to reject, to ignore, or to neglect our irreplaceable value. It is to think of ourselves as far less than we are. Without God as part of our outlook, only a few people are thought to be important, so that what they do, think, and want are covered by the media, discussed by pundits, written about by historians, and the like. Only a few, a very few people out of billions elicit much interest, and even those often considered to be significant have to make a great effort to retain the limelight. God's world is quite different. God attends to each of us. God attends to every act, every thought, every desire of each of us. What we do, think, and wish matters to God. Only to God does every person matter profoundly and unforgettably.

The divine basis of our worth can easily be seen from an important crisis in the Western world. Since the rise of modern thought, there have been frequent and persistent efforts to give a nonreligious basis for our ethical, political, and legal theories. Since the eighteenth century, efforts to establish our worth on a nonreligious basis have failed. Every ethical and political theory that has been put forward as a basis of our worth has suffered devastating criticism. (See once again Basil Mitchell's book just cited). Today our universities and schools often openly tell us that they do not teach values, for the simple reason that they don't think there are any that they can justify. Everything is considered to be a matter of personal preference and cultural norms. But the conviction that we all matter still haunts us. Hence comes the agony at pulling the plug on people, the resistance to euthanasia, the ongoing debate over whether embryos are human—because human beings should not, except perhaps in extreme cases, be killed or destroyed. All this is an echo of a conviction we have lived with for a long time, the conviction that all people matter profoundly. Yet we are increasingly realizing that this conviction can find no secular or nonreligious basis.

This lack of a nonreligious basis for our significance should not actually be a surprise. It does not take much effort to learn that the ultimate significance of every person was introduced into the world by Jesus. It takes only a little thought to realize that the only intelligible basis of our significance is God's love. Our indefeasible value is intelligible only by reference to God, not any deity, but the God and father of our Lord Jesus Christ. For God so loves us that he sent his Son into the world as a humble human being to seek us, teach us, and to die on our behalf, and finally to rise so that our destiny is not to become dust and ashes and part of the earth, but to live with God now and eternally (cf. John 3:16).

Each of us is of irreplaceable value. This is because God loves each one of us and desires each of us to turn to God and to live as beloved, obedient children, who as his children will inherit the kingdom. Nothing makes us of irreplaceable value but God's love. Consider this simple comparison: None of my children is the best looking, the brightest, the most accomplished person in the world. Yet I would not take the best looking, the brightest, the most accomplished person in their place. Nothing can be a substitute or a replacement for any one of them. Why? Because I love them, and nothing else will do but each one of them. So too I am not the best father, the wisest father, the most considerate father, and so forth. But happily, I am irreplaceable to my children; when I used to reach home, it was my voice they wanted to hear, it was me they wanted to be with.

This is all true of God. The yearning of a shepherd for a lost and helpless sheep, in peril of its life, and the shepherd's joy at recovering it; the frantic search by a housewife for a lost coin; a broken-hearted father who waits and endures great suffering for his son—all these are but figures and images of that profound yearning, searching, patient love of God that has its culmination in his cruci-fied Son. For the suffering of the Son on our behalf is a grief taken into the very heart of the Father, as he endures with his Son the cost of human indifference, rejection, and folly.

But do we think of ourselves as lost? As in need of being found? One way to approach this question is for us to ask ourselves whether we think of ourselves as of irreplaceable value. If we don't, then we are selling ourselves short, and to that extent we are lost, unable to find our true selves. Pascal once wrote that many of us do not suffer from self-love but struggle with misery because we cannot find enough in ourselves to love.[4] We find ourselves rather disappointing, and even in some cases it is sometimes unbearable to be ourselves. That is one way to be lost and in need of being found: not to know a love that makes us care for ourselves, not to know a love that makes us of irreplaceable value, not to know a love that loves us because we are who we are.

Some people seem to think highly of themselves and have quite a lot of reasons to be pleased with themselves. They are rather like the prodigal, who took his endowment and lived it up. But just as he ran out of resources and was reduced to utter insignificance, so too are those who take their talents and achievements and rest themselves on them; they too will run out of resources, for time devours all, and even all memory of them will disappear. Fortunately, the prodigal "came to himself," which is a polite way to say that he realized he had been a fool. Some people who think highly of themselves for the wrong reasons need to come to themselves, not to live as fools who do not recognize the most obvious truth about themselves: By relying on ourselves, we end up as a pile of dust. The prodigal son came to himself, realized his foolishness, and decided to return home to the one who loved him. So whether we feel lowly about ourselves or think more highly of ourselves than we ought, the same truth applies: Because of God and only because of God are we of irreplaceable value. Not to respond to God's love in our lives is to be lost.

Another way to be lost is to be like the elder brother. He rejected his brother's restoration. By denying the irreplaceable value of his brother, he at the same time rejected his own value. For we have such value ourselves if and only if everyone else has it as well. Our attitude and treatment of others is a good way to determine whether we ourselves are lost. Whenever we hold others in disdain, whenever we treat others unjustly, and do not repent of it, we simply reaffirm our own lostness.

It is hard to believe that everyone is of irreplaceable value. Perhaps the analogy drawn by Teresa of Avila (1515–82) will help. In her book *The Interior Castle*, she says that just as a castle has many rooms, so too there are many rooms inside each of us. One of those rooms is "the image of God." Many do not live in that, the most splendid of rooms, but in lesser rooms. Some of us even use filth and dirt to smear the outside of the room that is the image of God. But it is still there, however much it is defaced. So too every person retains their irreplaceable value to God, even when they have so defaced themselves that they are worthless on every earthly measure of value.

This account of God as seeking us illustrates the way our ideas of God affect our view of ourselves and our behavior. Indeed, it shows their relevance to our daily lives; for not only do we have to deal with ourselves and the way we think of ourselves; we also have to deal with other people all the time.

In this book as I give an account of theology, I will strive to be as accessible as the Prodigal Son is to people without a long, technical training in theology, and to show the way our ideas of God affect our view of ourselves and our behavior. Even though, like all theology, it will not be in the form of a narrative story, as is the Bible, I will frequently connect the theological topics covered to the biblical story, as in the example just given of the Prodigal Son. I will also show that a Christian understanding of God is credible, or makes sense, as I have just done by pointing out how Jesus' teachings form the basis of the widespread conviction in our civilization and beyond that each of us is of irreplaceable or absolute value.

PART ONE
THE NATURE OF GOD

Chapter 1

The Holy One of Israel

Usually an introduction to Christian theology begins with the doctrine of creation, following the order of the Bible. But the present biblical order does not follow the *actual* chronology of the religion of the people of Israel. As we will see in the next chapter, Israel first believed in a God, called Yahweh, who had made them a people and was their personal God. They were henotheist, not yet monotheist: in contrast to other peoples around them, they themselves had only one God, but they recognized the reality of the gods of other people. Only sometime in the eighth century did the view prevail among them that their God Yahweh was not just their God, but also the God of all peoples, and that other people's gods were idols. They expressed this conviction by affirming that their God Yahweh was the creator of all people and indeed the creator of all that existed. So we will consider their belief in God as creator after we have looked at an earlier period in their history in which God forms them into a nation by calling Moses to lead them out of slavery in Egypt.

Taking things in this order will enable us to understand how the very notion of creation is transformed by the Jewish[1] claim that *Yahweh* made the heavens and earth. What Yahweh is affects what creation is understood to mean. Creation is not a mere cosmic event that stands at the start of history. Rather, when creation is made the work of Yahweh, who is concerned with the plight of the Jews and redeems them from slavery, the creation of the universe becomes part of the story of God's redemption. Creation is understood to be a part of history, and God's creation is seen as itself a saving activity that prevents the return of chaos. By treating God's redemptive activity first, we can then see how remarkable this daring understanding of creation is.

To begin with creation first would make it appear that the Jewish faith begins from speculation about the natural world. It would make it appear that belief in God began with reflection on the origin of the universe, so that the Jewish religion is fundamentally a religion based on the natural world. But Jewish religion not only begins with God's concern for them as a people; redemption also always remains the center around which all else in their religion turns. Failure to realize this has led modern philosophers to treat all monotheistic religions as based on an inference to God's existence from the existence and order of the natural world. When philosophers show that such an inference fails (the so-called traditional proofs of God's existence), they then erroneously claim that belief in God has no rational basis.

I have chosen to begin my account with Moses' experience of God speaking to him in a burning bush rather than the earlier event of God's making a covenant with Abraham.[2] This is because throughout this study, I stress the dual characteristics of God as transcendent and immanent. God's transcendent nature is not properly understood by the usual philosophic characterization of God as omnipotent, omniscient, and all-good. Without a proper understanding of God's transcendent nature, all we say of God is utterly inadequate, indeed not God at all. Yet at the same time, God makes Godself accessible to us. An examination of God's holiness as experienced by Moses and, in the next chapter, by Isaiah, enables us in a brief compass to characterize both God's transcendence and God's immanence.

The story of God's calling Moses to go to Egypt and lead the Jewish people out of slavery comes to us through a great deal of recasting of a story about the Jewish people being formed into a nation. It was originally in oral form and in several versions for some time before it was committed to writing and reedited several times. So the present Exodus text has the later conviction that Yahweh, their God, is creator, and that the gods of other people are idols. So the story of Moses as it is written is not straightforward history. What matters is the conception of deity that we find in the story of Moses and the Jewish people. It is an extraordinary understanding of God: the way God is understood is our primary concern here. We will consider why one should believe in such a God later, as we gain in understanding of who the biblical God is.

In the biblical story of Exodus, the ancient Hebrew people are slaves in Egypt over a thousand years before the birth of Jesus. They have become so numerous that an Egyptian ruler orders every newborn Hebrew boy to be killed. To evade the authorities, Moses' mother hides him until he is three months old, then puts him in a small waterproof basket and places it among the reeds in the river. While bathing, Pharaoh's daughter finds the baby. Out of pity, she takes the baby home and raises him as her own child. Although raised as an Egyptian, Moses feels an affinity with his oppressed people. When he sees an Egyptian beating a Hebrew, Moses kills the Egyptian and hides the body in the sand. The next day when he sees two Hebrews fighting, he tries to intervene, but they turn on him and taunt him as a murderer. When Pharaoh hears of what Moses has done, Moses is forced to flee for his life.

Moses settles in the nearby land of Midian, and there he marries. After some years of working for his father-in-law, Moses receives a call from God to return to Egypt in order to lead the Hebrews out of slavery. The text is as follows:

> Moses was keeping the flock of his father-in-law Jethro, the priest of Midian; he led his flock beyond the wilderness, and came to Horeb, the mountain of God [also called Mount Sinai, traditionally in the eastern part of the Sinai peninsula, where later the covenant and law were given to Moses and the escaping Hebrew people]. There the angel of the LORD appeared to him in a flame of fire out of a bush; he looked, and the bush was blazing, yet it was not consumed. Then Moses said, "I must turn aside and look at this great sight, and see why the bush is not burned up." When the LORD saw that he had turned aside to see, God called to him out of the bush, "Moses, Moses!" And he said, "Here I am." Then he said, "Come no closer! Remove the sandals from your feet, for the place on which you are standing is holy ground." He said further, "I am the God of your father, the God of Abraham, the God of Isaac, and the God of Jacob." And Moses hid his face, for he was afraid to look at God. (Exod. 3:1–6)

In the story God is not visible, but God is present in a burning bush. God warns Moses not to come closer and to remove his sandals in order to show reverence for the divine presence. Then God identifies himself as the God of Moses' ancestors. In fear Moses hides his face, rather than looking at the bush in which God is present. In the story holiness itself is not described directly. Rather, its nature is indicated indirectly by the order not to come closer, to remove his sandals, and by Moses' reaction of terror and dread at the mysterious power that threatens him.

One of the most cited studies of holiness is Rudolf Otto's *The Idea of the Holy*,[3] which covers the experience of holiness in various religions of the world. Otto argues that the experience of the holy or the "numinous," as he calls it, is a unique, awe-inspiring experience of a phenomenon that both repels and attracts, a *mysterium tremendum et fascinans*, as he puts it. The holy is separate, wholly other, transcendent. It has no place in our scheme of reality but belongs to an absolutely different reality. In these respects Otto's account of the experience of the holy coheres with what we have read about Moses' encounter with God. But Otto also claims that there is no moral content, no notion of goodness, in the primary and original experience of holiness, so that goodness is not an integral part of the experience of God or holiness. Goodness is a later addition to the notion of holiness.

Norman H. Snaith, however, in his *Distinctive Ideas of the Old Testament*, emphatically rejects Otto's claim:

> It is true that in primitive religion "the idea of sin, in any proper sense of the word, did not exist at all." But it is also true that there was no proper sense of Deity either. Further, as soon as there was any idea of an Other, however well or ill conceived, there was also a recognition of danger and "wrongness" (in a broad, almost pre-ethical sense) of breaking a *taboo*, of infringing some tribal sanction. . . . We are dealing with embryo notions of *quodish* [*qodesh*] (holiness), and equally embryo notions of ethics. We maintain that the embryo *quodish* (holiness) involves an embryo ethical content and an embryo idea of sin. The word *quodish* originally had no moral content in our developed sense of the word "moral," but it did involve pre-ethical restrictions, as undeveloped in content as itself.[4]

In the case of Moses' experience of God's holiness, the goodness of God is prominent. The holy God, whom Moses encounters, gives Moses a task: He is to lead the Hebrews out of bondage in Egypt. This is the focal point of the story. Moses indeed responds with awe, dread, and fear before God; he removes his sandals since the very ground has become holy because of the nearness of God. But the full and proper response is to do what God commands him to do, for the story turns immediately from Moses' reaction of awe and fear to God's concern for the misery of his people in bondage. Moses is appointed to go to Egypt in order to lead the people to Mount Horeb, where they are to worship God (Exod. 3:7–12). Indeed, as we read the Exodus text from this point onward (from 3:7–12 through 4:31), we learn that the people are to be freed from bondage to the Egyptians so that God can make a covenant with them and, through Moses, give them the law that is to be obeyed as their response to the covenant. Finally, they are to be led by Moses to the land that God has promised to them as Abraham's descendants. As we continue to read the story from the initial encounter with God's holiness, Moses' awe and fear seem to recede into the background. It is as if the intensity of the divine presence has been greatly toned down, so that for the rest of the chapter 3 and on into chapter 4, Moses' discomfort arises solely from what he has been called to do and deals with how he is to achieve his task. One by one, all three of his excuses for evading his call are met:

- If the Hebrews ask me, "Who has sent you," what shall I say? God reveals his name to Moses, "I AM WHO I AM."
- What if Pharaoh will not let the Hebrews go? God gives Moses the power to perform awesome signs.
- Finally, Moses complains that he is not a good speaker. God assigns Moses' brother, Aaron, to be his spokesperson.

Then the holy God manifests or reveals Godself as a savior of God's people from slavery, and God's permanent involvement with them is through a sacred covenant. In addition, with this covenant God calls God's people to be holy:

to be dedicated to God and thus set apart from all other people. According to God's foundational promises to Abraham (Gen. 12:1–4), this is in order for God through them to fulfill God's purposes for all humanity. Their response to the covenant is to become righteous: to follow the law that God reveals to Moses on Mount Horeb, or Sinai. Thus, the holiness of God *shows itself* in God's righteous and saving action in response to the oppression and distress of his people, in God's call to them to be righteous or obedient, and in God's ultimate aim to bless all peoples of the earth through them. Holiness is not to be understood simply in terms of experiences of awe and fear that God's presence evokes, but also includes what the holy God seeks to do.

Notice the difference in method between Rudolf Otto's study of holiness and the one I have followed here. To learn what holiness means, Otto turns to comparative religion and seeks for what is common in the experiences of holiness found in various religions, dropping what is distinctive to each religion. In contrast to this approach, I have looked at how God reveals himself to Moses. It is the holiness *of the God of Israel,* as God reveals God's purposes, that specifies for me (and others) what holiness is. As Geoffrey Wainwright bluntly puts it, "God is holy and by that fact defines holiness."[5]

The same difference in method is evident in the treatment of the proof for God's existence and my approach to the witness of nature. For example, Antony Flew—in his foundational paper read to the Socratic Society in Oxford in 1950, "Theology and Falsification" (and published in virtually every anthology on the philosophy of religion since first read)—argues that the order of the world is ambiguous. It is rather like a clearing in a jungle upon which two explorers stumble. One observes what seems to be signs that the clearing was made by a gardener; the other explorer claims that the clearing has other features showing that it is the result of natural causes. They decide to settle the matter by putting up a fence around the clearing and watching to see if anyone climbs in to care for the clearing. No one does. After a while, one of the explorers suggests that perhaps the gardener is invisible. So they patrol the perimeter of the fence with bloodhounds. But the dogs give no indications of an intruder. These and all other empirical tests fail to detect a gardener. So the implication is that there is none.

Rather than conduct empirical tests on the pattern of modern empirical science, Flew and others like him could have turned to an examination of the story of God's revelation to people in the Bible. By not doing so, they ignore the holiness of God and so the essential hiddenness of God. God is treated as a member of the universe, subject to the same kind of treatment as anything else that resides within the universe. The biblical revelation is utterly ignored. So nature's order, which should serve as a witness—a witness that should lead one to examine biblical revelation, an examination that can take one well beyond what nature by itself can reveal—is instead turned in an alien and fruitless direction.

Some fifty years after his seminal paper, Flew recognizes this point as well. In an appendix to his *There Is a God,* titled "The Self-Revelation of God in Human History: A Dialogue on Jesus with N. T. Wright," Flew and Wright discuss several questions: How do we know Jesus existed? What are the grounds that Jesus is God incarnate? What is the evidence for the resurrection of Christ? After a lifetime of militant atheism, Flew concludes the discussion with these amazing remarks:

> I am very much impressed with Bishop Wright's approach, which is absolutely fresh. He presents the case for Christianity as something new for the first time. This is enormously important, especially in the United Kingdom, where the Christian religion has virtually disappeared. It is absolutely wonderful, absolutely radical, and very powerful.[6]

Even though God has revealed Godself as holy, righteous, and savior, God still remains hidden in God's essence or being. This is stressed in Moses' reaction to God's call. As we mentioned in passing, Moses is deeply anxious over how he will persuade the Hebrews to accept him as their leader, especially after the failure of his earlier attempt to intervene on their behalf. Even though Moses has been told that the Holy One is the God of his ancestors, Abraham, Isaac, and Jacob, Moses wants to know the identity of the God in terms of God's inmost being. What God has done for his ancestors is not enough for Moses. He thinks that he must show a knowledge of God superior to that which the Hebrews have if he is to have sufficient authority among them to be their leader. "If I come to the Israelites and say to them, 'The God of your ancestors has sent me to you,' and they ask me, 'What is his name?' what shall I say to them?" (Exod. 3:13–14). In antiquity, selfhood is expressed in the name given to a person, and people's names were sometimes changed to express their personality, status, or natures. To know a person's name may give one power over what is named.

Then God cryptically replies, "I AM WHO I AM" (also translated as "I AM WHAT I AM" or "I WILL BE WHAT I WILL BE"; Exod. 3:14). Much ink has been spilled trying to sort out this reply. But this much is clear. It implies that even when God's name is revealed, God's inmost nature is impenetrable to us, since the meaning of "I AM WHO I AM" baffles us. This is also true of the Hebrew "YHWH," the divine name in the third person, which may mean "He CAUSES TO BE." YHWH, He CAUSES TO BE, tells us something about God: we learn that God is the cause of things, but all we can perceive are the *effects* of God's causality. God in Godself remains hidden. It is also clear that YHWH becomes the cultic name for the God of Israel. It is spelled "Yahweh" and likely pronounced "YAH-way" (written Hebrew originally had no vowel points), but since it was so sacred that it was never spoken, we cannot be sure. In speech, "Adonai," meaning "the Lord" or "my Lord," was substituted for Yahweh, and often in writing as well.

As I will explain more fully later, holiness expresses the transcendence of God, while glory is God's presence to the world. In virtually every episode in the Gospel of John, the glory or the presence of God is made manifest in Jesus. The divine reality—the Word that is with God and that is God—manifests itself in the incarnation. One way this is presented in John's Gospel is the use of "I am" by Jesus (although John did not invent the use, since there are examples in the other Gospels that verge on it, such as Matt. 14:27; Mark 6:50). By so speaking, Jesus claims to have the same status as the Holy One who called Moses to lead God's people out of slavery, status as one who has the authority and the power to save. The most important and supreme act of God's love is the giving of Godself in the incarnation. This action, John tells us, is a measure of God's love. "God so loved the world that he gave his only Son, so that everyone who believes in him may not perish but may have eternal life" (John 3:16).

The essential hiddenness of God is charmingly expressed in the interpretation given to Exodus 33:18–23 by Gregory of Nyssa and his friend Gregory of Nazianzus, in which Moses asks, "Show me your glory, I pray." God explains that no one can see him and live. But God says, "While my glory [presence] passes by I will put you in a cleft of the rock, and I will cover you with my hand until I have passed by; then I will take away my hand, and you shall see my back; but my face shall not be seen." The two great bishops explain that God is unbounded (there is no Greek word for infinite) and holy, so that God is forever beyond our grasp. But even in this life we can know the back of God: we experience God's holiness and know God's power, wisdom, goodness, providence, and righteousness or justice from his "operations," as they put it, or actions, as we say it today. We will forever learn more and more of God, and grow in knowledge, virtue, and love as we follow behind the unbounded, inexhaustible Lord forever. This is why God shows Moses only his back; for Moses too is following God and can never catch up to see God's face.

Moses' claim of authority stems from his having contact with God, who appoints him leader of the Jews, gives him the law to transmit to the people, and provides the design for the tabernacle as a place of worship. The Hebrew Scripture is somewhat ambiguous on whether Moses ever sees God. As we just saw in Exodus 33:18–20, when Moses asks to see God's glory, God agrees but says, "You cannot see my face and live." But in Deuteronomy 34:10 we find that Moses has seen God face to face. Later rabbinic interpreters reconcile this passage with the others by saying that the prophets saw God through many panes of glass (presumably not as clear as our glass today), but Moses saw him through only one, and hence Moses has superior authority. Jesus' authority is also said to come from contact with the Father, but Jesus has greater intimacy with God than Moses. "No one has ever seen God. It is God the only Son, who is close to the Father's heart, who has made him known" (John 1:18). So Jesus' authority and knowledge are greater than Moses' and all others.

An aspect of holiness that reflects an early and primitive understanding of the incomprehensibility of God and the danger of approaching God too closely is recorded in 1 Chronicles 13 (cf. 2 Sam. 6). The ark of the covenant, which contains the copy of the law given to Moses on Mount Sinai and represents God's presence among the people of Israel, has been neglected during the reign of Saul, Israel's first king (c. 1000 BC). Saul's successor, David, proposes to revive the cultic worship focused on the ark. The ark is carried on a cart from its place of storage, driven by Uzzah and his brother. When the oxen stumble and the ark is tilting off the cart, Uzzah puts his hand on the ark to steady it. Immediately he is struck dead. It is as if the holiness of God is an impersonal force like electricity: highly beneficial, but may be lethal when touched.

This aspect of holiness was present in the cultic worship of God. God's worship developed into an increasingly elaborate and even idolatrous attitude to holiness. Not only was a ritual purity in the sacrifices offered by the priests in the temple quite rigorous: probably also unique to the religion of Israel was the extension of ritual purity beyond the priestly circle to the general population, expressed in such things as ritual washing and food restrictions. The eighth-century prophets often fiercely condemned such a focus on ritual purity because they believed that ritual holiness had become a substitute for righteousness in the community's life. Leviticus 19 contains the so-called Holiness Code, expressing concern for the poor, disadvantaged, handicapped, and aged, as well as calling for honesty in action, word, and judgment; but by the time of the prophets, that code had been largely lost from view. For example, in Isaiah we read,

> What to me is the multitude of your sacrifices?
>   says the LORD;
> I have had enough of burnt offerings of rams
>   and the fat of fed beasts;
> I do not delight in the blood of bulls,
>   or of lambs, or of goats.
> When you come to appear before me,
>   who asked this from your hand?
>   Trample my courts no more;
> bringing offerings is futile;
>   incense is an abomination to me.
> New moons and sabbath and calling of convocations—
>   I cannot endure solemn assemblies with iniquity.
> Your new moons and your appointed festivals
>   my soul hates;
> they have become a burden to me,
>   I am weary of bearing them.
> When you stretch out your hands,
>   I will hide my eyes from you;
> even though you make many prayers,
>   I will not listen;
>   your hands are full of blood.
> Wash yourselves; make yourselves clean;
>   remove the evil of your doings
>   from before my eyes;
> cease to do evil,
>   learn to do good;
> seek justice,
>   rescue the oppressed,
> defend the orphan,
>   plead for the widow.
>   (Isa. 1:11–17)

The relation between our worship of God and our daily lives is well-captured in Jesus' teaching: "But the hour is coming, and is now here, when the true worshipers will worship the Father in spirit and truth, for the Father seeks such as these to worship him. God is spirit, and those who worship him must worship in spirit and truth" (John 4:23–24). This passage concludes Jesus' discussion with the Samaritan woman at the well. She has pointed to the dispute between the Samaritans and Jews over the place of worship. The Samaritans worship at a temple on Mount Gerizim and refuse to recognize the temple worship in Jerusalem. The woman at the well thinks that Jesus as a prophet ought to be able to settle rival religious claims. Jesus points out that the place of worship is not of primary importance. Worship in spirit is our response to God's gift of Godself, and worship in truth (as John implies) is to worship in accord with God's nature as seen in Christ.

The Sisters of the Community of the Holy Spirit (an Anglican order of nuns in New York City) make a connection between worship in spirit and our work. Each Tuesday they pray that all people may find God in their active work. They wish for people to carry out the duties of their daily life in such a way that God may be present through their actions and to offer their worship in the joy and restfulness of true worship. Validation of worship is, therefore, not to be sought in feelings of elevation and the like during worship, however welcome they are. And we may hope for and expect guidance, comfort, and inspiration for our daily life in and through our worship. But it is in a life in accord with God's will, in our work and service to those in need, that we are truly able to worship God in spirit and in truth.

In the New Testament it is quite revealing that when Peter, following Jesus' advice, makes an enormous catch of fish, he becomes aware of the holiness of Jesus. (Luke [as in 4:14] stresses that Jesus is filled with the Holy Spirit.) Peter then says, "Go away from me, Lord, for I am a sinful man!" (Luke 5:8). Probably Peter does not mean that he is guilty of gross moral sins. Rather, in order to earn his living as a fisherman, he cannot keep the elaborate ritual laws of cleanliness that have developed. Rather than agreeing with Peter, Jesus recruits Peter to join him: "Do not be afraid; from now on you will be catching people" (5:10b). So too can we understand Jesus' uncoupling of ritual holiness from righteousness in his appeal: "Come to me, all you that are weary and are carrying heavy burdens, and I will give you rest. Take my yoke upon you, and learn from me; for I am gentle and humble in heart, and you will find rest for your souls. For my yoke is easy, and my burden is light" (Matt. 11:28–30). We also find Jesus rejecting ritual cleanliness for himself and his disciples by such acts as healing on the Sabbath, eating with "sinners" and without washing his hands in the prescribed manner, and telling parables, such as the Good Samaritan, in which the person who loves his neighbor is a Samaritan (a person who refuses to worship in the Jerusalem temple) in contrast to a priest and Levite who failed to do so. In these actions and teachings, Jesus incurs the bitter opposition of the priests, scribes, and the Pharisees.

Paul's view that salvation is given by God apart from the law, and the agreement among the apostles and other leaders in the church in Jerusalem to greatly limit the application of rituals for Gentile (non-Jewish) Christians—these triumphed in the primitive church. Christianity rejected the entire system of Jewish ritual cleanliness. In its place were instituted the rite of baptism, understood to be our participation in Christ's death and resurrection, and the ritual of Holy Communion, which recalls Jesus' Last Supper with his disciples and is a regular renewal of our participation in his death and resurrection. Both are understood to be eschatological events: events that in the present time represent and anticipate the realization of God's kingdom that will be fully established with Christ's return in glory.

In Christianity are two other important liturgical actions that involve the holiness of God. First, in every service of Holy Communion is the reenactment of the cry of the seraphs before the throne of God, "Holy, Holy, Holy, Lord God of Hosts; Heaven and earth are full of thy glory," which is taken from Isaiah's vision of God (6:3; we will examine Isaiah's vision in the next chapter). In the ritual it is referred to as "the Sanctus," from the Latin for "holy." (Sometimes "Lord God of Hosts" is rendered as "Lord, God of power and might.") "Holy" is repeated three times because there is no way to express the superlative in the Hebrew language except by repetition. The entire congregation, not just the choir, sings the Sanctus in praise of God, because the people share in the song that is continually sung by the heavenly host and by the whole company of heaven. Holy Communion is thus a *joining* in the heavenly praise of God.

The other great liturgical use is in the Lord's Prayer, the primary and most important example Jesus gave his disciples for how we are to pray (Matt. 6:9–10). The clause "Hallowed be thy name" is a prayer that the intrinsic holiness of God be established and recognized within creation, that God's kingdom would come and God's will be done.[7]

This prayer is also usually said or sung by the entire congregation. It signifies that we are called to be a holy people: called out by God to recognize God's rule, and at the same time commissioned to call others to join in that recognition. In relation to ourselves, holiness also means that through God's forgiveness and conferring of the Holy Spirit in baptism, we have been freed of the burden of evil and filled with God's Spirit of love or charity toward all. God's holiness is not capable of being received all at once by us, but the capacity to grow more fully into it is conferred upon us. This is part of our journey into God. In rituals of worship we proclaim, celebrate, and even anticipate the world of God's kingdom and our participation in it.

The biblical God is a transcendent being whom we are unable to understand fully, yet God is also immanent, making Godself present to us so that we do have some understanding of God. As we have mentioned, the Bible refers to God's immanence or presence as God's glory. God's transcendence and immanence are like two sides of a coin. The side that is present to us is the immanence of God as God manifests Godself to us. But the other side of the coin is always hidden from us, since God's infinite nature is forever beyond our comprehension or grasp. What God is in God's transcendent nature does not contradict or detract from what God shows God's self to be in God's manifestations. Rather, the mystery of God heightens the manifestations by drawing our minds and spirits from anthropomorphism toward the infinity of God. The story of God's manifestation through a burning bush to Moses is a lovely example of the simultaneous immanence and transcendence of God. God manifests God's self in a burning bush and speaks to Moses, but Moses is unable to go nearer to God than that. Even when God reveals God's name, "I AM WHO I AM," God's full nature is not understood: it remains hidden in God's glory. This ought to make us quite uncomfortable with the inadequacy of any piety that lacks a proper sense of reverence and that exhibits overfamiliarity with God, as is the case in quite a bit of American religion.

In this and the next chapter, I will continue to discuss the ancient Jewish belief that God is holy, utterly transcendent, not part of this world, a reality that depends on nothing else for its being, and the source of all that is or can be. This understanding of God by the ancient Israelites is in marked distinction to that of their neighbors. Scholars of Israelite religion, such as Yehezkel Kaufmann and Michael Fishbane, have been struck by the Bible's break with what they call the prevalent Near Eastern "mythical consciousness."[8]

The Deity of the Hebrew Bible is not part of a pantheon (one among several gods) and is not described as having any sexual relations with any consort, nor does he impregnate animals as does Baal. He is not a dying-and-rising god like the Canaanite Baal or Egyptian Osiris. As Theodore J. Lewis puts it, "This new paradigm was characterized by a 'creator-creature distinction' in which an autonomous God is portrayed as distinct from the created world. . . . God is not dependent on any outside power."[9] This understanding of God led Pascal to write, "Any religion which does not say that God is hidden is not true, and any religion which does not explain why does not instruct."[10]

Since the Enlightenment of the seventeenth century, the notion of mystery has been considered invalid. Whatever is presently not known is something that we can seek to understand, because nothing is incomprehensible to the human mind and its methods of investigation, in Enlightenment's view. This attitude to the *natural* world was actually encouraged by Christian doctrine, since nature is a creature and, unlike God, is comprehensible. (If nature should finally be beyond our full understanding, this is because of the limits of the human intellect, not because nature itself is inherently a mystery.) Among those who rejected mystery in religion as well as in nature, some developed a new religion based on reason and nature alone, often called natural religion or deism, which rejected miracles, the divinity of Christ, and the Trinity. With a religion of reason, neither faith nor the Bible are needed. However splendid the results in science proceeding from this new attitude toward nature, it cannot deal adequately with the biblical God. Unfortunately, some theologians and clergy also reject mystery, in theory or in practice; in their attempts to meet what they consider to be rational standards, they reduce Christianity to what they think is suitable for a modern mind.

A quite different attitude is needed to approach and try to understand God. The hidden God is not available to our unaided intellect. God must make Godself available to us. Not only an attitude of moral repentance is needed to approach God; as Michael Foster put it in his masterful book *Mystery and Philosophy,* we need a kind of *intellectual* repentance as well.[11] Not only do we have moral failings, but we are also prone to believe that we can approach God without any intellectual preparation whatsoever. Yet our hearts and minds need considerable transformation or renewal not once but each time we seek to deal with God. Consider the reflections of Anselm (d. 1109), one of the greatest intellects and theologians of all time, as he begins his intellectual inquiry into the nature of God in the first chapter of his *Proslogion*:

> Come now, little man,
> turn aside for a while from your daily employment,
> escape for a moment from the tumult of your thoughts,
> Put aside your weighty cares,
> let your burdensome distractions wait,
> free yourself a while for God
> and rest awhile in him.
> Enter the inner chamber of your soul,
> shut out everything except God
> and that which can help you in seeking him,
> and when you have shut the door, seek him.
> Now, my whole heart, say to God,
> "I seek your face,
> Lord, it is your face I seek."[12]

Anselm believed that to increase our knowledge of God through intellectual inquiry, we must on *each occasion* of inquiry begin by seeking to free ourselves from all distractions so that we may desire God with our whole heart. Rather than having our mind and heart filled with a multitude of desires, pulling us in different directions, we must focus on God, whom we do not see, but whom we hope to come to know better by increasing our understanding of God. The mind is to be aroused from its torpor "to the contemplation of God" (chap. 1) by being reminded that God is not a member of the created order, but dwells "in light inaccessible" (chap. 1). Accordingly, Anselm confesses, "I cannot seek you unless you show me how, and I will never find you unless you show yourself to me" (chap. 1). These remarks—as well as lamentations over the effects of our disobedience, which hinders our search, and expressions of a fervent hope based on our redemption by Christ—fill about nine times as much space as the above-quoted passage. Anselm concludes this meditation with the remark that in our intellectual inquiry we are not to expect fully to understand God. "I am not trying to make my way to your height, for my understanding is in no way equal to that, but I do desire to understand a little of your truth which my heart already believes and loves" (chap. 1).

This heartfelt meditation occurs *before* Anselm's reflection on the nature of God's existence. In his reflections, Anselm comes to understand a fundamental truth with his intellect, not just to believe: God's existence is not like the existence of everything else that does or might exist. God's existence is a "necessary existence." The things that are, do in fact exist, but they might not have existed and might cease to exist. This is not true of God. God is, and it is not possible that God might not have existed, or that God might cease to exist. This understanding of God as a necessary being is now widely accepted in the philosophy of religion, even by those who reject Anselm's "ontological argument" for God's existence, part of which is his view of God as a necessary being.

The ontological argument is treated by philosophers as one of the so-called traditional proofs of God's existence. I have not treated it as a proof of God's existence, but as a proof that God's being is necessary rather than contingent. This is an increase in our understanding of God's nature. Until about 1960, most philosophers followed Hume's criticism that no being could be a necessary being, because it is a self-contradictory notion. Logical necessity belongs to statements (or more technically, propositions), not to beings. But in recent years philosophers of religion have come to agree that Hume's criticism is misguided. It does not apply to Anselm because Anselm uses a different sense of "necessary" than "logically necessary." The distinction is subtle and so easily overlooked, but the distinction is clear.

Anselm's achievement is that he has found an intellectually precise way to distinguish God from the universe, and he thereby can help prevent us from confusing God with what is not God, such as happened with the gods in ancient paganism. With this understanding, Anselm has drawn closer to God, whom he has been seeking. His theological reasoning is an excellent example of what Augustine means by theological inquiry:[13] Anselm calls it "faith seeking understanding." Anselm already believes in God because of his free response of faith to God's self-giving *before* he begins his inquiry, and he must prepare himself to approach inquiry into God, both morally or spiritually, and intellectually. Only so can he, by use of his reason, hope to increase his understanding of what he believes by faith.

God is hidden from the senses and is above the level of the mind's ability *fully* to comprehend, so both spiritual and intellectual repentance are required to approach God, who is holy above all. Atheists and philosophers quite commonly regard God simply as omnipotent, omniscient, and all-good. Such a limited conception of deity is widely called "theism," and it is claimed that theism gives us the essential character of God as found in Judaism, Christianity, and Islam. But such a characterization fails to realize the critical characterization that God is holy, and that God's holiness is an *integral* part of understanding what God's power, wisdom, and goodness themselves are. Without holiness, we do not properly characterize any of God's other properties or actions.

Holiness is not even mentioned in atheists' and philosophers' examination of the grounds for biblical religion, which they assume is simply the same as the grounds for theism: the so-called traditional proofs of God's existence. Yet, the central part of the Jewish temple in ancient Israel was called the Holy of Holies. It was where God was said to be especially present. Significantly, the Holy of Holies was empty of any representation of God. Unlike all the nations that surrounded ancient Israel, and the non-Jews within the nation of Israel, who had many pictures and statues of their gods, the ancient Jews realized that the only, best, and proper representation of God was no representation, for as the Holy One of Israel, God transcended all creatures: nothing in heaven and earth can be used to represent God. Rather than God, any representation would be an idol. "Imageless worship of the Lord made Israel's faith unique in the ancient world."[14] The second of the Ten Commandments explicitly prohibits any representation of God—"You shall not make for yourself an idol, whether in the form of anything that is in heaven above, or that is on the earth beneath, or that is in the water under the earth" (Exod. 20:4)—precisely because any representation of God *in himself* is impossible. This prohibition is modified in Christianity, in which icons of Christ are used because of the incarnation of the Son of God, whereby the Holy One "became matter for my sake, and accepted to dwell in matter, and through matter worked my salvation."[15] The final justification is that the icon depicts the person rather than the nature of Christ. Even so, the transcendence of God is so strongly held in Christianity that several times in Christian history, there have been strong rejections and even the destruction of pictures, statues, stained-glass windows, and the like. The most violent ones have been the iconoclasm (breaking of religious images) imposed by imperial edict in the Eastern Church in the eighth and ninth centuries, leaving few existing icons from before that date, and the popular iconoclasm of the Puritans in Britain during the sixteenth-century Reformation.

The absence of any representations in the temple indicates simultaneously both God's transcendence—a being utterly apart from all creatures—and also his holy presence. Often his presence is described as his glory. So while holiness expresses God's transcendence, his glory concerns his immanence or presence to the world. Thus when we say we are doing something for God's glory, we mean we are doing something with the hope that it may make God present in a situation or place. Given the prevalence in the cultures around Israel of polytheism, religions saturated with imitating sexual reproductions, and birth and decay in nature, it is no wonder that Israel was so fiercely protective of its monotheism and utterly opposed to idols. To equate the biblical God with any ancient mythological religion, such as God with Zeus, as has been done by some prominent atheists, goes against all the scholarly evidence.

No wonder the man with whose letter we began was troubled about answering the question "Do I believe in God?" Since God in Godself is not accessible to the senses, he rightly approached the question of God's existence by considering the attributes of power (omnipotence), knowledge (omniscience), and goodness. These, he found, did not pass the test of the Holocaust nor the death of a child. He was, nonetheless, on the right track in not trying to picture God, but to start with things we say about God, such as God's power, knowledge, and goodness.

For in spite of God's incomprehensible nature, we can know some things *about* God, because God makes Godself known or reveals Godself *in what God does.* That is why I did not start, as did our letter writer, with the abstractions of God's power (omnipotence), knowledge (omniscience), or goodness, but with God in action, with God's revelation of Godself as holy. And as we will see more fully, God's holiness, or transcendence, crucially modifies our understanding of God's power, knowledge, and goodness.

"Holiness" may not seem to be an attractive notion to some people because of the negative associations the word has for them, such as in the expression "holier than thou." They may have the notion that holiness is to strive grimly and joyously to be perfect in moral behavior.

So let me first give an example of what holiness means in our lives. Once in a public lecture I said that in our lives holiness meant to be free of the burden of evil, and full of godly love toward others. I pointed out that one way we deal with the evil we do is to point to others and say, "I am not nearly as bad as so-and-so." We act as though a great chasm separates us from such a person. Yet we actually differ from others only in a matter of degree. We are both on the wrong side of a chasm that separates a life with injustices committed against others and a life free of such evils. For example, when we have trouble getting our way, the means we use can be as simple and apparently as innocent as a charming smile, or it can be as unpleasant as pressing a contract to the letter of the law, or to telling a lie, until at the bottom of the scale we have the use of violence. A charming smile is not the same as a violent blow, but they are not separated by a gulf or chasm. These two acts, and all that lies between them, are connected, however distantly, by the fact each operates on the principle of getting what is desired—getting it unjustly.

All injustice, however mild its appearance, is connected to a frightful king-dom. An extreme instance of injustice helps us see clearly the chasm that sepa-rates justice from injustice and, more important, to see that we have a decision to make regarding the way we shall seek to have our desires met. That is all that we need to see in order to decide where to place our allegiance—with that frightful kingdom, or with another. To seek to live justly leads to an increasing awareness, no matter how incomplete, of what holiness is. This awareness is the first step toward participation in that holiness. Soon after that lecture I received a letter from Joel Mattison, a well-known surgeon in Tampa, Florida:

> Your crystallization of holiness (a word which I seldom use and which I now consider as a vacuum in my vocabulary) as freedom from evil has meaning to me both theologically and now medically.
>
> When I served as surgeon at the Florida State Prison, I found that there were basically two kinds of "convicts" there: the thieves and the murder-ers. Each group was inordinately proud not to be like the other. It was best summarized by the man who would say, "I may have killed a man or two, but I ain't no thief, and I wouldn't lie to you." The next, in turn would proudly admit, "I may steal, but I ain't never killed nobody." Both of them, incidentally, looked down on the sex offenders and especially the

child molesters. I find myself doing the same thing, imaging that my own collection of the manifestations of sin are somehow more easily excusable than those of someone else.

Holiness looks neither so strange nor unattractive when seen as giving liberation from bondage to one's egocentricity, self-righteousness, and above all, superiority to others, rather than as one who shares with all others the need from mercy, forgiveness, and restoration to life in God's kingdom.

Chapter 2

Holiness for Today

The second biblical example of the experience of holiness that I want to examine is that of the eighth-century prophet Isaiah. I selected the passage of Moses' call because it concerns the foundation of the Jewish people as a nation. Isaiah represents the height of the prophetic period, and indeed the height of Israel's understanding of God. With Isaiah we have the various features of God's nature revealed in Moses' encounter with God reinforced, but also some new features. The experience of God's transcendent power and presence in glory is even more overwhelming in Isaiah's encounter. Initially, it fills Isaiah with despair. Yet he comes to see that God's display of power finds its focus in a concern for people who are oppressed and treated unjustly, and God's purity shows itself in mercy. What power and purity signify are far richer in meaning when described in the setting of a biblical story, in contrast to being abstracted from their roots into philosophical concepts such as omnipotence and omniscience. Concern for the oppressed and for mercy certainly do not spring to mind from the notions of sheer power and knowledge.

Here is the account of Isaiah's vision:

> In the year that King Uzziah died, I saw the Lord sitting on a throne, high and lofty; and the hem of his robe filled the temple. Seraphs were in attendance above him; each had six wings: with two they covered their faces, and with two they covered their feet [nakedness], and with two they flew. And one called to another and said:
>
> "Holy, holy, holy is the Lord of hosts;
>   the whole earth is full of his glory."
>
> The pivots [meaning of the Hebrew is uncertain] on the threshold shook at the voices of those who called, and the house filled with smoke. And I said: "Woe is me! I am lost, for I am a man of unclean lips, and I live among a people of unclean lips; yet my eyes have seen the King, the Lord of hosts!"
>   Then one of the seraphs flew to me, holding a live coal that had been taken from the altar with a pair of tongs. The seraph touched my mouth with it and said: "Now that this has touched your lips, your guilt has departed and your sin is blotted out." Then I heard the voice of the Lord saying, "Whom shall I send, and who will go for us?" And I said, "Here am I; send me!" And he said, "Go and say to the people: . . ." (Isa. 6:1–9a)

This vision occurred about 742 BC, some 500 years after the call of Moses, and some 250 years after Israel's greatest age under King David. The Jews were bitterly divided into two kingdoms: Israel and Judah (the northern and southern kingdoms) each with their own monarchical dynasties, sometimes at war with each other and sometimes united against a common enemy. Throughout their histories, both are in greater or lesser danger from foreign nations; ultimately, both nations fail to heed the prophetic message of God to repent of unrighteousness. Isaiah is in the temple, taking part in a worship service as an official prophet. He is looking from the sanctuary that was ringing with music and filled with the swirling smoke of incense, and toward the innermost chamber of the Holy of Holies, where the Lord is especially present, when the vision of God occurs. He sees the reality symbolized by the ritual. Superimposed onto an annual reenactment of the king's enthronement was Isaiah's momentary vision of the throne of God, the true throne, rather than the one occupied by his earthly representative, the king of Israel. In and through the earthly music and singing, Isaiah hears the seraphs cry, "Holy, holy, holy is the Lord of hosts; / the whole earth is full of his glory." Once again we see that holiness is the essential quality of the Deity, and his glory or splendor is his manifestation in the world. In this instance, Yahweh manifests himself as the God of the whole earth. Yahweh is far more than merely the God of the Hebrew people. In the next chapter we will have more to say about the realization that the God who called the people of Israel to be a holy people is the universal God, whether recognized as such by all nations or not. Here we will focus on the significance of God's holiness for the nature of justice.

Isaiah's initial reaction to the holy presence of God is similar to that of Moses, except that Isaiah's awareness of uncleanness before God, which is expressed by

Moses in awe and fear, is made explicit. Isaiah has intruded into the holiest of all sanctuaries and immediately realizes that mortals have no place there.

> Ethical "holiness" marked the most significant distinction between God and man [people]. . . . However well he might have purified himself according to cultic requirements, however well he might have kept the customary rules of morality, in the presence of holiness exalted in righteousness he and all men [people] were unclean.[1]

> His human lips are not fit to join in the ritual song. He realizes that he and all his people. . . . are debarred from the highest worship by the moral uncleanness of their nature (cf. vs. 7); the gulf between God and man [humans], between the holy and unclean, is created by an ultimate distinction between supreme ethical holiness and the corruption of human nature.[2]

> But with this recognition of creatureliness and unworthiness there also came a cleansing by a sovereign act of grace, and a commission to obey and a judgment upon the inevitable disobedience of those who were satisfied to be "unclean."[3]

Although it is not possible to perceive God by the senses, God does make Godself available in visions (Ezek. 1:26–27; Dan. 7:9; 2 Chr. 18:18). In Isaiah's vision "it is only a glimpse, a sudden overpowering realization that he is in the presence of Majesty on high; the throne, the royal robe, and the attendant beings are described, but not the appearance of the One upon the throne."[4] The focus of the action is on an overwhelming sense of moral uncleanness before God that is answered by a gracious cleansing made possible by Isaiah's awareness of the nature of God's holiness, followed by a new capacity to hear God's word, "an immediate spontaneous response of willing obedience,"[5] and a commission to speak God's word to the Israelite nation. *Holiness* shows itself in the *gracious cleansing* of Isaiah, and in a call to give relief to the poor, the widows, orphans, and more generally for justice in government, commerce, and social relations.

Not only is holiness to be understood in terms of this graciousness and righteousness, but also as the nature of God's power, wisdom, and goodness. "If God inspires fear, it is on account of his power and purity; if God attracts, it is by his creating love and redeeming grace. More precisely, God's power shows itself as love for the creature; God's purity shows itself as grace to transform the sinner."[6]

The oppression that God sought to relieve in Moses' time was the oppression of the Hebrew people by the Egyptians. Here in Isaiah it is the oppression of those Jews who are unable to defend themselves from fellow Jews. God so cares for the poor, the widows, and the orphans, as well as the conduct of government, commerce, and social relations, that he will destroy both kingdoms, unless they listen to the prophets and repent. It is in such terms that righteousness or justice is understood in contrast to the ancient Greeks, whose conceptions of justice, even in the most exalted form as found in Plato, fail even to notice the distress of the helpless in a society in which 90 percent of people were slaves. This understanding of righteousness or justice and the severity of the threatened consequences of failure (consequences that were in fact eventually carried out) marks off the prophets not only from their Middle Eastern neighbors, but also from the ancient Greeks and Romans.

In his teachings Jesus adds new dimensions to God's justice that mark it off from present-day Western democracy and Marxism. In Western democracy every person has inalienable rights to life, liberty, and property. No government is supposed to violate these rights or take them away from us unjustly. Every person has equality before the law. As far as this goes, it is in accord with Jesus' teachings and indeed has its ultimate source in his teachings. In economic terms, however, there is a difference. If you work and are paid for your work what supply and demand establish, your rights are not violated. No injustice has been committed.

Marx criticized Western democracy's view of justice because it exploits the worker. He claimed that the worker alone is the producer of wealth, yet the worker receives only a wage—a part of the wealth. The rest of the wealth is taken as profit by the owners of the means of production. The worker is thus exploited because the workers' right to the entire product of their labor is violated.

Western democracy's and Marx's theories have different views of what human rights are; yet in both systems, people have value in terms of what they produce. The theory of modern democracy allows the marketplace to determine the value of a person's labor; the Marxist value labor differently.[7] But neither political or economic theory shows that people themselves have an absolute or irreplaceable value. Their value is relative to their work; their value is relative to each other. Not only is the absolute or irreplaceable value of people—which, as pointed out in the introduction, is the Christian understanding—not even broached by these theories; these two theories also do not even consider the depth of harm and injury that can be done to a person. For this we must consider Jesus' teaching about love of neighbor.

When a lawyer, seeking to trip Jesus up, asks him, "Teacher, what must I do to inherit eternal life?" Jesus asks him in return what is written in the law. The lawyer replies, "You shall love the Lord your God with all your heart, and with all your soul, and with all your strength, and with all your mind; and your neighbor as yourself." Jesus gives his approval: "You have given the right answer; do this, and you will live." The lawyer, wanting to justify himself (to show himself to be righteous or acceptable to God by defining limits to who is a neighbor), asks Jesus, "And who is my neighbor?" For an answer Jesus tells the story of the Good Samaritan (Luke 10:25–37), which expands the Jewish restricted view of neighbor as fellow Jew and perhaps resident aliens to include anyone who is in deep distress.

In the parable Jesus has a priest, who represents the highest religious leadership among the Jews, and a Levite, the lay-associate of the priests, pass by a stricken man. (They may think the man is dead. To touch a dead body would incur ritual defilement. If so, we have an indirect criticism of such practices, since Jesus is not afraid to break ritual taboos in order to help persons in physical distress or outcasts.) Outrageously, Jesus says that a Samaritan, a hated foreigner, who is not expected to show sympathy to Jews, assists the stricken man. The Samaritan not only binds up his wounds but also takes him to an inn, pays for his care, and promises to reimburse the innkeeper on his next journey if the expense for his care is greater than expected. To drive home his teaching, Jesus then asks the lawyer, "Which of these three, do you think, was a neighbor to the man who fell among robbers?" He thus forces the lawyer to admit that it is the despised Samaritan. For Jesus, love of neighbor extends beyond our human barriers and boundaries to include anyone in distress. He teaches that to act as the Good Samaritan has acted is to act as a neighbor, and that this is the way to eternal life.

Simone Weil (1909–1943), the philosopher and mystic, brings out an often-neglected dimension of the parable. She asks whether the priest or Levite who pass by a man who has been robbed and left as a naked and battered piece of flesh has violated the injured man's rights. Could anyone have taken them to court for not helping? Could they be said to have acted unjustly? A theory of inalienable rights, which a government must protect, would not convict the priest or Levite of injustice. Yet Jesus once made the basis of the separation of the sheep and goats (the righteous and unrighteous at the last judgment) those who gave drink to the thirsty, fed the hungry, clothed the naked, and visited prisoners—and those who did not do so (Matt. 25:31–46). The "sheep" are not called merciful, but righteous or just. According to Jesus, they have performed acts of justice.

In the New Testament the Greek word *dikaios* is translated as "just" or "righteous." We are usually lulled to sleep with the usual English translation of the Greek word as "righteous" and would probably be surprised if it were translated as "just," since then we would realize that the Good Samaritan is portrayed by Jesus as having performed a just act. This story and the story of the sheep and the goats reflect a different view of justice from that of modern democracy. The New Testament view of justice is not limited to the protection of rights. Its view of justice is deeper because it has a deeper view of what people are and what is owing to them in distress. This is why we who live in democracies find it strange to consider the act of the Good Samaritan and the acts of the "sheep" in the parable of the Sheep and Goats as acts of justice. To those who think in terms of democratic societies, it is an act of mercy, not justice. Can sense be made of Jesus' teaching?

The man who is beaten and robbed no longer has any possessions to cause anyone to take notice of him. He has no clothes to indicate his social position; if he were a person of distinction, perhaps notice would be taken of him. Since his *relative* value cannot be estimated, what claim does he have to consideration? If his claim were based on rights, if rights were the bottom line, then he has no claim. What applies to him applies to all of us. Any of us can be left without family, money, friends. This happens in our day to many people who have become refugees or victims of natural disasters. What basis do such people have for making a claim on anyone? All such people can do is to beg, beg for mercy. People may listen, or they may turn away. But if rights are the final and ultimate ground for a claim to consideration by others, no injustice has been committed even if they are not helped.

Weil argues that people in distress do have a claim on others because we all have absolute value. Since we have absolute value, we have reason to cry out in adversity: Why? Why must we bear lives of great deprivation? It is unjust not to answer such a cry. It is unjust to allow what is of absolute value to be wretched, mangled, twisted, neglected, unnoticed, unwanted, resented, hated. To believe that we are *obliged* to respond to those who are in distress, as many Western governments and individuals often do, indicates that Christ's teachings have in practice superseded our secular theory of justice. That there is such a strong and widespread sense of obligation to help people in distress in Western society, and even in the United Nations, is the effect of Jesus' teaching of the absolute value of people.

But what gives us absolute value? Nothing earthly can do so. In every way we are unequal: in ability, good fortune, health, and the like. We have only relative value, limited value, conditional value. Our value is determined by our standing compared to other people. Weil claims that only what is utterly and wholly good of itself, utterly and wholly pure of itself, utterly and wholly free of corruption of itself—only that has absolute value. Only such a being can give us irreplaceable value by loving us, as we saw in the introduction, and absolute value by having made us to receive absolute good. Apart from the good that is God, we have no absolute value, and we must keep our eyes closed to what is around us and before us: a physical universe that is utterly indifferent to us and a great, deep, empty abyss toward which we are headed.

The absolute value of every human being adds an important ingredient to the question about the death of a lovely seven-year-old child, the question raised in the letter I received from the man wrestling with the question of whether he believed in God. We do not know why the child died so young, and we automatically react to innocent suffering with grief and even anger. We feel that it is outrageous that an innocent child should die. If we reflect on these automatic feelings, we may realize that we feel as we do apart from any teachings about God, including that God is omnipotent, omniscient, and all-good. Those qualities of God are used to construct the philosophic "problem of evil," but they are not the immediate source of our grief, anger, and sense of outrage. I think these feelings must spring from an unspoken and even unconscious sense that the child has absolute value and has been violated by dying so young. Such an automatic reaction is somewhat on the same order as the compassion we feel in just hearing the story of a man left beaten on the side of the road by robbers. Any walk down a hospital corridor can stir us deeply and after a while make us feel rather numb. In loss and tragedy, in the sorrow, anger, and outrage we feel, we seem to have an awareness, whether articulated or not, of the absolute value of people. If we had no sense of the child's absolute value, and no hint whatsoever of it, would we be particularly troubled about the reality of an all-powerful, all-knowing, all-good God? Those three abstract characteristics of all-power, all-knowledge, all-good are not sufficient to account for the depth of the shock that her death, and other human suffering, causes us. But a sense, implicit or explicit, of people's absolute value does account for why we are so shocked and troubled. As we have pointed out, our absolute value seems to rest on the love of God. How she, and others like her, will receive the absolute good is based on our faith in Christ's promise that with his return in glory, the dead shall be raised, and those who have followed his ways (whether, as we have seen in Matt. 25:31–46, realizing it or not, and including certainly innocent children) will be with him in glory.

The cry of the human heart—which makes sense only if we are being violated or when we witness violation as in the case of this child—is met with silence when we look to anything earthly. Only those who recognize in their own hearts the harm we can suffer, the anguish of what it is to be a frail and vulnerable human being, paradoxically actually experience in their anguish the reality of God's gift of absolute value by its very absence. Since the absolute value that God confers has no earthly source, it cannot be destroyed by anything that happens to us. This is explicitly stated by Jesus when he contrasts the attempt to accumulate earthly goods and heavenly treasure.

> Do not store up for yourselves treasures on earth, where moth and rust consume and where thieves break in and steal; but store up for yourselves treasures in heaven, where neither moth nor rust consumes and where thieves do not break in and steal. For where your treasure is, there your heart will be also. (Matt. 6:19–21)

It is also evident to a significant degree in the story of the Good Samaritan. The stricken man's relative value is rather well taken away, but he retains absolute value, as the action of the Good Samaritan shows. He sees that it is unjust to allow such great distress to be unanswered. He recognizes that it is an outrage to allow such brokenness to lie unnoticed and unattended. In the face of death, we are helpless to act. All we can do is feel the numbness and bafflement of the destruction of one who has absolute value. But in that experience also we are implicitly aware of the absolute value God can give.

Jean Vanier, founder of the L'Arche movement, which now has over 120 residences for the intimate, personal care of the severely disabled, found that the care of such people leads to a sense of community and a profound joy. "Paths taken by the ordinary able-bodied person . . . are not open to the severely disabled. In order for them to live, to be fulfilled, they need relationships," Vanier says. "They need communion more than generosity." This is a distinction he is fond of making: generosity, while worthy, is when someone superior gives to someone inferior; communion involves conversion and vulnerability. The particular gift of the disabled, Vanier has learned, is to "lead us into communion." This is the conversion being experienced by the Good Samaritan, who is first moved by generosity, then by compassion, then by amazement and joy. "Something must have happened," says Vanier, "when the man woke up and saw he had been saved by an enemy, and says, 'You're my brother!'"[8]

Why do people who care for the helpless and near helpless feel or experience such positive gifts? According to Matthew (25:31–46), Jesus identifies himself with the afflicted. To care for them as human beings is to care not only for them but also to be in contact with them, and unexpectedly to benefit from that communion.

The demand for a more just distribution of the goods of this world, and the call for recognition of the absolute value of human beings—these are not identical. Their difference and their connection can be illustrated by the early twentieth-century struggle of the labor movement in Britain. Ernest Bevin, who led the dockworkers' union in Britain in the 1920s and 1930s, stressed that the most important goal of the labor movement was for the workers to gain a sense of human dignity and to stop feeling like second-class citizens. Better working conditions and better wages were both ends and means to this more elevated end. In the 1930s a Parliamentary Commission was appointed to hear the case of the dockworkers. The management was represented by an eminent King's Counsel. Even though Bevin had little formal education and no legal or economic training, the dockers chose him to argue their case. Bevin mastered the immensely complicated economic and legal facts relevant to the inquiry in a short time and presented their case magnificently. He became known as the "Dockers' K.C." It became a point of pride among the dockers that one of their own was able to make their case. Weil would have recognized this as a manifestation of the absolute good in human lives.

According to Weil, Marx's theory of oppression does not show a full awareness of the real nature of oppression. This is because the harm people suffer is not finally expressible in economic terms. In far too many situations, it is the experience of work itself that oppresses. She bases this claim in large part on her firsthand experience of factory work in the 1930s. In a quite different setting, the same noneconomic oppression is powerfully portrayed by Arthur Miller in his play *The Death of a Salesman,* in which we see how humiliating it can be to be a salesperson.[9] Also in management, humiliation must usually be endured to move up or stay in place, and dismissal can mean utter collapse. A theory of oppression that is only or primarily economic does not allow the depths of oppression to be articulated and thereby actually leads to perpetuating and even increasing human oppression.

Weil believed that Jesus' attitudes, teachings, and actions can open our eyes to the depths of harm that human beings often endure, harm that cannot be articulated without an understanding of the absolute value of human beings. For example, consider the emphasis on lepers in the Gospels. Lepers were socially uprooted from the fabric of society. They were forced to live outside of towns and villages and to call out "Unclean!" as a warning to anyone who approached them, to avoid others' infection and also ritual defilement. So it is not an accident that the Gospels frequently mention and even emphasize that Jesus heals lepers—people especially socially uprooted and suffering the immense harm of such an existence—and that he restores them to the social fabric. Nor is it an accident that his great follower, Francis of Assisi, kissed the sores of lepers. By that quite disgusting act, Francis restored to the outcast the status of personhood. Francis affirmed the absolute value of those whose social value was less than nothing: They were a social nuisance. Would we even be aware of the nature and extent of the suffering that leprosy caused to people in the ancient world (and in some places today) if it were not for Jesus' actions and his teachings about the love of God?

These are but a few concrete examples of what it means to claim that human beings are significant, have dignity, and have absolute value. We can say that human beings are sacred, set apart by God to be recipients of Godself. Indeed, they illustrate that people are of indefeasible value: they have an absolute worth that cannot be annulled or undone by whatever happens to them, even death. They also illustrate that even though God cannot be perceived with our senses, and in his essence is above the power of our reason to grasp, nonetheless God in his holy, saving righteousness is accessible to us.

Chapter 3

The Maker of Heaven and Earth

"In the beginning God created the heavens and the earth" (Gen. 1:1 RSV). This is the traditional translation, following the Greek version prepared by Jewish scholars in the third century BC, translating the original Hebrew text. The English (and Greek) versions treat this verse as a thematic sentence for all that follows, forming a title for the first chapter. This is linguistically defensible, and to me it has the added authority of being the translation favored by the ancient Jews in translating a Hebrew verse into their Greek version of the Old Testament, for use by Jews who had lost the ability to read Hebrew.

In Hebrew, it could also read, "When God began to create, the earth was a formless void and darkness covered the face of the deep"; or, "In the beginning when God created, the earth was a formless void . . ." (cf. NJPS). These two renderings imply that there was a formless earth and a chaos of water *already* existing when God began to create. But the traditional translation, "In the beginning God created the heavens and the earth," says that there is nothing already existing. God's initial creation of the earth was as "a formless void and darkness covered the face of the deep" (Gen. 1:2a), and God proceeds to order the formless void and watery chaos into a habitation for the living creatures, which he creates

Creation out of nothing

afterward (Gen. 1:3–25). It culminates with the creation of human beings as the crown of creation (Gen. 1:26–27).

Regardless of the ambiguity of the first verse in the Hebrew language, centuries before the verse was written, the Jewish people had the firm belief that God was absolutely sovereign. This is clearly expressed in verses 3–5, in which by God's effortless speech, light and darkness come into existence: "Then God said, 'Let there be light'; and there was light. And God saw that the light was good; and God separated the light from the darkness. God called the light Day, and the darkness he called Night. And there was evening and there was morning, the first day." These verses anticipate the formula later used in 2 Maccabees 7:28 to express the uniqueness of the Jewish doctrine of creation: creation out of nothing, ex nihilo. So even though there are several *linguistically* permissible translations of the first verse of Genesis (and it is translated in various ways in different English versions of the Bible), since the Jewish conviction is that God depends on nothing to be and that nothing can exist or endure independently of God, we will use the translation, "In the beginning God created the heavens and the earth," because it expresses the Jewish belief about the nature of creation in the rest of the Bible. We will shortly see how radically distinctive that conviction is.

Although this is the first verse of the Bible in its final edited form, it is not the first verse that was written. It was written sometime in the sixth century before Christ, when the Jews were in captivity in Babylon; that was some seven hundred years after their successful escape from captivity in Egypt. No doubt the conviction that their God was the creator of all that exists gave great encouragement to the Jewish people in Babylon, who had survived the destruction of their temple and their nation. The creation story of Genesis 1 is in the form of a hymn or poem used in worship services. It reminded them, as did earlier psalms, that their God was not only their God, a mere tribal god like the gods of other peoples, but also the absolute sovereign creator and ruler of all that exists. "The earth is the LORD's and all that is in it, / the world, and those who live in it" (Ps. 24:1). Their God, the Holy One of Israel, is the *primary* reality, from which the heavens and earth and all that is in them depend for their reality.

> By the word of the LORD the heavens were made,
>   and all their host by the breath of his mouth.
> He gathered the waters of the sea as in a bottle;
>   he put the deeps in storehouses.
>
> Let all the earth fear the LORD;
>   let all the inhabitants of the world stand in awe of him.
>   (Ps. 33:6–8a).

Not only is the present first verse of the Bible not the first verse that was written, but even the theme it announces for the opening three chapters of Genesis—that creation theme comes later in Israel's faith. The Jewish people believed in God *before* they realized that he was the creator of heaven and earth.

This sequence, belief in God before belief in God as creator, undermines an important part of the ground that has been used in modern times to reject belief in God in the name of reason. Among eighteenth-century deists, atheists, and in present-day philosophy of religion, it is widely held that the only possible rational basis for belief in God would be by arguments that the existence and order of the world prove the existence of God. If such proofs are not possible, then belief in God is dismissed as irrational. This is often done without examining any other reasons people may have for belief in God. Belief in God is treated as a blind faith, based solely on emotions. But as we have just pointed out, the ancient Jews had a belief in God before they believed that he created the world. So the notion that belief in God mistakenly arose from an invalid inference from the existence and order of the universe to God's existence is historically wrong. Among the ancient Jews, the earliest and most widely used confession about God is that he brought Israel out of bondage in Egypt. Their initial belief in God is based on a saving act in their *history,* in contrast to the *cosmic* event of creation. Among the earliest and most important confessional statements about God's acts in saving Israel is Deuteronomy 26:5–9:

> A wandering Aramean was my ancestor; he went down into Egypt and lived there as an alien, few in number, and there he became a great nation, mighty and populous. When the Egyptians treated us harshly and afflicted us, by imposing hard labor on us, we cried to the LORD, the God of our ancestors; the LORD heard our voice and saw our affliction, our toil, and our oppression. The LORD brought us our of Egypt with a mighty hand and an outstretched arm, with a terrifying display of power, and with signs and wonders; and he brought us into this place and gave us this land, a land flowing with milk and honey.

In his monumental work *Old Testament Theology,* Gerhard von Rad calls this a Credo: a creed that states Israel's faith.[1] This particular span of history was regarded as the time of saving history par excellence. It is what made the Hebrews a people, and they used this creedal statement to celebrate the fulfillment of the promise given to Abraham in Genesis 12:1–3 that they would be given a land of their own.

The ancient Jews were not initially monotheist, in the sense that there is only one God. Yahweh was indeed *their* God, but they also recognized the reality of the gods worshiped by the original inhabitants of the land they had conquered, as well as the reality of the gods of the surrounding peoples—what is called "henotheism." Sometimes the ancient Jews worshiped these "foreign" deities alongside Yahweh, even though they were not supposed to do so. Only with the eighth-century prophets do we have an explicit monotheism that denies the reality of the gods of other nations. Jeremiah compares other deities to "cracked cisterns that can hold no water" (2:13), and Isaiah 45:5 bluntly declares, "I am the LORD [Yahweh], and there is no other; besides me there is no god." As we pointed out, the affirmation that Yahweh is creator of the world expressed the ancient Jews' realization that Yahweh was not just their own personal God, but the also absolute sovereign over all peoples, and even more strikingly that he was the primal reality from which the heavens and earth derived their existence. They expressed their convictions by adding the stories of Yahweh's *cosmic* action of creation as a preface to their earlier confessions of God's saving acts in their *history*. As creation logically and temporally precedes God's saving actions in history, the creation stories of Genesis 1 and 2 come before his actions in history. Or better yet, as we will see, God's creation is brought *within* history because history began with the creation of the universe.

Although we do not know the process by which Israel connected Yahweh, its savior and benefactor, with the creation of the world, von Rad indicates what was involved in bringing the two together:

> It is hard to imagine that, in the environment of Canaan, whose religious atmosphere was saturated with creation myths, it would not have occurred to Israel to connect creation—that is, heaven, earth, the stars, the sea, plants, and animals—with Yahweh. Probably the sole reason for the lateness of the emergence of the doctrine of creation was that it took Israel a fairly long time to bring older beliefs which she actually already possessed about it into proper theological relationship with the tradition which was her very own, that is, with what she believed about the saving acts done by Yahweh in history. In an old cultic creed [Deut. 26:5–9] there was nothing about Creation. And Israel only discovered the correct theological relationship between the two when she learned to see Creation too as connected theologically *with saving history*.[2]

This Jewish stress on salvation in history, what happens in time, as the substance of their religion is quite different from the kind of truth presented in myths. Myths are timeless truths and are not rooted in the events of history. This is what we find in the local Canaanite religion and in the other religions that surrounded the territory of ancient Israel. It is also different from the timeless cosmic principles, such as those the greatest of ancient Greek thinkers sought. Von Rad stresses that to bring the cosmic into relation with the historical was no light task:

> What had been opened up for her through Yahweh's revelation was the realm of history, and it was in light of this as starting-point that the term creation had first to be defined. Theologically it was a great achievement that Israel was actually able to make a connexion between Creation and the saving history—and not with a [timeless] present conceived in terms of myth.[3]

Von Rad illustrates the way that Yahwism, which had been *exclusively* a religion of salvation, was connected to creation in Isaiah:

> Thus says the LORD, your Redeemer,
>   who formed you in the womb:

> I am the LORD, who made all things,
>   who alone stretched out the heavens,
>   who by myself spread out the earth.
>   (Isa. 44:24)

Yahweh, who *created* Israel, also created the world. In Isaiah 51:9–10 the two creative acts are almost made to coincide:

> Was it not you who cut Rahab in pieces,
>   who pierced the dragon?
> Was it not you who dried up the sea,
>   the waters of the great deep;
> who made the depths of the sea a way
>   for the redeemed to cross over?

Von Rad observes:

> Hardly has he [Isaiah] spoken about the driving back of the waters, in the language of the mythical struggle with the dragon of Chaos [Rahab in the Canaanite myth], than he jumps to the miracle of the Red Sea where Yahweh again held the waters back "for the redeemed to pass through." Here creation and redemption . . . can almost be looked on as one act of dramatic divine saving in the picture of the struggle with the dragon of Chaos.[4]

After citing several other passages that connect Israel's saving history to God as creator, von Rad concludes:

> In the light of all this, it is extremely likely that this soteriological [salvation] understanding of Creation also lies at the basis of the creation stories in J [Gen. 2] and P [Gen. 1]. In neither of these documents of course is Yahweh's work in Creation considered for its own sake: instead it is incorporated within a course of history leading to the call of Abraham and ending with Israel's entry into Palestine. . . . The beginning of this divine history was now put back in time to Creation. But this pushing back of the beginning of the saving history was only possible because Creation itself was regarded as a *saving work* of Yahweh's.[5]

Earlier we saw that the Jewish people in exile in Babylon were encouraged by Isaiah to be hopeful because their God was not just their God, one among many, but also the ruler of heaven and earth, and so God was able to redeem them as he had redeemed their ancestors in Egypt. But von Rad points out that the encouragement is stronger than would come from the simple realization that Yahweh is creator and so he has ample power to save them. Rather, it is that his very act of creation itself was a saving act. "The reason why the allusion to Creation strengthens confidence is that Deutero-Isaiah obviously sees a saving event in the creation itself."[6]

The cosmology used and transformed in the first chapter of Genesis highlights the way the creation of the universe is not just a bare fact; it is also intimately connected to Yahweh's saving care of Israel, and indeed of all humanity. The creation story of Genesis 1 drastically revised the mythical idiom of the day in order to express Israel's mature belief in Yahweh's sovereignty. It retained the commonly held view in the Middle East that the earth is surrounded by waters held back by a solid dome or vault, called "Sky," that separates the waters that are above the dome from those below it, and which has the earth shaped liked a disc, mounted on pillars (Gen. 1:2, 6–8). We hear an echo of this commonly held understanding in Isaiah 51:9–10, the passage we just mentioned, which refers to the slain Rahab. This is an allusion to the Babylonian monster of chaos, which God destroyed by God's word in Genesis. The novel element here is that it is by God's word, a physically effortless action, that the inhabited world is made safe and kept safe from the surrounding waters of chaos. Only from time to time is water allowed beneficently to seep in from above in the form of rain and also from below as springs. (Only much later in the story of Noah, when human disobedience has become hopeless of redress, is the water allowed to flood the entire earth so that God is able to renew the human race from Noah's family.) So the creation of the universe is far more than an account of the origin of the universe as such.

The ancient Middle East's commonly held view of the basic structure of the universe and even the Babylonian views of nature gods, such as Rahab, are related to God's cosmic power and care by making God's creation a *preface* to the story of God's call of Abraham, the father of the Jewish people, and so to the story of the saving history of Israel. Ultimately, through God's blessing of Israel, God will be a benefactor of all humanity. The climax of the Genesis 1 creation story is the creation of human beings, male and female, in the divine image, in which they are given dominion over or care of all creatures (vv. 26–30). This is expressed in detail in the Genesis 2 creation story. Adam and Eve are made partners with God in taking care of the garden of Eden so it does not turn into a wilderness (a form of chaos or disorder). After their disobedience, the story of God's efforts to restore humankind reaches a climax with the call of Abraham in Genesis 12. This marks the beginning of the Jewish people, and so the beginning of the long story of God and his people Israel. All this and more shows that the understanding of creation in Israel is far more than a bare account of the origin of our universe. Creation is intimately linked to God's never-failing efforts to bless Israel and humankind, to mitigate human disobedience, and ultimately to achieve God's purposes for human beings as revealed in Jesus Christ.

Although not as picturesque as the creation stories, the connection of creation to history is also evident and made fundamental in the first words of Genesis: "In the beginning." With this phrase the world is put under the category of an event, something that happens. In ancient Greek thought, which has so influenced our science and philosophy, the world is something that "just is" and has been so always. Aristotle and the other Greek philosophers, and until very recently our sciences and philosophy, took the world's existence as something permanent, with no beginning, however much change there is within it. But Genesis 1:1

boldly says that the world had a beginning, and it distinguished its source from all else: God is, and all else has come to be by his word. And that part of the creation that has been made habitable, continues to be habitable, rather than falling into chaos, only because of God's will and command, by his word.

When Christianity spread the idea across the Roman Empire that the world was created, it was ridiculed. The Manicheans, a rival religious group to which Augustine had once belonged, considered the notion to be absurd. They asked, "If God created the world and created it out of nothing, why did God create it at the time God did and not sooner or later? What was God doing before it was created?"

In book 11 of his *Confessions,* Augustine points out that it is true to say that the universe did not begin *in time* but nonetheless it did *begin.* Time is created *with* the creation of all things. Time does not exist on its own apart from any universe. So however far you go back *in* time, you never come to a time that existed before the universe began. Although we use the motions of the sun, stars, and planets to *measure* time, their motions do not constitute time: time is not to be identified with the motions of the heavens. So the universe indeed began, as Genesis reveals, but not because it is preceded by a time, so that there is a time "before" it began. Rather, there is an *absolute* beginning of time and the universe. So if you go back in time, there is no first moment *of* time when the universe began; however far back you go in time, there will always be more time. So the universe has an *absolute* beginning, beginning with its creation, *with* time itself. Because the universe began, it is not the ultimate or prime reality, but one that is dependent on God. Only God, who is eternal, is without beginning or end. Time and the universe exist within God's eternity. The Manicheans' questions were raised only because of an erroneous notion of time as an independent reality. However strange Augustine's remarks on time may seem at first sight, they are much in line with theoretical work on time since the discovery of relativity theory in the early twentieth century. Augustine's way of thinking about time does not seem at all strange to the philosophers of science who have considered his thoughts.

In Augustine's examination of time, he also considered what it is to be *conscious* of time. He is the first person who described what it is to be a historical being. For us, there is a present, past, and future. The present flows through our consciousness and becomes past; and the future comes into our consciousness and becomes present, then past. But once the future has passed through us and become past, it is no more, just as when it was future, it was not yet. The past then exists as memory, the future exists as expectation, and the present exists as attention. For us to exist as temporal or historical beings, then, is for us to act now, with memory and anticipation. We act with an understanding of the significance of the past for our present, and of the future for our present. But unlike us, God is not a temporal being. He is eternal, and time exists as his creature. The Scriptures often talk of God in temporal terms, because although eternal, God can act in time. His eternity encompasses time. But for God, in contrast to ourselves, there is nothing that passes away or comes to be in his life.

Because God is eternal, we cannot comprehend the divine. We may make true statements about God's relation to time such as that he is creator and called Israel into a covenant, and we can make correct statements about God's eternity, such that his life is not subject to the passage of time, but full comprehension is beyond us. We cannot fully understand how temporal categories do not apply to God's essential nature. Our very thinking is subject to a temporal order of before, now, and after. This is why some have said that intuition (an immediate grasp) and visions, in which there is neither before and after in our awareness but only a temporally extended present, are much more adequate ways to have an awareness of God than discursive thoughts that are ordered in a sequence of before and after. This may be part of the reason Thomas Aquinas gave up writing his massive *Summa theologica*. He had frequent visions, and he felt that through them he had a more adequate understanding of God than he could achieve in his conceptual thought. He is reported to have said that by comparison with what he had experienced in his visions, what he had written was straw.

Augustine's profound views on time enable him, and those who came after him, to break with the theory of time as the circular motion of the everlasting universe, with endless repetition. "In the beginning," an absolute beginning, opened the way for Israel intuitively, and later for Augustine conceptually, to develop a view of history as having a direction and purpose. This was utterly novel in the ancient Near Eastern and Greek cultures. So the very creation as an event could be related to the call of Israel and the incarnation of the Word of God, and so the cosmos itself could be given direction and purpose. Rather than the circular motion of an everlasting universe, with events swallowed up into a purposeless, repetitive, circular stream, events are moving toward the goal of the kingdom of God.

For centuries our sciences operated with the assumption that the universe is everlasting or permanent. To many scientists and philosophers the biblical notion of creation, an absolute event, seemed childishly absurd. But in the late 1920s it was realized that the universe is expanding. After much debate about what this signified, the big bang theory was developed. According to this theory, our universe has not always been in its present form. It began as a very small, highly dense mass, which exploded and which is still expanding. To develop this theory, scientists used concepts that are consonant with the notion of the universe as having a beginning, indeed an absolute beginning. At the very least, developments in contemporary cosmology mean that the theological claim that our universe began no longer looks absurd to those cosmologists and others who had assumed that our universe has always been here. Israel's treatment of creation as an event, when it connected creation to their story of the divine saving history, is thus not philosophically nor scientifically absurd.

The tie between creation and salvation is taken to new heights in the New Testament. John begins his Gospel with the very same Greek words as the Jewish translators had rendered Genesis 1:1, "In the beginning." In one of the most quoted passages of Scripture, John wrote, "In the beginning was the Word, and the Word was with God, and the Word was God. He was in the beginning with God. All things came into being through him, and without him not one thing came into being. What has come into being in him was life, and the life was the light of all people" (John 1:1–4). He then makes a breathtaking connection: "And the Word became flesh and lived among us, and we have seen his glory, the glory as of a father's only son, full of grace and truth" (1:14). So God's creative word at creation is the saving word that became incarnate, Jesus Christ.

Something of the significance of this remarkable conjunction of the power that created and ordered the universe with the incarnation was pointed out by John Turkevich. He was both a chemist and a priest, combining in his own life a study of the natural world with a commitment to the incarnate Lord. In a memorable remark at a science and religion conference, he pointed out that it is not difficult for a Christian to look at nature's order and in it recognize God's power, wisdom, and goodness. But God so perceived is "a God of very large numbers." This is a graphic way to refer to the astounding size and age of the universe on a macrolevel, and the restriction to statistical at the microlevel. We exist between the immensely large and immensely small. That the creator of such a massive universe, intricate in its details, should be aware of us, even with a personal care, does not arise from nature itself, but with the affirmation of the incarnation of the Logos. Because it is by and through the Word of God that all things are made, God, whose mind is manifest to us in very large numbers of the cosmos, is also present to us humanly and personally in Jesus Christ.

Chapter 4

The Limits of Science

The biblical understanding of creation clearly presents us with a religion in which God is concerned *primarily* with human redemption. But its affirmation that the universe is created is not the result of a scientific attempt to explain the existence and order of the universe, the origin of life, or human life. Science seeks to understand natural processes, and its claims are based solely on how well laws, theories, and hypotheses explain those processes. The existence of the processes of nature is taken as a given. The question of the ultimate source of nature's processes and nature's very existence is widely recognized as being beyond the scope of science.

This difference between the biblical claim that the universe is created and ordered by God and scientific claims that deal with natural processes is well captured in the contrast C. S. Lewis drew between the biblical doctrine of creation and pagan creation-stories:

> When the curtain rises in these myths there are always some "properties" on the stage and some sort of drama is proceeding. You may say they answer the question, "How did the play begin?" But that is an ambiguous question. Asked by the man who arrived ten minutes late it would be properly

answered, say, with the words, "Oh, the first three witches came in, and then there was a scene between an old king and a wounded soldier." That is the sort of question the myths are in fact answering. But the very different question: "How does a play originate? Does it write itself? Do the actors make it up as they go along? Or is there someone—not on stage, not like the people on the stage—someone we don't see—who invented it all and caused it to be?"[1]

The opening chapters of Genesis, for all their superficial similarity to pagan creation myths and indeed even the employment of parts of a Babylonian creation myth, are talking about ultimate origins, not natural processes as are pagan myths. Lewis makes the distinction between Genesis and pagan creation stories a distinction between the origins of a play and the members of its cast. In talking about God, the Genesis stories are not talking about a member of the cast, so to speak, but the author of the play. In contrast, pagan creation myths are about members of the cast. Their god or gods emerge out of water, or an abyss, or from ice and snow, or from time and heaven, and then produce still other gods, who in turn make new parts of the world from preexisting materials. Wherever you have preexisting materials or beings, you do not have creation, but the description of a *process of development* in which events that come earlier in the process have produced events that come later in the process. Both earlier and later events are part of the same process. These so-called creation myths, then, are stories about the *relations* of the various members or parts of the universe. Even though some parts of the universe are gods, the stories are about processes *within* the universe. And as we see and will show more fully in the next chapter, the biblical God is not a member of the universe, but the source of all that exists.

Insofar as science is concerned with ongoing processes, it is to that extent like pagan creation stories. Science and pagan creation stories differ drastically in other respects, but in this one, critical respect they are alike: They both are concerned with relations between the members of the universe. Because of this likeness, although science is vastly superior in its knowledge of the relations between the members of the universe than are the pagan myths, it is just as far from the notion of creation as are pagan myths. However much our scientific knowledge of the relations between the members of the universe increases, it will still be knowledge about the relations between the members. So when the discovery of the expansion of the universe led to the big bang theory, it soon became clear that the science of cosmology had reached a limit. It had reached the end of natural processes. Although the theological implication was evident— the big bang raised the issue of ultimate origins—science itself had to remain silent before the issue of the ultimate origin of the universe.

This distinction helps us understand the misguided claim that there is a conflict between science and religion. The gods of pagan religion are replaceable by modern science because science has discovered that other natural members of the universe perform in natural processes the tasks mistakenly assigned to the pagan gods before the rise of science. The advance of science does indeed undermine the pagan gods, who historically had already been driven out by early Christianity. But atheists and some historians seem to think that the Christian God was put forward to account for natural processes in the same way as were the pagan gods. Since science removed the role played by the pagan gods in antiquity, it is assumed that science replaces God as well.

But modern science does not replace the biblical God, because the biblical God, unlike pagan gods, does not perform the functions that members of the universe perform. Rather, God's power is what keeps in existence all the various members of the universe that perform their functions by his never-ceasing creative action. Only from the perversion of biblical religion in the late seventeenth and early eighteenth centuries by some thinkers and scientists, such as Isaac Newton (1642–1727), who used God as a member of the universe and as a gap-filler within natural explanations—only from that perversion do we find a conflict between science and religion. For example, it was thought that some energy is lost in every collision of particles. This troubled Newton because it meant that the universe was running down. So he claimed that God injected more energy into the universe to keep it stable. Later scientists realized that energy is not lost in a collision but is transferred to the molecular level. By using deity as a filler for an apparent gap within natural processes, Newton's theological blunder made it look as though science had replaced God as an explanation for a natural process.

The same thing happened with the irregularities in the motion of the planets. Newton postulated that God gave the planets a nudge, so to speak, so that their irregularities of motion would not lead to the collapse of the solar system. Later scientists found that the alleged irregularities, which so troubled Newton, were actually periodic: they righted themselves in the long run so that the solar system is inherently stable. This is why Pierre Laplace (1749–1827), the champion of the inherent stability of the world machine, replied to Napoleon's complaint that Laplace, in his book on celestial mechanics, had neglected to mention God, "Sire, I have no need of that hypothesis." The removal of God from various alleged gaps within natural processes with the advance of science led to the erroneous impression that there is an inherent incompatibility between science and religion. Such a replacement of God can only happen if God is incorrectly treated as a member of the universe (one of the actors *on stage in the play,* so to speak). Such a replacement can never rightly happen with the biblical conception of God as creator, since science is at its limits with the issue of the ultimate origin of the universe and the ultimate origin of its order.

Guenther Höwe, a pioneer in nuclear physics in the 1930s, had his attitude toward theology transformed when he learned of this elementary but fundamental distinction between God and the universe. He, like many scientists and philosophers, had simply taken it for granted that in ignorance God had been naively postulated as a natural force in order to account for some aspect of the workings of the universe. When Höwe learned how mistaken he had been, he immediately invited Karl Barth (1886–1968), then the leading Protestant theologian in Germany, to take part in discussions with him and other scientists on science and religion.

Höwe's earlier mistaken assumption is made by many scientists, philosophers, and historians. They rightly believe that all scientific attempts to understand the world's operations must be based on accounts that involve only the members of the universe. But they do not realize that biblical religion agrees with them. As we have seen, God is not a member of the universe, and any attempt to have God involved within the processes that science studies is theologically utterly unacceptable. And almost as important, we need to realize that biblical religion does not affirm God's reality because its writers were trying to explain the working of the natural world. Biblical faith is a *response* to God's initiative, rather than the result of an *investigation* of nature. Thus not only is God not part of the world, but the grounds for belief in God are also quite different from that found in science. Pascal, Kierkegaard, and Karl Barth never tired of stressing both these points.

Barth, however, went so far as utterly to reject all natural theology. He described natural theology as an attempt to go unaided "from below" up to God, in contrast to God coming to us "from above." It is true that we can only reach God with God's aid, as we saw graphically in Anselm's prayer before he began his intellectual inquiry into the nature of God's existence. Nature, however, can and does have a legitimate role in our reflection on God. Although the ancient Israelites stressed that they knew God only because of God's self-revelation to them, above all in the calls of Abraham and Moses, we may nonetheless raise the question, "Is there *anything* about the universe, its order and its very existence, which gives some indication or suggestion that it is created, and that reveals something about God?"

This question is not the same as seeking to prove God's existence from the natural world. It does not seek to replace the Bible's witness by moving solely from nature to God, seeking to go "from below" to prove God's existence by reason alone, or even to prove God's existence. In addition, the world does actually bear some marks of its dependence on God. These marks are not how Israel came to the conviction that God is the creator, nor to their initial belief in God as their people's deity in contrast to other gods. Nor do they prove God's existence in the deductive fashion that forces one to accept the conclusion of a proof or be faced with a contradiction. But they do point toward God and so support the faith we have in the biblical revelation that God is creator. It would indeed be strange if nature and our human nature were created but gave no indication whatsoever that they are created. Today we also live in a world in which our knowledge of the natural world has greatly increased. It is only reasonable to seek to connect what a scientific study of the natural world presently indicates to us with the biblical conviction that God created and orders our world.

In the eighteenth century, at the very birth of modern science, Gottfried Wilhelm Leibniz (1646–1716), one of the greatest philosophers of all time, realized that science was inherently limited. He himself vigorously promoted science not only with his inventions of the calculus (independently of Newton), the binary system used in modern computers, and a calculating machine, as well the discovery of kinetic energy; he also founded the Prussian (later German), Austrian, and Russian Academies of Science. Yet in spite of all this, he tried to convince people that science is inherently limited. He argued that science could hope to find the laws that governed our universe, but that science could not explain why we have the laws we have. All scientific discoveries are about the *actual* laws we have, but from the laws we have, we cannot explain why we have those laws and not others.

It took some time for Leibniz's view of the limits of science to be accepted generally. At the rise of modern science, most scientists believed that nature's laws were necessary, so that the actual laws we have are the only possible ones. It was widely believed that Newton and others had discovered the immutable, absolute truth. But David Hume in his *Treatise concerning Human Understanding* (1738) argued that nature actually operates in an orderly way, but that its so-called laws are not necessary: they are not logically necessary. (They can be denied without any logical contradiction.) Nor could Hume find any physical necessity in natural processes. Nature's laws actually do hold, but they are not necessary. No one gave serious attention to Hume until Kant realized the significance of his claims. Kant agreed that experience can only show us what *is* the case, and not what *must* be the case. Yet Kant was convinced that the principles of Newtonian physics were necessary. His futile attempt to prove that they were necessary was the last great attempt to establish the laws of nature as necessary.

Most working scientists, however, do not pay much attention to the views of philosophers. It was not until the work of Albert Einstein (1879–1955) that it was realized that Newton's laws of motion, which had reigned supreme for two hundred years, were not the laws of nature after all. Einstein's work, taken together with the previous work of Max Planck, was the birth of modern science, in contrast to the classical science of Newton. Scientists realized that the laws they formulate are not necessary, but are always open to revision. So we do not have any guarantee that the formulations we have will not require fundamental revision; and even if the major laws turn out not to be revised in fundamental ways on the order of Einstein or Planck, they are not necessary. So Leibniz has been vindicated by our understanding of the nature of scientific explanations.

On the basis of science, all we can do is try to determine what laws nature has (knowing that any formulation may need revising or be wrong), but we can say nothing about why nature has these laws, nor indeed why we have a universe at all. Scientifically speaking, nature's existence and order may or may not have a reason. On the basis of science or philosophy, on the one hand, no one is in a position to maintain that nature's existence and laws are just brute facts; but on the other hand, we can clearly say that nature's existence and order are not *self-explanatory*. Scientifically speaking, nature's existence and order raise the ultimate questions of why there is a universe and why this particular one. We can go even further. We can also say that the only sort of answer to the kind of question that nature's existence and order raise—the only answer would have to be because of something beyond or outside the universe itself that accounts for its own being: a transcendent, intelligent God, or as Anselm put it, a necessary being. So the existence and order of the universe do pose a real question to our intellects: Is there a reason for the universe's existence and order? We cannot tell from science or philosophy. That much is evident to reason. Our reason can also tell us that since nature is not self-explanatory (science is limited), nature's existence and order, even though they do not prove God's existence, point beyond themselves to a transcendent, intelligent God as the only explanation.

In the past few decades a number of books on cosmology and biology by eminent scientists have pointed out how in various ways the operations of nature point toward God. We have already mentioned the big bang theory, which traces the origins of our universe to a very rapid expansion some twelve or more (perhaps nearly 14) billion years ago from a very tiny, dense mass of energy. Less well known, but also widely used is what has been called the anthropic principle. It is as if our universe were crafted in order for human beings to come into existence. If only one of some thirty basic laws of physics, or constants of nature, had been only to the very slightest different—say the mass of an electron—then no planet capable of permitting the evolution of human life would have been possible. To avoid the obvious theological implications, some scientists and philosophers have speculated that our universe is only one of a large number of universes that have no contact with each other. Ours just happens to belong to the subset of universes that are conductive to the appearance of human life. This is generally viewed as a rather ad hoc hypothesis, with no evidence, devised simply to avoid the obvious implications of the fine-tuning of our laws of physics to allow for human life.

Less well-received but not without merit is the claim made by Fred Hoyle and later by Antony Flew that our planet and indeed our universe are simply not old enough for life as we know it to have arisen by chance. Both have abandoned their atheism to postulate an intelligent being as involved in some way in the design of conditions that would allow for life to arise and evolve. This has encouraged still others to argue that Darwin's theory of natural selection does not account for the origin of species, and instead argue for intelligent design. According to the theory of intelligent design, there are instances of "irreducible complexity" that Darwin's theory of natural selection is logically incapable of explaining. But some religious biologists firmly resist this claim. They hold that alleged instances of irreducible complexity are in principle susceptible to Darwin accounts.

These claims from the big bang through intelligent design are of a different type than the point made by Leibniz. Science is forever incapable of dealing with the ultimate questions of the existence and order of the universe. The big bang, the fine-tuning that leads to the anthropic principle, and various interpretations of the significance of Darwinism in accounting for the origin of species—all these are in a different category. They are all subject to fundamental revision, even replacement. Whatever happens to them in the future, Leibniz's point still holds. But it is nonetheless rather encouraging to have recent developments in science that point in the direction of God, especially after so many centuries in modern history when atheists utilized science to attack religion. Still we should not build our faith solely on the science of the day. And we should also remember that if science in the future should be less hospitable to religion than it now is, we should not abandon our faith either. For we now know that scientific theories and explanations are not absolute, inscribed in stone, but are revisable in fundamental ways, and what is unfavorable at one time may give way in another time.

The ancient Jews were not concerned with these questions about nature's existence and order when they affirmed that their God who saved them from slavery in Egypt was creator. They were not trying to explain nature's existence and order *in the sense* of being engaged in scientific or philosophic investigation, or even naively simply wondering where everything came from. But their claim was to affirm that their saving God was much more than their God only, was universal in his scope, and was indeed Almighty. Their creation stories actually provide an answer to our questions about the reason for the existence and order of the universe, but our questions are not what they were seeking to answer. Besides, in claiming that the cosmos is created, they are concerned to identify *who* it was who intended the existence and order of the universe as a saving action. "Say among the nations, 'The Lord [Yahweh] is king! / The world is firmly established; it shall never be moved. / He will judge the peoples with equity'" (Ps. 96:10).

Their stories thus concern not only the origin of the universe, but also the *purpose* of the creation by connecting creation to the divine saving history of Israel. In God's promises to Abraham and Sarah is included a promise that all the peoples of the world will eventually be blessed by their progeny. So the Genesis account of creation, by being a prelude to the call of Abraham and Sarah, is not just a story of origins; it is also an account of our significance and the promise that God has a goal for us.

Chapter 5

What Is Meant by "God"

In this chapter I am primarily concerned to examine more fully what is *meant* by "God" in Christian theology to free us from several misconceptions that we will examine. Whether one believes in such a God is a different issue, which we will address briefly in this chapter but much more fully later. It is important to be clear about what is meant by God in Christianity because of various widespread misconceptions that treat God as part of or a member of the universe. This can be seen in the ambiguity of the word "universe." It can mean all that there is, including God. Although this is correct for the pagan gods and the god whose existence is enshrined in the so-called traditional proofs of god's existence from nature's order and existence, it is not true of the Christian understanding of who God is. In the Christian understanding of God, God is not a member of the universe, but God is its creator. As creator, God transcends the universe and thus is not a member of it. "Universe" means all that there is except God. As we will see, whoever rejects God because the traditional proofs of God's existence fail is like someone fishing in the ocean. Such people fail to catch God in their nets, not because their nets are too small, nor because their nets are torn, but because God is not in the ocean. At every moment of time God is the creator and sustainer of the "ocean." God continuously generates everything that exists. This is why God is everywhere, present as the continuous generator of everything that is, present to everything as their source.

Now the subject matter of theology is God. But when you try to picture God, what comes to mind? A blank? If so, that is as it should be. We cannot picture God, and we should not try to do so. God is not available to the senses; for God generates the existence of all things, continually, including all that can be sensed. This is what makes so absurd the statement of the first Russian astronaut who circled the earth: "I did not see God." If he had claimed to see God, we would have to say that whatever he did see, it was not God and could not have been God; for God cannot be detected by the senses. Nonetheless, this troubles some people, even the former British Bishop of Southwark, J. A. T. Robinson, who made a name for himself among the public with his confession that God is not "out there." He then rather clumsily tried to work out where God was.[1] No doubt a lot of people are troubled by not being able to picture God and assumed that bishops somehow must be able to do so; hence, for a bishop publicly to say he could not was for a while newsworthy.

Many people realize that God cannot be perceived by our sense organs, but they believe that we can conceive of God with our mind. This is very true. We can understand some very important things about God, such as God being creator of the universe.

Nonetheless, God is also beyond our minds. God's own being, in contrast to what God does, such as create and sustain the universe, cannot fully be grasped by the human mind. God as the source of all that exists or might exist has no source. Nothing can cause God to be or to cease to exist. God has no need for the existence of anything else to be full and complete in God. Sometimes this is expressed by saying that God is a necessary being and thus not dependent on anything else to be, in contrast to every other being, which is contingent and thus dependent on something else for its being. In these ways, God is distinct from all other beings, so that God does not belong to the class of created beings that make up the universe. God's nature is essentially different from every creature, so that God is not a part of the universe or a member of the universe.

No wonder that God is not "out there" in space somewhere, since God is the source of space itself; and since God depends on nothing else to be himself, God can exist without there being any space at all. As it is often put, God's nature and being transcend the universe. When we are aware of God's presence, one of the crucial features of God's being that we experience is holiness, so that God is spoken of as "wholly other," an expression indicating that God is both transcendent (not in the universe) and also of a *quality* that sets God utterly or wholly apart from all else. As "wholly other," God is above the power of our creaturely intellects to comprehend God's essential being. Sometime this is expressed by saying that God is "hidden" in God's essential nature. So when God reveals Godself to us so that we know some vitally important things about God, and even when we experience God's holy presence, God remains beyond the powers of our minds fully to comprehend. As the old Welsh hymn puts it so well, "Immortal, Invisible, God only wise, / in light inaccessible, hid from our eyes, . . .O help us to see 'tis only the splendor of light hideth thee" (Walter C. Smith). So to try to fully comprehend God by our minds is rather like trying to look at the sun. We can see things of this world because of the sun's light rays, and these rays are properties of the sun, but we cannot look at the sun itself with our naked eyes because the light is so great that it dazzles us. So too our minds are overwhelmed by the being of God.

Put abstractly, a finite mind cannot fully grasp an infinite being; only an infinite mind can fully comprehend an infinite being. The hiddenness of God should not cause us any anxiety. It is actually a mark of the unsurpassable greatness of God that God is hidden in God's essential nature from us. Indeed, it should give us immense assurance of God's goodness toward us. That a being of unsurpassable greatness, utterly full of life and lacking in nothing, should desire to create other creatures, is an act of utter love, because there is nothing this being needs for itself. And that God desires to have us as God's beloved companions, to share in God's eternal life and being, should fill us with wonder and unceasing thanksgiving. In addition, God's greatness explains why, when God makes Godself available to us, God must reduce God's intensity, so to speak, so as not to overwhelm us utterly. It also accounts for the craving of people who know God's goodness to a degree to desire more and more to have God's presence in their lives, and to persistently seek to enter into the life of God more deeply. The journey into God is never ending, because of God's utter fullness of being; it results in our entering more and more into a glorious never-ending joy.

It might be helpful to give some analogies besides the one above about God's very light hiding God's fullness from us. That God is beyond our intellect fully to comprehend can be compared to a blackboard with writing on it. If you focus on the blackboard itself, there is nothing for us to grasp. If you focus on what is written, you have a meaning you can grasp. But there could be no letters even formed to give us a meaning we can grasp if there were not a blackboard with spaces of darkness to write on. So too with the way God remains hidden even when he reveals himself to us. We can also make an analogy from music. Music is a combination of sound and silence; if there were no silence, however slight, we would not have notes.

So when in theology it is stressed that God is beyond all our conceptions, so that we need to set aside all our thoughts of God (called the *via positiva*) and say that God in Godself is utterly unknowable (called the *via negativa*), we must be careful. This is especially true of the spiritual writers whom we usually call mystics, since they seek to know God as God is in Godself, and so they stress that God is unknowable. This may give us the impression that all we say of God, because it concerns a transcendent being, is really to be discarded since it does not yield God's essence to us. Rather, what such theologians of the *via negativa* and mystical spiritual writers are doing is concentrating on the blank spaces of the blackboard exclusively, or to the silences between the notes, so to speak. But such a focus, which can be important in reminding us that our minds cannot fully comprehend God, does not mean that we know nothing about God at all. God has revealed God's self to us through God's creation and in God's call of Israel and the sending of God's Son, Jesus. What God is in Godself does not contradict or negate what God has chosen to reveal of Godself and God's purposes, even though God in fullness is beyond our powers to grasp.

God's difference in being from all creatures, however, is a major reason we often do not find it easy to experience God's presence. It takes practice, discipline, and patience to be able to learn how to approach and to receive the life of God, just as it takes a lot of practice, discipline, and patience to learn how to play tennis or golf well. This comparison with sports is not to trivialize the practice of learning to approach God when one recalls how much effort people are willing to put into becoming even moderately proficient in these sports compared to the commonly feeble effort people make to learn of and to seek God. We do not expect to be proficient in golf in three lessons. But many would not think it absurd to say, "I went to church three times, but nothing happened. So I quit."

The failure to take into account the essential hiddenness of God's nature enables some atheists to claim that since the proofs of God's existence fail, it is irrational to believe in God. They assume that the only possible *rational* reason people could have for believing in God are the so-called traditional proofs of God's existence; their failure means it is irrational to believe in God. These proofs are not in the Bible, and they were not even formulated until over a thousand years after Christ. Rather than examining the Bible to see why the Bible is silent over proofs, and why people have believed in the biblical God without proofs, they simply assume that these so-called traditional proofs of God's existence must be the only possible *rational* grounds for not only Christianity, but also Judaism and Islam. Since the proofs fail to prove God's existence, they conclude that there is no rational basis for belief in God.   ·

Now even though the Bible has no such proofs, by a brief examination of two of the so-called traditional proofs, we can gain a better understanding of how God transcends the being of all creatures. If they were sound arguments, what they would prove to exist would not be a transcendent God, and the reason they fail is because God is transcendent. This is perhaps most easily seen with the argument from design, or the teleological argument (*telos* is the Greek word for "end" or "goal"; for some Greek philosophers, all things seemed to be goal-directed, and so were said to have been designed). The various forms of the argument from design aim to show that the order of the universe implies that it has been designed. But it is obvious that this does not show that this great mind or designer *created* the universe from no previously existing materials. It also only gives us a designer that is a member or a part of the universe. We certainly do not have a holy God that transcends the universe. All the order of our universe could possible prove is a being that does not transcend the universe. This is why Fred Hoyle, the great astrophysicist, and Antony Flew, the well-known philosopher, even though they changed their minds and now believe that the universe shows evidence of design, still do not believe in the biblical God. Formerly, they believed that the order of the universe did not imply an intelligent designer. But after studying the theory of evolution, they both concluded that this theory, though sound as far as it goes, was by itself not sufficient to account for life as we know it. For us to have life as we know it implies some sort of intelligence and implies that the designer is simply a member or a part of the universe itself. The designer does not transcend the universe, in their view.[2]

Process theologians, such as Charles Hartshorne and John Cobb, for whom the bottom line is not the Bible, are happy to call this designer the deity, even though the designer is part of the universe. But to believe in such a god is really to return to Greek and Roman paganism, in which the gods are fellow members of the universe and are simply more powerful beings. In fact, the ultimate source of process theology, the philosopher-mathematician Alfred North Whitehead, had as his inspiration Plato's *Timaeus,* in which Plato postulates a designer who took preexisting time, space, and matter and organized them. However much the early church fathers admired Plato and employed him in their work, the Bible was always their bottom line, and they never lost their conviction in the transcendence and holiness of God.

Nevertheless, Hoyle and Flew's recognition of design in the evolution of various forms of life is of considerable interest. For a biblical Christian, the order of the entire universe is a witness to God. As we will see in the next chapter, the concept of a witness is a rich and important one, and the witness to God found in the order of the universe is of considerable importance. Order is a mark or sign of God's handiwork. Although belief among the ancient Hebrews did not arise from a study of the natural world, as we have seen, nature does give us an indication or sign that nature depends on another reality for its order and existence. But at this point we want to emphasize that order does not and cannot prove the existence of the biblical God, who is transcendent and holy. The order of the universe points toward God and yet cannot reach the biblical God; thus God is a different kind of reality from any member of the universe.

Even more helpful in understanding the transcendence of God are the failures of the cosmological argument. This argument seeks to infer the existence of God from the existence of the universe; hence "cosmological" comes from the Greek word for the universe, *cosmos.* The cosmological argument's basic idea is that every thing that exists has a cause, and so for the universe to exist, there must be a first cause. The first cause itself has no cause; otherwise the series of causes and effects would be unexplained. The argument has two forms. In the first form, the series of causes and effects is finite. We may picture this by having x represent a being with a cause; and as its cause, we would generate a series of caused beings and their causes as $x1 < x2 < x3 <$ and so on until we come to the first cause $x\infty$, which has no cause, $<$. But the x which has no cause is either a member of the series or it is not. If the first cause is a member of the series, and so part of the universe, we may ask, What caused it? It must have a cause, otherwise it violates the causal principle that everything has a cause. The alternative is to say that the first cause is *not* a member of the series. Without a first cause as a member of the series, the series of caused beings would be an infinite series.

Now an infinite series of caused beings *may* or may not have a cause that transcends, or is outside, the infinite series of caused beings. We cannot prove that it does or does not have a transcendent cause. We cannot use the causal principle that holds between members of the universe because the transcendent cause is not a member of the universe, and so its causality is not like that which holds between members of the universe. It does not act by physical impact, by chemical change, gravitational force, magnetism, or any other kind of cause that we study in physics and chemistry. We do not know that there is any other kind of causality than these to say that the universe needs it in order to exist.

Precisely because God transcends the universe and thus is not a member of the universe, the cosmological argument cannot reach him. The cosmological argument in its various formulations fails to prove that there *must* be a cause of the universe. But this failure is actually required by the very notion of the biblical God. Ironically, the *primary* reason for the utter inadequacy of the cosmological argument to establish God's existence actually is because God is a transcendent being.

Usually, in the philosophy of religion the failure of these two so-called traditional proofs of God's existence is said to show that there is no rational basis for the existence of God. Many theology textbooks rightly point out that the biblical God cannot be the conclusion of any proof based on the cosmos. But they neglect to point out the primary reason for their failure. As we have said, the proofs are like nets that cannot catch God. It is not so much that the nets are torn in many places, that many forms of the arguments contain logical fallacies that philosophers and atheists never tire of pointing out, nor even that the nets are simply too small to catch God. Rather, God is not even in the ocean, because God transcends all that God has made. God is constantly and continually producing the entire universe by a power utterly different from any that we study in physics and chemistry. God is undetectable by the tools we have or that we will ever develop in our study of the universe because God and God's causal power are not part of the universe. Even a brief examination such as we have given of these two proofs should enable us to better understand what it means to say that God is transcendent and hidden. Such an understanding is absolutely fundamental for all theology and indeed fundamental for our daily religious life as we seek to live our lives in God and for God's Spirit to live in us.

A skeptic could say that God is a human conception, an invention, a personal and unprovable conceit. But as I said at the beginning of this chapter, we are concerned with what is *meant* by "God" in Christianity, and to set aside several mistaken conceptions. All that we have said so far is implied by the very biblical notion of God. In the 1950s, when the philosophy of Ludwig Wittgenstein dominated the English-speaking world, what we have said would have been called "grammatical remarks": they are about the very *meaning* of what is meant by "God" in the Bible. It would have to be admitted by anyone who understands what is *meant* by "God" in the Bible as correct characterizations of God. But it has important implications. When we understand that God is not part of the universe, we realize that to be unable to prove God's existence is not a defect; for whatever is proved or sought to be proved to exist by the design and cosmological arguments would be a member of the universe and so would not be God. Precisely because God's nature is unique and unsurpassable, we can neither prove nor disprove God's existence from the natural world. To understand why this is the case is a positive gain: From God's very essential hidden nature, we know something about God. We know that God is not a member or part of the universe, but transcendent, "wholly other" than creatures.

An atheism that relies on the failure of the two traditional proofs of God's existence that we have considered assumes that God is part of the universe. These proofs have a pagan understanding of the divine, an understanding that is in a different category than God. For example, pagans were usually polytheists. But "gods" is not the plural form of "God," because God is not a member of the universe as are the pagan gods. Christianity is not a revised pagan polytheism, reducing the number of gods to God. Such monotheism is not Christianity. Atheism is an easy creed when the divine you are talking about is not the biblical God.

Most philosophers and atheists who consider the order and existence of the universe to be the only basis for a rational belief in God are ignorant of the actual relation of nature to God as God is understood in biblical faith. From the earliest days of theology, there was a distinction between the two books of God: the book of Scripture and the book of nature.[3] Our knowledge of God is above all based on the Bible, which is a witness to God's revelation of Godself and God's purposes to the people of Israel, especially through the patriarchs (Abraham and his progeny), Moses, the prophets, and above all Jesus Christ. The natural world is also a witness to God's power, wisdom, and goodness. So nature can be "read," so to speak, as we read the Bible. But the Bible is an indispensable guide for us to our reading of nature, as we can see from the inadequate reading of nature by the non-Jews in the ancient Middle East and by the ancient Greeks and Romans. Guided by Scripture, nature supplements and confirms the Bible's witness to God's power, wisdom, and goodness. Nature gives us a way of appreciating the immense power, wisdom, and goodness of God. But the book of nature was always a greatly inferior source of our knowledge of God, and always used in conjunction with the book of Scripture. Nature was not used to move from unbelief to belief. Nature was always used by people who had *already* been moved by God's grace to a life of faith as a way to gain a better idea of God's power, wisdom, and goodness from nature's immense size, intricate order, and usefulness for human life.

In the sixteenth and seventeenth centuries, the roles of the two books of God were radically changed. The incessant rivalry and sometimes violent religious conflicts between Roman Catholics and Protestants, and among Protestants themselves, over the interpretation of the Bible led some intellectuals to seek a noncontroversial basis for religion. The scientific revolution that transformed our understanding of nature seemed to give them just what they wanted. They turned from the Bible and looked exclusively to the book of nature. They believed that the new philosophic and scientific view of the physical universe as a great self-sustaining machine required that there be a first mover to give the world motion, and to establish the laws of motion. This first mover and lawgiver then left the world alone to run itself. This understanding of nature and God was thought to be an ample and uncontroversial rational basis for religion, a natural religion or religion of reason, in contrast to the controversial interpretation of the Bible. They believed that they had captured the rational core of religion. So the Bible was dropped. Their postulated deity was an ingredient in their scientific explanation. That is to say, god was used to deal with the *unanswered* questions of science. Without realizing it, they made this god a captive to science. By the end of the eighteenth century, as science progressed, scientific answers were found to hitherto unanswered question in Newtonian celestial mechanics. The need for god to plug the gaps in scientific explanations evaporated. This led to the view that is still with us today that as science progresses, religion retreats. Yet intellectuals and the public at large often do not notice that the retreating religion was a natural religion, a religion postulated on nature alone. The retreat of natural religion is a major part of the case to reject all religion—Christian, Jewish, Muslim—by many atheists today.

The exclusive use of the book of nature led to a strong protest from the great mathematician-philosopher Blaise Pascal. Although Pascal cogently and conclusively rejected nature as the basis of Christian belief, he could not stem the adherence of many intellectuals of the seventeenth century to natural religion, and even the use of natural religion to attack biblical religion as full of superstition and inferior to a religion based solely on reason.

The exclusive use of the book of nature by many intellectuals propelled the so-called traditional proofs of God's existence into previously unheard-of dominance. In the second half of the eighteenth century, however, the inability of the commonly used forms of the argument from design and the cosmological argument to establish natural religion became apparent. The reasons for their failure are enshrined in classical form in David Hume's *Dialogues concerning Natural Religion* (1781) and Immanuel Kant's *Critique of Pure Reason* (1781).[4] These refutations of the traditional proofs of God's existence are still the core of courses in the philosophy of religion, and they are regularly used as a basis of the atheists' claim that belief in God's existence has no rational basis. In addition, atheists rely on a view of God as a "god of the gaps," whose existence the progress of science has shown to have been asserted on the basis of ignorance of the natural causes of previously unexplained physical processes. But in Christianity, the book of nature had served (and continues to serve) only as a *modest supplement* to the understanding of God for those who believe in God on the basis of a life of faith through the grace of God (and not initially because of the book of nature), for those whose God is not a part of the universe (not a "god of the gaps" in scientific explanations). Yet the biblical God has incorrectly and firmly become identified in the minds of many philosophers, scientists, and atheists with the god of natural religion, and they often think that nature is the sole possible basis for a rational belief in any deity. Unfortunately, in order to distance themselves from these misconceptions, many Protestant theologians have completely ignored the book of nature. Usually a knowledge of science and a positive relation of science to theology was restricted to theologians who were on the margins.

There is also an irony in the exclusive reliance on proofs in the philosophy of religion. No other field of inquiry relies on proofs of the kind sought for God's existence. Beginning in the seventeenth century, it has been increasingly recognized that the older Aristotelian ideal of knowledge as proof or demonstration is simply unattainable in any of the sciences. We do not go from premises to conclusions that "are so and cannot be otherwise." Probability is the standard, and in the case of atomic physics, only statistical probability is possible. With the replacement of Newtonian physics, scholars have realized that all hypotheses and even well-established theories are subject to revision and even, in extreme cases, rejection. The futility of trying to find new methods that would enable us to attain knowledge that was *necessary* was gradually realized in modern philosophy through its long development from Descartes to Kant. It became far more generally realized during the revolution in modern physics with the discovery that energy does not radiate uniformly but in units called "quanta," the development of quantum theory, and with Einstein's theories of relativity. Only pure mathematics remains as a field where proofs are still the standard. But even pure mathematics was revolutionized by Kurt Gödel's theorems (1930s), which showed that any system of mathematics that is complex enough will always generate propositions whose truth or falsity cannot be demonstrated within the system.

In spite of the abandonment of proofs or demonstrations as the standard in all of our branches of science, and in other academic fields as well, in the case of God's existence many philosophers and atheists continue to hold to the standard of proof or demonstration, and anything less makes religious belief irrational. Yet nothing else is held to this standard. Why then should the existence of God be held to this unworkable and discarded standard? Courses in the philosophy of religion that examine the so-called traditional proofs of God's existence rarely, if ever, mention that "proofs" are not used in other fields of inquiry or consider the implications of this for the field of philosophy of religion.

In addition, when atheists find that God's existence cannot be proved, they assume that they have considered the only rational reasons for belief, ignoring all the indications of God that nature and human nature provide, as well as the witness to revelation presented by the Bible. Faith is treated as equivalent to having no rational reason for belief, as utterly emotional and irrational. All you have to do is mention the word "faith," and many philosophers and atheists immediately jump to the false conclusion that this is equivalent to saying that there are no rational reasons for belief. This excuses them from making an examination of the actual reasons people have for holding to belief in the biblical God by faith, or even considering the possibility that faith might perhaps be the right response to God, who in interaction with the people of Israel and in Jesus gives us many indications of God's reality and purposes. Belief in God is not something *below* the level of reason, and so irrational. Rather, it is something that is *above* reason, suprarational. By God's very nature, God is unbounded, without limits, or infinite, and God's fullness is incomprehensible to anything less than the mind of God itself. But God through God's loving actions on us enables the mind and heart to rise above their normal ability, and to respond with faith toward God, who reveals Godself to various people known to us in the Bible and above all in Jesus. In the next chapter we will examine how nature is a witness to God.[5]

PART TWO
SUFFERING

Chapter 6

Nature as a Witness and Innocent Suffering

Although the ancient Jews themselves were not engaged in science or philosophy, they did believe that the natural world formed a witness to God. "Witness" has at least three elements. First, a witness is something that reveals a fork, indicating at least two possible directions to follow. Second, a witness makes it incumbent on a person to act: either to follow or not to follow a particular direction. The decision may be made consciously or unconsciously. Our practices indicate the nature of our decision. Third, a witness is often, but not always, expressed verbally. In the Old Testament, for example, prophets frequently chastised the people of Israel for some specific evils, and called upon them to return to the ways of God.[1]

The natural world, however, does not address us verbally. But this does not disqualify it from being a witness. Consider, for example,

> The heavens are telling the glory of God;
>   and the firmament proclaims his handiwork.
> Day to day pours forth speech,
>   And night to night declares knowledge.
> There is no speech, nor are there words;
>   Their voice is not heard;

> yet their voice goes out through all the earth,
>   and their words to the end of the world.
>   (Ps. 19:1–4)

As we have seen, nature's order and existence are not self-explanatory. Its order and existence thus raise an ultimate question. A choice must be made between regarding the universe as just a brute fact that has no explanation, or following another direction by seriously examining the possibility that the natural world is dependent on God. To consider that possibility seriously and with persistence is in fact to have begun to follow one of the paths indicated by nature's witness. The creation stories of the pagan gods do not function as a witness because the question of the ultimate status of the universe is not raised by them. The pagan gods are simply part of the universe. The very notion that God is the creator of all that there is, however, can function as a witness because the very notion of God raises the ultimate question of nature's dependence. The fact that nature is not self-explanatory should make the reality of God an inescapable and vitally important possibility with which to wrestle.

Nature's witness, once encountered, leaves us without the excuse of total ignorance for failure to begin an exploration of one of the directions it indicates that can in time and with persistence lead us to find God's grace; for the notion of creation is not a bare fact: it points to One who seeks us in many other ways than just through the witness of the natural world. Paul claims that the witness of nature itself, however, makes one eternally responsible before God for one's way of life.

> For the wrath of God is revealed from heaven against all ungodliness and wickedness of those who by their wickedness suppress the truth. For what can be known about God is plain to them, because God has shown it to them. Ever since the creation of the world his eternal power and divine nature, invisible though they are, have been understood and seen through the things he has made. So they are without excuse; for though they knew God, they did not honor him as God or give thanks to him, but they became futile in their thinking, and their senseless minds were darkened. Claiming to be wise, they became fools; and they exchanged the glory of the immortal God for images resembling a mortal human being or birds or four-footed animals or reptiles.
>
> Therefore God gave them up in the lusts of their hearts to impurity, to degrading their bodies among themselves, because they exchanged the truth about God for a lie and worshiped and served the creature rather than the Creator, who is blessed forever! Amen. (Rom. 1:18–25)

Paul is not saying that the universe is proof that God is creator, but that it forms a witness. All people (not just Jews, who for Paul have had the benefit of God's special revelation) have a witness in nature. They can worship the universe or parts of it, or turn from it and look beyond it and its members. In addition, nature is orderly. Even though non-Jews did not have the law revealed to them as did the Jews, the very fact that nature is orderly ought to be sufficient for people to realize that they ought to live with others in an orderly, not lawless, way. Instead, "They were filled with every kind of wickedness, evil, covetousness, malice. Full of envy, murder, strife, deceit, craftiness . . . " (Rom. 1:29). Any of us today can see that this is not a good way for us to live together, and yet like people in the past, we continue to do these things, and more.

In his letter to the Christians in Rome, Paul stresses that non-Jews (or Gentiles, as they are called by Jews) have suffered dreadful consequences from ignoring nature's witness; yet in his sermon at Athens (which probably exemplifies Paul's typical way of approaching Gentiles), Paul says that the city's numerous idols indicate that its people have been groping for God. Even though Paul is deeply distressed by the numerous idols in the city (Acts 17:16), he tells his Gentile listeners that the time has come for them to learn the truth about the one to whom they had dedicated an altar as "an unknown god" (17:23b). Paul says that while previous misconduct due to human ignorance has been overlooked, people are now called to receive forgiveness in Christ. Nature's witness is enough to prevent people from the worst consequences of a lawless life, and the worship of heathen gods indicates that, according to Paul, at least some response to nature's witness must have been seen to some extent.

Besides nature's witness, there is also what can be called "an inner witness" that is available to all people. This can be illustrated from Genesis 3. After Adam and the woman (the terms in Hebrew mean "man" and "from man," so they stand as representatives of humanity, not just Jews; "Eve" resembles the Hebrew word "living" [3:20]) disobeyed God, they hide themselves when they hear God walking in the garden. God calls, "Adam, where are you?" It is not that God does not know where Adam is. Rather, after Adam and Eve disobeyed God, they do not know where they are. They have lost their orientation toward God, which is the fundamental meaning of sin, or original sin. In place of God, we have invented idols around which to orient ourselves. This may be in the form of an orientation of our lives around our nation, some cause, our cultural heritage, the guidance of intellectuals, or by imitating the lifestyle of celebrities. But whatever we have done, God's call can still be heard, as it was for Adam and Eve in spite of their disobedience and disorientation: Where are you?

Each of us encounters and ponders this question in one form or another at various times in our lives, often in unexpected moments. In pondering this question, without having heard a voice, and whether we are thinking of God or not, we are "hearing" God's call. The questioning of the basis or the fundamental orientation of our lives is a witness. When we become troubled that we do not know where we are, we have actually made an initial move toward God, whether we realize it or not. To persist with that pondering is to become open to nature's witness, and other witnesses as well.

If anything, we today have even clearer witnesses than people in Paul's day. We have the witness of the Old and New Testaments ("Testament" means "witness"), and the witness of the church, as well as the benefit of the modern study of the natural world and considerable philosophical reflection on the natural world. We can state with great precision, much greater than could either the psalmist or Paul (though their reflections are sufficient to be perfectly adequate as witnesses in their own days to their particular audiences), that the world's existence and order are unexplained by its members. Unless people are responsive to some degree to one or another of God's witnesses, it is unlikely that they will respond positively to the witness of nature. The fact that the world's existence and order are unexplained by its members is then often dismissed as a speculative matter. Some dismiss it by claiming that we do not need to concern ourselves with this remote fact in order to continue to do science and by its applications to improve life on earth. Some consider nature only in terms of whether its existence and order actually proves God's existence.

People are responsive to different witnesses. As we saw in the preface, some people respond to the biblical witness because they are seeking help for their broken and ensnarled lives. Some respond because of a powerful spiritual experience, along the lines of Moses and Isaiah. Some respond to God because they seek to understand the world and their lives within it. And others respond for other reasons we have mentioned. But whatever route is followed, nature's witness can help to confirm and strengthen a person's faith.

In ancient Israel, once it was realized that nature was God's creation, nature was understood to exhibit God's power, wisdom, and goodness. We have seen that Isaiah encouraged the people of Israel to take heart by reminding them that Yahweh was the creator of the universe. God easily had the power to restore their fallen nation now in captivity and to fulfill God's promises given to Abraham. The same juxtaposition of God's creative power and care of the people of Israel occurs in more than fifty psalms. Yahweh's power as creator reinforces their confidence in God's ability and desire to fulfill God's promises to God's people. For example, in captivity in Babylon Isaiah proclaims:

> Comfort, O comfort my people,
>   says your God.
> Speak tenderly to Jerusalem,
>   and cry to her
> that she has served her term,
>   that her penalty is paid,
> that she has received from the LORD's hand
>   double for all her sins.
>
>   (40:1–2)

After nine more verses along these lines, Isaiah sets aside any possible doubts by referring to the immense power of God as creator of all that there is:

> Who has measured the waters in the hollow of his hand
>   and marked off the heavens with a span?
>
>   (40:12a)

> Even the nations are like a drop from a bucket,
>   and are counted as dust on the scales.
>
>   (40:15a).

In Psalm 33 we find the same message of God's universal sovereignty:

> Let all the earth fear the LORD;
>   let all the inhabitants of the world stand in awe of him.
> For he spoke, and it came to be;
>   he commanded, and it stood firm.
>
> The LORD brings the counsel of the nations to nothing;
>   he frustrates the plans of the peoples.
> . . . .
> Happy is the nation whose God is the LORD,
>   the people whom he has chosen as his heritage.
>   (33:8–10, 12)

Nature also reveals God's wisdom in the wonderful order of the world. This is especially stressed in the creation story of Genesis 1, in which the world is ordered in a sequence of six days, with the frequent refrain, "And God saw that it was good" (vv. 4, 10, 12, 18, 21, 25), and concludes in verse 31 with "God saw everything that he had made, and indeed, it was very good." The wisdom of God is especially stressed in the Wisdom literature of the Old Testament in such books as Proverbs, which in short pithy sayings records the wisdom that can be gained from obedience to God. Wisdom is knowledge of how to live rightly. For example, "Whoever sows injustice will reap calamity. . . . Those who are generous are blessed" (Prov. 22:8–9).

God's wisdom is treated in a quite different and vitally important way in the book of Job. The book of Job is a collection of poems that wrestle with a widespread human problem: innocent suffering. In many societies surrounding Israel, stretching from Greece and Egypt to India and beyond, we find ancient texts wrestling in one way or another with the question of human suffering. Could all that happens to people be deserved?

The book of Job represents an attempt to make a break with the Jewish tradition of its day. It insists that sometimes people suffer innocently. This is not glibly asserted. It takes a great deal of wrestling and a back-and-forth argument in the heart-wrenching debates between Job, who has lost everything and is physically in dire straits, and his friends who come to counsel him. Job's orthodox friends, for all their sympathy, continually appeal to Job to confess his wrongdoing, which they are certain is the cause of his loss and suffering, and to rely on God's forgiveness. Relentlessly they press Job to yield, and with vehemence, anger, frustration, and firmness Job resists them. He insists that he is innocent.

Job becomes so frustrated at never breaking through the orthodox conviction that suffering is always a matter of punishment that he appeals in desperation to future generations for an ultimate vindication. He cries out, "O that my words were written! O that they were inscribed in a book!" (Job 19:23). He wants his words preserved for future generations to read, so that they can agree with him that there is such a thing as innocent suffering. But the life of a scroll (since papyrus decays) will not be long enough for Israel to break out of its orthodox shell. So Job cries out, "O that with an iron pen and with lead they were engraved on a rock forever!" (19:24). Iron and lead mixed together make a hard alloy stylus, and Job would like such a stylus to carve his words into the face of a cliff; for his words must last a very long time before the Jewish people, indeed the human race, overcome their prejudice.

Yet Job was right. The Jewish prejudice continued right into Jesus' time and was very strong in Jesus' day. Again and again, Jesus had to teach that there was not a one-to-one link between our suffering and our deserts. For example, once when Jesus healed a man who had been born blind, his disciples were puzzled. "Rabbi, who sinned, this man or his parents, that he was born blind?" Jesus answered, "Neither this man nor his parents sinned" (John 9:2–3). His blindness had nothing to do with punishment. Yet in spite of Jesus, the notion lingers. The present-day Jew is baffled by the Holocaust, struggling to understand how it happened, because their suffering, indeed the attempted extermination of them, was far too outsized to be put down to their failure to be faithful to the covenant. So they are at a loss. Even we Christians, with the benefit of Christ's clear teaching, are not wholly free of the connection of suffering and desert. Many people who suffer ask their clergy, "What did I ever do to deserve this?"

Job, present-day Jews, and Christians are all caught in a bind. On the one hand, we believe in God's wisdom and justice, yet there seems to be a great deal of injustice in the distribution of suffering. On the other hand, we can see the dire consequences of holding firmly and strictly to justice simply by a brief look at classical Hinduism. There justice is so firmly stamped into the fabric of reality that no good deed is unrewarded and no wrong is unpunished. Clearly this does not happen in this life. So according to classical Hinduism, there is a reincarnation, and everyone's place in life is a result of their deeds in a previous life. There is perfect justice. Unfortunately, this implies that those who suffer, who are poor, in lesser castes, or even born as animals or less, deserve their fate.

Abruptly Job turns from the consolation he seeks in the hope that he will be vindicated in the distant future by a change in people's attitudes toward suffering. He turns from all earthly hope. His final plea involves the most momentous expression of faith in the entire series of poems, perhaps in the entire Old Testament. With it he breaks out of the shell of the traditional explanation of suffering as deserved—indeed, from all explanations of suffering. With resounding conviction he exclaims, "I know that my Redeemer lives, and that at the last he will stand upon the earth; and after my skin has been thus destroyed, then from my flesh I shall see God, whom I shall see on my side [or *for myself*], and my eyes shall behold, and not another" (Job 19:25).

His fellow Jews, rehearsing the orthodox tenets of their faith, have utterly failed to help him in his dire distress. The hope of vindication in the distant future by generations yet to come offers him no comfort. But driven back into his deepest levels, Job finds his footing. For beyond his death and decay, he will be ushered into the holy presence. In his own flesh he will gaze on the fullness of the divine glory.

Now there is not even a hint about God's recognition of his innocence. Before God, Job expects neither reward nor clearance. He will be raised from the dead, and he will rejoice in the presence of God. The world of rewards for piety and punishment for failures has been left behind. The divine presence is enough.

There was an agelong reluctance in the Jewish faith to think beyond earthly death. Indeed, for centuries after the poems of Job were written, only some of the Jewish community believed in a resurrection. For example, in the New Testament we find the Sadducees, who did not believe in the resurrection, baiting Jesus with a quibble (Luke 20:27–38). They ask him about a theoretical woman who has been widowed seven times. After resurrection, whose wife will she be? But Job is not playing games. In what has widely been seen in Christian circles as an anticipation of Christ, Job breaks through the agelong Jewish reluctance to look beyond earthly death. Job bursts through not in the name of immortality of the soul, a natural ability to survive bodily death. The reluctance is overcome solely and only for the sake of communion with God. God is a good so utterly transcending the goods of this life, the goods that we so often sell our souls to possess that God disappears from our outlook. But there is a good, the good that is God's own person, which Jesus later compares to a pearl of great price. A merchant sells all he possesses in order to obtain it (Matt. 13:45–46). Without realizing it, Job has stumbled onto a path that leads to the realization of the great good that God is along the hard road of loss, suffering, and isolation from all human and earthly comfort. Job surrenders all claims to be publicly found innocent, all desire to claim his worth before the world of friends or future generations. It is God who is his redeemer, who by God's power, not by Job's power, lifts him into the recognition of God's goodness.

Job has found his way home the hard way—through the path of being reduced to nothing but his bare skin and bones. In that condition—when he suddenly abandons all claims to establish his own good name, all claims to justice—he is raised by God's Spirit to the soaring conviction that no matter what happens to him, he belongs to God, and God will bring him to God's presence in glory.

Alas, this flash of conviction, like so many of our own flashes of faith in the reality of God, is momentary. Although for a moment he is gripped and grasped by the sufficiency of God's grace, able to set aside any and every calamity he has suffered, he relapses into his former ways. The heavens close. God is absent because Job has become filled again with his old grievance that life has not been fair to him.

In his grievance Job once again calls out, "Let the Almighty answer me!" (Job 31:35). And so has Job's rebuke continued to this day, concretely by those who suffer, and abstractly by philosophers and playwrights in their writings: The God of religious faith has failed to answer the questions raised by innocent suffering. This is true even of some biblical scholars. Because the poems of the book of Job do not philosophically solve the problem of innocent suffering, some biblical scholars have expressed their disappointment with the poems. They regard the book of Job as a noble failure.

But the poet or poets of the book of Job do not finally present Job himself as one who is disappointed. After his lapse from his conviction in the goodness of God, Job is not given a direct answer. Rather, he himself is questioned by God: "Where were you when I laid the foundation of the earth? . . . Who determined its measurements? . . . Have you commanded the morning since your days began? . . . Have you entered into the springs of the sea, or walked in the recesses of the deep?" (38:4, 5, 12, 16). And on and on the questions fly for four chapters, filling several pages and containing such charming touches as this: "Do you give the horse its might? Do you clothe its neck with a mane?" (39:19).

Is the Lord being heavy-handed by reminding Job of God's immense, incomparable creative power and Job's smallness? Is God overwhelming Job with a reminder of whom he is dealing with? Is God bullying Job? Some may think so. But not those who recall that this great, mighty one, who far exceeds our ability to imagine, nonetheless from his infinite height inclines himself toward his creature Job, and so touches him that for a moment Job rises into the glorious light and proclaims, "I know that my Redeemer [or *Vindicator*] lives!" (19:25). The Holy One of Israel set aside Job's lapse and came to him again. This time, however, he came with questions that raised Job from the prison of his limited understanding and the enclosure of self-righteousness. With those questions, Job came to himself again, and this time with far more staying power as he yielded himself in adoration.

In the book of Job we find a remarkable resolution of Job's search for the reason for his innocent suffering when God exhibits to him the great order and beauty of the universe that has come to be from God's power and wisdom. Indeed, God shows Job his cosmic responsibilities in such a way as to confess his burdens to Job and thus also his profound concern for human beings enmeshed in the cosmic order. If the order and its life were not beautiful, submission to God would be a submission to sheer necessity. Job could hardly praise and even admire such a cosmic order if it were not so beautiful. God's responsibility for all creatures and the beauty of the order of the cosmos reduce Job's laments over his own unmerited loss and suffering to silence (Job 40:3–5). As God continues to call attention to the various creatures of his domain, Job is lifted out of his own personal and unresolved distress by Lord's glory exhibited by God's creation. God's wisdom far surpasses Job's understanding, "I have uttered what I did not understand, things too wonderful for me, which I did not know" (42:3b). Job is moved from what he has been taught about God by his "comforters"—moved to the experience of communion with God through the vision of nature, seen from God's point of view, not Job's own personal situation. "I had heard of you by the hearing of the ear, but now my eye sees you" (42:5). He is reduced to utter humility. "Therefore I despise myself, and repent in dust and ashes" (42:6).

William Temple, perhaps the most beloved of all the archbishops of Canterbury, once wrote:

> In his fellowship with God, Job has found that nothing matters in comparison with that fellowship. . . . The person who has found fellowship with God is rich though he possesses nothing. Fellowship—this is the real solution, not an answer to a riddle, but the attainment of a state of mind in which there is no need to ask.[2]

Job recognizes that the Creator is worthy of admiration regardless of his own condition and his inability to account for his suffering. God is worthy of worship, apart from our blessing or our woe, just as a painting of great beauty or a work of brilliant design is worthy of respect and admiration apart of any benefit it may bring to us.

All too often in our worship ("worship" is based on the Anglo-Saxon word meaning "to ascribe worth") we praise God for what he has done for us perhaps as a people, but mostly for ourselves as individuals, and all too often we fail to realize that God—apart from our well-being, for which we should indeed offer God thanks—is worthy of admiration and praise. This ought to be part of our worship too, and indeed, if it forms part of our being, it can enable us to bear inexplicable loss and harm. This is explicit in one of the opening prayers in the Anglican Book of Common Prayer in which we ask that we may "perfectly love thee, and worthily magnify thy holy Name."[3] We ask not just to love, but to love perfectly. Thus we are not to consider only what we may hope to gain from obedience to God, such as health, prosperity, and protection from harm. But we praise God for what God is, not what we have gained or hope to gain from God. Our praise should carry at least an element of sheer admiration above and beyond all that we as a people or as a person receive in the way of earthly benefits. Job's praise of God is a mark of integrity, of a recognition of God's worth apart from personal gain or loss. With his perfect love, Job has reached an outlook that is called a pure religious faith

Yet the fact that God is worthy of praise in Godself is not indicated by the commonly used description of God as omnipotent, omniscient, and all-good. It may have been implicit in the thought of the man with whose letter we began; for in spite of being unable to relate the Holocaust and the death of a young child to these three abstractions, he concludes his letter with "I think it was René Descartes who said: 'I think, therefore I exist.' Whoever said it, it makes sense and I understand it. I would like to add: 'I pray, therefore I believe, whether I understand it or not.'" Like Job, this man has sensed and probably is moved by the love of God arising inside himself. Job is able to affirm, "Though he slay me, yet will I trust in him" (Job 13:15 KJV). In light of all that Job has suffered, this exclamation is apparently wholly irrational to one arguing about how to fit the pieces of omnipotence, omniscience, and goodness together with great and tragic loss and suffering. Yet it makes sense if indeed we are like a fountain with an inexhaustible spring of water gushing through our being. Such a love arises in us as we hold to God and turn to God in prayer and openness before the suffering that we cannot explain. That love for God, flowing through us, can enable us to recognize and to respond to the beauty of the universe, and to love it and its maker, even though in time we will all be reduced to dust.

I hope that as we go along, especially in the next chapter, we can retain the admiration we have for God from the witness of nature, and add a greater degree of understanding than was available to Job, because of what is revealed to us by Jesus and his crucifixion. It is a matter of a greater degree of understanding, and not full understanding of the distribution of good and evil in this life, as Jesus made clear, for example, in his parable of the Laborers in the Vineyard (Matt. 20:1–15).

Although we have considered nature as a witness to God's goodness in our earlier remarks, there is one more point to be made. The goodness of God that nature reveals and for which God is praised is the making of a *habitable* universe, a place for us *and* all other creatures. This is reflected in the cosmology in which God separates and holds back the waters. God's goodness, as far as it concerns the natural world, does not refer to any special or specific benefit, such as God's call of Israel. We find, as in Psalm 104, an unsentimental praise of God's goodness in providing for us *and* all other creatures a world in which our basic needs can be met:

> You make springs gush forth in the valleys;
>   they flow between the hills,
> giving drink to every wild animal.
> . . . .
> You cause the grass to grow for the cattle,
>   and plants for people to use
> to bring forth food from the earth,
>   and wine to gladden the human heart,
> oil to make the face shine,
>   and bread to strengthen the human heart.
> The trees of the LORD are watered abundantly,
>   the cedars of Lebanon that he planted.
> In them the birds build their nests;
>   the stork has its home in the fir trees.
> The high mountains are for the wild goats;
>   the rocks are a refuge for the coneys.
> . . . .
> These [and many more named in the psalm] all look to you
>   to give them their food in due season;
> when you give to them, they gather it up;
>   when you open your hand, they are filled with good things.
> When you hide your face, they are dismayed;
>   when you take away their breath, they die
>   and return to their dust.
> When you send forth your spirit, they are created;
>   and you renew the face of the ground.
> May the glory of the LORD endure forever.
>   (104:10–11a, 14–18, 27–31)

It is particularly striking that the death of creatures is taken in stride as normal and as in no way detracting from God's goodness in making creatures and in providing a habitation for them.

Although God is admirable in Godself, God's power, wisdom, and goodness, even when celebrated as they are exhibited in nature, are always understood to be connected to his call of Israel and God's promises to Israel. As we have seen, God's power is to encourage Israel that in spite of its suffering, God is sovereign and will save the people; God's wisdom is evident in the existence and order of the world and merits admiration and praise, regardless of our personal circumstances. But as we saw with Job, God's wisdom also means that our personal circumstances are in God's hands as well. God's goodness also refers to God's proving a habitable place for all creatures, which in the normal course of things come to be and pass away. This understanding of power, wisdom, and goodness cannot be derived from the general terms "omnipotence, omniscient, and all-good," just as we earlier noted is also the case with holiness. Yet the philosophical invention called "theism," which purports to deal with the only rational basis for three major historic religions (Judaism, Christianity, and Islam), uses the three terms, "omnipotence, omniscience, and all-good," quite abstractly and as though they are all that is needed as a description of God when we set out to make an evaluation of the truth or falsity of these historic religions. Inferences are made along the same lines as we saw in the letter with which we began, inferences as to the incompatibility of these abstractions with the Holocaust, the death of a child, and the like—all without any reference to the understanding supplied by the biblical witness as to who God is and how God has dealt with the Jewish people or become incarnate in Jesus. We will see more fully in the next chapter how a fuller, biblical knowledge affects our response to evil and suffering.

Chapter 7

Innocent Suffering
and Life beyond Death

I have stressed that God's power, knowledge, and goodness are to be understood in the light of the covenant and saving history of the Jewish people, not in terms of theism's philosophical abstractions: omnipotence, omniscience, and goodness. Now let us consider how the understanding we have of God is affected by the New Testament conviction that the Son of God became a human being. We will find that our understanding of suffering is transformed by the life, teachings, death, and resurrection of Jesus. In this chapter we will consider some of Jesus' teachings.

As we saw in the last chapter, at one time the Jewish people believed that all adversity they suffered as a people and individually was a punishment for sin. They often praised God for his mercy in not punishing them as much as they deserved. But in time some people began to question whether all adversity was a punishment. We saw that the book of Job wrestles with the issue of innocent suffering. When Job was accused of having committed great sins, even if unknown to other people, he defends himself passionately, insisting on his innocence again and again. Because he believes in the justice of God, he powerfully affirms, "I know that my redeemer [or *Vindicator*] lives" (Job 19:25a). He was convinced that somehow in spite of all that has happened to him, and without understanding why it has happened, God is just and will vindicate him from all charges of sin. The book of Job reaches beyond the previous boundaries of Israel's understanding of suffering. By doing so it lifts the burden from innocent people. No longer do they have to accept the automatic accusation of wrongdoing that results from an inadequate understanding of God's justice, in which suffering is always a just punishment of sin.

As we saw in the last chapter, Jesus also firmly repudiates the view that all suffering is a just punishment. We have mentioned that in John's Gospel, to the disciples' question about who has sinned in the instance of a man born blind, Jesus answers that his blindness has nothing to do with anyone's sin (John 9:2–3). Since the Gospels treat this issue several times, and since it grips many people even today, we need to consider a few more of Jesus' repudiations of the older Jewish view.

Once Jesus bluntly asks, in reference to the death of eighteen people upon whom the tower of Siloam fell, "Do you think that they were worse offenders than all the others living in Jerusalem? No, I tell you" (Luke 13:4).

With the parable of the Rich Man and Lazarus (Luke 16:19–31), Jesus again firmly repudiates the view that all suffering is a just punishment and that prosperity is a mark of righteousness. All we know of each person in the parable is that one is very rich and the other is in abject poverty. The poor man lives on the garbage thrown out by the rich man, and he is so weak that he cannot drive off the dogs that lick his sores, which cause him to be ritually polluted. In the parable Jesus makes it clear that the fact that the rich man enjoys all the goods and comforts of this life does not mean he is righteous, and the fact that Lazarus knows nothing but abject poverty does not mean that Lazarus is unrighteous. For after they die and are in Hades, waiting for the final judgment, Lazarus (in the paradise part of Hades) is comforted in the bosom of Abraham. Since Abraham is the father of the Jewish people, this indicates that even though Lazarus has been wretchedly poor in this life, he is not rejected by God but all along has continued to be part of the covenant people. The rich man, however, is suffering in torment. Although he has been prosperous and enjoyed the best of life on earth, including a splendid funeral, in contrast to Lazarus, he is actually not righteous, even if for no other reason than for his utter neglect of Lazarus at his very gates. The name "Lazarus" means "God will help." Even though God helps Lazarus after his death, the rich man had the responsibility to help Lazarus before he died. Clearly in this parable, God's justice is not to be equated with how things are going for us in this life.

Probably Jesus' most powerful repudiation of this ancient view of justice is his parable of the Laborers in the Vineyard:

> For the kingdom of heaven is like a landowner who went out early in the morning to hire laborers for his vineyard. After agreeing with the laborers for the usual daily wage, he sent them into the vineyard. When he went out about nine o'clock, he saw others standing idle in the marketplace; and he said to them, "You also go into the vineyard, and I will pay you whatever is

right." So they went. When he went out again about noon and about three o'clock, he did the same. And about five o'clock he went out and found others standing around; and he said to them, "Why are you standing here idle all day?" They said to him, "Because no one has hired us." He said to them, "You also go into the vineyard." When evening came, the owner of the vineyard said to his manager, "Call the laborers and give them their pay, beginning with the last and then going on to the first." When those hired about five o'clock came, each of them received the usual daily wage. Now when the first came, they thought they would receive more; but each of them also received the usual daily wage. And when they received it, they grumbled against the landowner, saying, "These last worked only one hour, and you have made them equal to us who have borne the burden of the day and the scorching heat." But he replied to one of them, "Friend, I am doing you no wrong; did you not agree with me for the usual daily wage? Take what belongs to you and go; I choose to give to this last the same as I give to you. Am I not allowed to do what I choose with what belongs to me? Or are you envious because I am generous?" So the last will be first, and the first will be last. (Matt. 20:1–16)

My first reaction to this parable is to feel sympathy with the people who work all day. Either they should receive more, or those who have worked less should be paid less than they. To try to explain away the unfairness, as some people have done, is to miss the marvelous teaching of the parable. As Simone Weil humorously points out, the reason they are paid the same is because the landowner does not have any small change. That is to say, God gives Godself to everyone who hears his call and responds; for that is all that God has to give. Sharing in the life of God is God's purpose for us. Jesus realistically acknowledges that in this life there is not perfect justice. But God in his justice overturns all expectations; for God's justice is actually an act of overwhelming generosity, giving us communion with Godself. If we live fully in the light of God, his generous love and presence free us from envy and resentment even in this life. If we share in the life of God, we too become generous. For example, in the parable of the man forgiven debts far too great for him to repay, the man is severely rebuked when he fails to be generous to a person who owes him a far smaller debt; so he is condemned to live in his self-enclosed prison until he forgives his debtor from his heart (Matt. 18:23–35).

These last two parables introduce the notion of the injustices of this life being rectified in the life to come; they encourage us to live our life now in that light. The man whose letter we began with—after initially being unable to square human suffering with his understanding of God as omnipotent, omniscient, and wholly good—mentions that his mother told him that God wanted the little girl to be with him in heaven. This did not lighten his heart nor satisfy his mind, either as a child or an adult, even though as an adult he continues to pray. Following the logic of his mother's reply, he points out that if heaven is so wonderful, why don't we all go there now? To ease some of the tension between innocent suffering and the power, wisdom, and goodness of God, and to keep the assurance of an afterlife with God from making suffering and tragedy trivial, we need to gain a greater understanding of justice.

Innocent suffering and unrewarded merit have led some great thinkers who are profoundly committed to justice to a belief in life after death. Both Plato and Kant passionately believed in justice. They held that it is morally outrageous that the righteous should be wretched.[1] Plato believed that no one should be unjust and be able to get away with it undetected or unpunished. People should not be able to evade punishment for their evil just by dying; nor should people be denied rewards for the good they do, even though they are not moral in order to receive rewards. This conviction, not the inadequate proofs for the immortality of the soul (which he refutes in his dialogue *Phaedo*), is the main reason Plato believed in life after death. In a similar way Kant in his moral philosophy argues that in this world genuinely good behavior is rarely, if ever, properly rewarded. Indeed, moral people often suffer because of their virtue. If the universe is rational, it is rational to believe that there is another life in which justice will be done. I personally believe that Plato and Kant are correct and that a profound devotion to justice can give a person a reason to believe in a life beyond death and strengthen belief in the resurrection of Jesus.

But there are some issues that must be negotiated to follow this path. Nowadays there is a great clamor for justice and human rights. But to call for justice, even quite actively, does not show that justice itself is loved. Often it may merely be a demand for a better life for oneself. To determine whether we love justice itself as Jesus taught us to do ("Blessed are those who hunger and thirst for righteousness, for they will be filled"; Matt. 5:6), we can perform this simple test. To love justice itself is to desire with our whole heart (to "hunger and thirst") that the consequences of the wrong we have done fall fully and wholly on ourselves, and not on anyone else. All too often the consequences of our evil fall on others, and we generally seek, as much as we can, to evade the consequences of our evil from falling on ourselves. But when we regret and lament this injustice and even to strive to rectify it, we truly love justice itself.

Loving justice thus puts us into a horrible situation. We both want and do not really want justice. But to be so constrained is to open us to blessedness, because it would make us long for mercy and be receptive to the love of God in Christ. It also raises a belief in life after death above triviality. For to reach the conviction that there is life after death, one must follow the route of justice, which leads to a conflict between our desire for justice and our fear of it. Only with the acceptance of our personal failure before the standard of justice and the reception of God's mercy are we able to hold to belief in a life after death when we encounter innocent suffering. Life after death is not offered as a solution to innocent suffering; instead, it is accepted because of a belief in justice. But do we hunger and thirst for righteousness to a sufficient degree to experience the blessedness of God? Until we do, the claim of a life after death will not give any relief in the face of innocent suffering. But the love of justice itself and the need for mercy is absent in the philosophical discussion of the problem of evil.

Yet we must go even deeper than we have so far. Let us examine one of the major terms used in the philosophy of religion in its consideration of the problem of evil: the concept of omnipotence. The Bible does not claim that God is omnipotent, even though philosophy and theology usually say that God is omnipotent. "Omnipotent" is the translation of the biblical Hebrew and Greek words for "almighty." But "almighty" and "omnipotent" do not mean the same thing. "Almighty" means to have authority over all things; "omnipotent" means to be able to do all things. "Almighty," not "omnipotent," is used in all the great creeds, such as the Apostles' Creed, which begins, "I believe in God the Father, Almighty, maker of heaven and earth," and the Nicene Creed, which begins, "We believe in one God, the Father, the Almighty, maker of heaven and earth, and of all that is, seen and unseen." In the Eastern Church the domes of churches symbolize the universe, and on the underside of each dome is an icon of Christ in glory as ruler of the universe. This icon is call "Christ the Pantocrator," "Christ the Almighty Ruler."

The word "omnipotence," which means "can do all things," is actually a philosophically indefensible concept. Peter Geach has shown that all attempts to prove that God is omnipotent or that he can do everything lead to all sorts of needless contradictions and absurdities, such as whether God can contradict his own will or change the past. With great care Geach shows that various efforts to find a coherent interpretation of the concept "have only landed themselves into intractable problems and hopeless confusions; no graspable sense has ever been given to this sentence [God can do everything] that did not lead to self-contradiction or at least to conclusions manifestly untenable from a Christian point of view."[2] By the time a theologian, such as Thomas Aquinas, has finished qualifying the word so that it may suitably be applied to God, it has actually been so redefined that it means the same as "almighty." So we may say that God is omnipotent only if we are careful to make sure it means the same as the word "almighty." Yet the word "omnipotent" is often used innocently to emphasize God's great power and not to mean that "God can do everything."

The use of the notion of "omnipotent," however, can be harmful. All too often when people suffer, or witness the death of a young person, such as did the man with whose letter we began, they cry out, "Why did God let this happen? Isn't he supposed to be able to do anything?" This is not surprising since God's omnipotence is so widely taught in churches, and since few people have been taught that "almighty" and "omnipotent" do not mean the same thing. But the notion "can do anything" simply does not and cannot apply to anything or anyone because it does not make sense. Even so, why an almighty God, one who rules over all things, allows so much evil and suffering still troubles us.

Although philosophers of religion use "omnipotent" when they treat the problem of evil, they have not been able to show that there is a contradiction between God and the existence of evil in the universe. This is because human beings have freedom to obey or disobey God. It is often claimed, and rightly so, that God chose to allow human beings to have freedom to choose to do evil, and that a great deal of human suffering, including innocent suffering, is the result of human actions. The alternative of making people without freedom to choose would be to create robots, not human beings. So even though the cost of human freedom is extremely high, that cost is the result of human action, not God's. This so-called free-will defense shows that there is no contradiction between God's attributes of power, wisdom, and goodness on the one hand, and human suffering on the other. But the free-will defense does not deal with the fact that a great deal of human suffering comes from the operations of the natural world in the form of disease and natural catastrophes, not directly or not primarily from human action. So we will have to deal with suffering that comes from the operations of the natural world, which is called "natural evil" in the philosophy of religion. Just as we had to go deeper into our understanding of justice and our love of justice in order to deal with belief in restitution after death, so too we will have to go much deeper into an understanding of God's relation to the natural world and the significance of Jesus' own suffering in order to understand human suffering at the hands of nature.

Chapter 8

Suffering from Nature and Extreme Human Cruelty

Earlier we saw that in the Bible, God is praised for his power, wisdom, and goodness. One aspect of his goodness is that he has created a habitable universe. But it was realized that nature's operations cause illness, accidents, aging, death, and decay. Some philosophers have claimed that it is impossible to believe in God's goodness from an examination of the natural world. One of their favorite texts is David Hume's *Dialogues concerning Natural Religion,* which is used in most philosophy of religion courses. Through his character Philo, Hume claims that the world order fails to cater sufficiently to our well-being and to that of animals for it to merit praise for its goodness:

> Look round this universe. What an immense profusion of beings, animated and organized, sensible and active! You admire this prodigious variety and fecundity. But inspect a little more narrowly these living existences, the only beings worth regarding. How hostile and destructive to each other! How insufficient all of them for their own happiness! How contemptible or odious to the spectator! The whole presents nothing but the idea of a blind nature, impregnated by a great vivifying principle, and pouring forth from her lap, without discernment or parental care, her maimed and abortive children.[1]

74

This runs counter to Job, who amid his suffering was able to find God's order admirable. The ancient Greek philosopher Epictetus, who had no knowledge of the Bible, also claims that "from everything that happens in the universe it is easy for a man to find occasion to praise providence."[2] If we discover how Epictetus came to this conclusion, we will see why he differs from Hume and agrees with Job, and it will also help us understand the religious significance of suffering.

Epictetus claims that "from everything that happens in the universe it is easy for a man to find occasion to praise providence." In the first instance this refers to the teleological order of nature. "Just as a sword is fitted to a scabbard and a scabbard to a sword, so too are colored objects and light fitted to our vision and our vision to them."[3] Everything in nature has some purpose, and so each item helps to make our universe a cosmos, a harmonious whole. Each creature fulfills its purpose by acting in accordance with its nature; human beings, because they have reason, have the task of discerning these purposes and rendering praise for the glory of the ordered whole.[4]

But all does not go well for human beings. Epictetus responds to this fact by asserting that we can make use of whatever befalls us.[5] The goodness of the cosmos is not that everything goes according to our will, with each of our desires catered for; but if we take a comprehensive view of the entire order of the universe, we will see that we are but one item among many in a vast interconnected whole. Many pleasant and unpleasant things occur to individuals because of the interconnections, but in every instance we have the ability to bear whatever happens to us "without being degraded or crushed thereby."[6] We can wipe our noses because we have hands; we can accept being lame, as Epictetus was, as a small sacrifice for the rest of the universe; we can even endure an unavoidable death from the hands of either nature or the social order without degradation.

This is achieved by recognizing "necessity" and by exercising the only real freedom we have. Our position in the physical and the social world is that of but one reality among many in a system of interconnected events, most of which are utterly beyond our control. What is beyond an individual's control can sometimes injure an individual's wealth, social position, body, and even bring utter destruction. In such circumstances an individual's only real freedom is the manner in which one responds to untoward events beyond one's control. We can complain about our misfortune; or without degradation we can bear whatever comes, even death, by seeing its necessity and yielding to it courageously and magnanimously.

One thus makes *use* of whatever befalls, by using it to bring out these qualities of character. A person can thus be grateful to providence, whatever happens to him, for providing one with the capacity to recognize the universe as an ordered whole and for the capacity to yield to the adversity it brings—even death—with courage and dignity. Thus Epictetus can exclaim, "Bring now, O Zeus, what difficulty Thou wilt; for I have an equipment given to me by Thee, and resources wherewith to distinguish myself by making use of the things that come to pass."[7]

But we might ask Epictetus: It may indeed be possible to make use of everything that happens to us and thus have reason to praise providence, but could not things have been better arranged than they are? If we try to follow up that question, two things result: (1) We find that we can never get it resolved. (2) We fail to learn from suffering.

We can never get this question resolved because things in the world are so connected that we do not know what consequences the alteration of any one factor might have for the rest of the universe. After some speculation, even Hume in his *Dialogues concerning Natural Religion* admits that we cannot pronounce with definiteness on the matter. The decision seems too presumptuous for creatures so blind and ignorant. Nonetheless, he insists that the world's order is such that it does not allow us to infer that its source is good. As we have seen, his character Philo is quite negative about nature's order. "How hostile and destructive to each other! How insufficient all of them for their own happiness! How contemptible or odious to the spectator!"[8]

But Epictetus believes that a world order is achieved by each thing following its nature, which involves, for example, being eaten and used. "Each of the animals God constitutes, one to be eaten, another to serve in farming, another to produce cheese."[9] Each fulfills its purpose by being itself. "For them it is sufficient to eat and drink and rest and procreate, and whatever else of these things within their own province the animals severally do."[10] Human beings also perform actions of this type, but we also have as our purpose the use of our understanding to discern the way things fit together and serve each other. "God has brought man into the world to be a spectator of Himself and His works, and not merely a spectator, but also an interpreter. Wherefore it is shameful for a man to begin and end just where irrational animals do."[11]

We are to render praise because of the abilities given to us. "Great is God that he hath given us hands, and power to swallow, and a belly and power to grow unconsciously, and to breathe while asleep."[12] We are also to render praise, as we have seen, for the ability to withstand whatever befalls us, without being crushed or degraded thereby. We follow our nature and fulfill our purpose, then, by our discernment of the orderliness of nature and by rendering praise.

"If, indeed, I were a nightingale, I should be singing as a nightingale; if a swan, as a swan. But as it is I am a rational being, therefore I must be singing hymns of praise to God."[13]

What is the significance of the disagreement between Hume's Philo and Epictetus over the goodness of nature? It is granted that we cannot settle the question of whether nature could have been better arranged than it is; yet the reason the question is raised is because one of them is dissatisfied with its actual arrangement. One of them is dissatisfied because he expects that everything that lives ought to be better looked after and ought not to suffer so much. Naturally the world order will then fail to provide such a person with a basis to praise the goodness of its designer. But to approach nature with the expectation that we ought to be better looked after, makes it unlikely that we will learn from suffering. Suffering can teach us that we are a very small part of the universe and that we are not to expect as much as we do from its workings. When this is learned, we can then see more soberly and accurately what it does provide for us. What it does provide gives us ample reason to be grateful, in spite of the tragedies its workings produce, whether for us or for others. Indeed, in our humbled and more realistic condition, we can see the glory of the entire world order and be grateful for our capacity to yield ourselves to it courageously and magnanimously even when we are caught in its workings. Let us examine this claim in some detail.

Most of our thoughts and actions are self-serving in various degrees. We stand at the center, with all other people and events in orbit around ourselves. Everything is seen from our perspective and is evaluated, understood, and thought about in such a way as to enhance or protect ourselves. But sometimes we rise above our egoism. However rarely, we do at times restrain our self-concern, even though perhaps not perfectly.

One way this can occur is in relation to the fact that we are material beings. We are part of the natural physical order, subject to its laws, subject to microbes and viruses, subject to aging and decay, subject to death. Here we encounter certain harmful realities that are not completely avoidable. We can mitigate them, as we ought to do whenever possible, but we cannot completely avoid them.

How do we react to the fact that we are material beings, subject to wear and tear? How do we react to illness, to accident, to decay, to death? Do we respond egoistically? Most of the time we do. But sometimes people do not; sometimes they transcend their egoism. This is done when people recognize their vulnerability, recognize it as part of the human condition, part of being a piece of matter.

But egoism is common. "Why did this happen to me? What did I ever do wrong?" This is often said or felt with a sense of indignation, outrage, offense, self-pity. At other times when we feel that we suffer adversity unfairly, we become mute with depression. These are just samples from a host of quite automatic and normal reactions to adversity.

But these automatic responses can be the occasion for *reflection*. They can be an occasion to ask oneself: "Why did I think that I was immune to such misfortune? Why did I think that good and evil are parceled out according to some scheme of merit?" Such reflection can lead us to recognize more fully something we already know: we are material, and as a piece of matter we are vulnerable to injury, illness, decay, and death. To realize this is to realize our status, our place—to realize what we are. It is to come to terms with a hard fact.

Yet with such reflection we also can transcend the psyche's egocentric mechanism. Egocentricity seeks to expand, to get its own way, to go as far as it can. But when the flow of our self-regard is painfully interrupted, reflection can lead to a new awareness of our limitations, and it may lead to an act of *acceptance* of such limitations. When we to any degree accept our status as a piece of matter, we paradoxically to that same extent transcend being merely a piece of matter. Any degree of humility means that one has performed an action that a piece of nonliving matter or nonhuman living matter does not perform.

Thus our automatic self-centered responses to suffering, which on reflection yield to a more realistic recognition of what we are (vulnerable pieces of matter), paradoxically enable us to recognize that we have by that very act transcended being *merely* a piece of matter; for we are not encompassed completely by the principles that govern the rest of matter. In this sense, we are spiritual beings. Our spirituality is found and is affirmed precisely in and with the fact that we are material: subject to the grinding wear and tear of matter. In facing the material facts of illness, accident, decay, and death, we can rise above our egoism and discover that we are spiritual beings.

Here is an example of such a response to the unavoidable price of being a piece of matter:

> Waiting for a lab report,
> Dependent on mysterious authorities,
> Gazing at my daughter in hospital,
> Her mother and I sharing a hard fellowship,
> I know a timeless, tribeless circumstance;
> I drive to the hospital in an eternal procession,
> I eat in the snack bar among the whole human race;
> My tears began 100,000 years ago
> And will never stop.[14]

The person in this poem moves from a mere concern for his child to join the human race. He sees her illness as part and parcel of humanity's vulnerability, and his tears as part of the tears of people throughout the ages. His drive to the hospital is not just his own journey, but part of an eternal procession; in the snack bar he eats among the whole human race. The title is *Common Life*—not a title that refers solely to his daughter's illness. He has transcended the mechanism of the self-centered psyche.

The fact of our material vulnerability can be the occasion to move us off center, to melt the illusion that we are of ourselves immensely significant, and to show us that we are formed of the clay of the earth. That is part of the truth about us. But in that very recognition, in the very act of being humbled, we can recognize that we are spiritual beings. By saying, in the face of hard realities, "Yes, it is so," we break out of the fetters of egocentricity and exhibit a capacity not found in the rest of matter.

Epictetus stresses the attainment of this kind of humility. He regards people, and himself specifically, as part of the cosmos, with no special privileges beyond the ability to perceive its order, to give thanks for its positive benefits, and to endure whatever happens to us without being crushed or degraded thereby. Only with such humility—a humility achieved by one's response to adversity—is it possible for a person to look at this world and to find it gloriously ordered and praiseworthy. Without such humility we do not perceive its goodness because its order often brings adversity to us.

Philosophical discussions of the problem of evil often treat suffering only as evidence that runs counter to a theistic worldview. If we regard suffering only as counterevidence, as did Hume, then we are unlikely to learn from suffering. Our egocentricity will remain intact. We then will judge the world without humility and thus be unable to see that it is praiseworthy despite the adversity it brings to us and other creatures. Nature is not good enough to warrant the gratitude and praise of a person who lacks such humility, who lacks a realistic view of oneself as but a small part of nature.

One might object that the world order may be good enough for a Stoic, but a Stoic is not a Christian. For a Stoic, the cosmos is ordered by an immanent principle, but there is no transcendent creator and ruler of nature. Are not people much more important in Christianity? Are they not the object of a perfect love? Their vulnerability to accident, disease, and tragic death from natural forces does not seem to cohere with the picture of a loving Father who cares for people more than he does for the birds of the air and the lilies of the field.

Actually, *belief* in a loving Father is precisely what enables a person to perform, in the face of adversity, a *second* act. This action enables a person to *experience* God's love in the midst of suffering. It can be performed only by a person who believes in a loving God and who also has the humility of the Stoic. The first act is a necessary condition for the performance of the second. Those who have found themselves not to be encompassed completely by the principles that operate in all matter, by yielding to nature's might, can yield themselves to its might *as a reality that obeys God.* We have been told that when we do this, we find ourselves experiencing God's love. Sister Basilea Schlink claims, "When you are in suffering say, 'Yes, Father,' and strength will flow into your heart."[15] She offers her claim not as a theory but as what actually happens when you so act. There are others who make the same claim that a gracious presence is thus experienced.[16]

Such a gracious presence cannot be known *theoretically*. It comes only by the *act* of affirming God's rule and way of ruling. For a Christian, nature operates as it does, following its intrinsic principles, not merely of its own accord, but because it is so created and presently sustained by God. In saying "Yes, Father" to the *unavoidable* effects of nature on us, we submit to nature's might as something that obeys Another, and not to it merely as a senseless destructive force. Through this act believers claim that the gracious presence of God is known; it flows into oneself and gives a felicity that is beyond the calculation of the pluses and minuses of the pleasant and unpleasant things of this life. The goodness of God is not understood solely in terms of the health and well-being that is enjoyed, and then set over against the untoward things that have happened or may happen to us. God is good in Godself, a unique good, whose value cannot be compared to the creaturely goods and evils we know. And it is God's own goodness, God's Spirit, it is claimed, that comes more fully into a person, and comes precisely through the untowardness of material things and a person's own response to their untowardness.

The act by which one says "Yes, Father"—yielding to nature's might as something that obeys God—is not necessarily a self-conscious act. It seems to have been done by Simone Weil when she was suffering from intense headaches and reciting George Herbert's poem "Love." She says she did not realize it, but she was actually praying, and

> Christ himself came down and took possession of me. . . . I had never fore-
> seen the possibility of that, of real contact, person to person, here below,
> between a human being and God. . . . Moreover, in this sudden possession
> of me by Christ, neither my senses nor my imagination had any part; I only
> felt in the midst of my suffering the presence of a love.[17]

Not only was the act that Weil describes not self-conscious; there also had been a long preparation for this reception of God's love, again not self-consciously. Part of that preparation was her learning, bit by bit, the lesson of our material vulnerability, the first action described above. But in no case is the act whereby one yields to nature's might *as someone who obeys God* simply a matter of reading about it and then saying on the next occasion of an illness, "Yes, Father." One must first learn to see that nature is an orderly whole, with each part operating as it does without any regard for any other part. One must face one's vulnerability to its workings, and not think that this essential vulnerability can be avoided by prayer, any more than Jesus could escape destruction by his prayers in the Garden of Gethsemane. Only when one has had one's egocentricity pierced by the work-ings of nature, and when the fact of vulnerability has become part of the sub-stance of one's character, is one perhaps ready actually to yield oneself to nature as a reality that obeys the Father—to yield not with one's lips but with one's entire self. That "Yes, Father" is what people such as Schlink, Barfoot, and Weil claim leads to a reception of a gracious love in the midst of suffering.

Philosophers surely would not accept at face value the claim of these women that *God* is experienced by yielding to the workings of nature as forces obedient to God. They would say that to believe in God and to act on that belief in the face of adversity *might* make a person feel marvelous whether there is a God or not. Indeed, without further investigation we cannot tell whether it is reasonable to say that God's presence is or is not being experienced by them.[18] But there is no reason to doubt that a felicity is experienced that transcends the normal pluses and minuses of life.

Suffering is almost always discussed primarily as counterevidence to a theistic worldview. It is thought that unless suffering's existence is explained, the presump-tion is against religious belief.[19] It is not noticed, however, that suffering may be a route to humility and hence a route to finding nature praiseworthy, as well as a route to experiencing God's love. We do not therefore need to have a complete account of why suffering exists before we can have a rational faith. A humble person finds nature good in spite of the serious adversities it brings; and a humble person can find God's love precisely by yielding to suffering as God's will.

We have dealt with some of the concerns of the man whose letter we have been considering. Although we do not know the circumstances of the death of the young girl that made such a powerful impression on him, our discussion of the way we are all subject to the workings of nature should help all of us deal with such human vulnerability, whether it affects the young or old. Now we want to discuss another question that he raised: the Holocaust, in which about six million Jews and five million others were exterminated by the Nazis and their sympathizers. This man mentioned his disappointment with the remark of the novelist Norman Mailer, "There was so much going on at the time that God was distracted."

Please remember the caution with which we began this book. I mentioned that a person in communication theory once told me that a speaker says, "Blue, blue, blue." The audience is thinking, "Yellow, yellow, yellow." What is heard is "Green, green, green." This caution is especially necessary when dealing with such an explosive matter as the Holocaust, when the most well-intentioned remark can often be heard as an insult.

I believe that since human freedom is so great, human beings may descend to such depths of evil that events like the Holocaust of World War II, the geno-cide of Armenian people in 1915–16 (plus some in 1922–23) in Turkey, and the 1994 genocide in Rwanda—these can all be attributed to human action. Nonetheless, these and other horrors do not put people and such events beyond the redemptive power of God. I want to point to a way in which we may join together to act redemptively.

Let us approach it this way. When we read about the Holocaust or see films of its victims, we frequently feel that we must ensure that it never happens again. I am afraid, however, that this resolve can be carried out only with a deeper moral and spiritual renewal than can be produced simply by an exposure to the horrors of the Holocaust. Furthermore, a Christian must think not only of the future, as important as it is, but also the past. For Christianity is concerned with the redemption of evil. Redemption from evil is the substance of its hope. Not only do we believe that God seeks to redeem us from evil, but Christian people also are to participate in that action. So my approach to the Holocaust is to ask how we Christians today can act redemptively, and in particular act redemp-tively vis-à-vis the victims themselves.

Crucial to my answer is the concept of a total event that I learned about in Iulia de Beausobre's book *Creative Suffering*.[20] She was arrested and tortured during the Stalinist purges and farm collectivization of the 1930s when some ten million peasants perished. She points out that the suffering inflicted on a person is not a complete event; a complete or total event must include a person's *response* to the suffering (and indeed the response of other people). The way a person responds affects the meaning and significance of the act. For example, a person who responds to torture with fear, self-pity, and hatred, and in no other way, makes the total event worse. But a creative response to the torture can bring a redemptive element into existence. Since the response is part of the total event, it affects the meaning and significance of the event.

The Holocaust, then, is not just an event of the late 1930s and early 1940s, an event over and done with. It includes people's *responses* to that event. How we react to it even now affects the meaning and significance of the event. If our response today is one of utter indifference, then the significance and meaning of the death of the victims differs from what it would be if our response is one of reconciliation with present-day Jews. These are just two possible responses to the event of the Holocaust; but they illustrate how the nature of a response becomes part of the total event and affects the meaning and significance of the event.[21]

With the concept of a total event, we can find a way of acting today so as to bring a redemptive element into existence. The events of the 1930s and 1940s need not remain past events about which we can do nothing except perhaps hope to prevent the like in the future. Instead, they are part of a past that we can affect by our present response. We can affect what that past is, and can even affect the victims of the Holocaust, by the way we act today. Our response cannot change the pain and degradation they endured, but it can change the meaning and significance of what they endured. The Holocaust need not simply be an event of unmitigated horror, a senseless and meaningless liquidation of millions of innocent people.

But how can we act today so as to bring to the total event a redemptive element? Here we need to look at the way presentations of the Holocaust generally affect people like you and me. We hear people refer to the Holocaust, perhaps read a book about it, or see a TV program about it. A normal human reaction to horrible suffering is to ask, "Who is responsible for it?" We want to know who is to blame. For we feel rage and hatred at the sight of cruelty, and we look around for its cause, since we want to focus our hatred on its source. But in the case of the Holocaust, people do not let us stop with the Nazis as the focus of our hatred, for they prod more deeply into the reasons for anti-Semitism and how it was that such acts were allowed to happen. It is frequently proposed that we non-Jews share the blame with the Nazis. This is suggested in many ways. Sometimes it is said that the Christian churches did not resist the Nazis; that the pope was silent when he could and should have spoken up, and it is even claimed that he had at least a tacit understanding that in return for his silence, the Nazis would not interfere with the Roman Catholic Church;[22] and more generally, that long-standing Christian anti-Semitism fostered the attitudes that led to the Holocaust. We present-day Christians are thus implicated indirectly because of our bonds to Christianity and its institutions, a creed that is said to bear heavy responsibility for the Holocaust.

This immediately puts us on the defensive. "I wasn't in Germany in the 1930s or 1940s; I wasn't even born," some will say. The horror of the suffering portrayed, which provokes the normal human reaction of blaming and hating those responsible for it, now clashes with a desire to declare our own innocence. That conflict can lead a Christian of today to feel *resentment*. In many of us, I believe, is a tendency to resent Jews for constantly "harking back" to the Holocaust—a tendency to say, "All right, all right. Jews in the past have suffered. But do you think you are the only ones? What about all the non-Jews who were liquidated by the Nazis? Why don't you talk about them too?" (in spite of the fact that the Jews often do).

This particular response may not always occur, and it may be present in different degrees of intensity, and indeed it is not the feeling that all persons have. But resentment is one of the feelings many Christians have over the frequent references to the Holocaust by present-day Jews. This response is not redemptive. It actually adds to the negative weight of the Holocaust and makes the total event worse.

As long as Christianity or Christians are perceived as bearing some degree of responsibility for the Holocaust, we Christians are likely to want to forget the Holocaust and not to be reminded of it. But present-day Jews cannot forget the Holocaust. They as Jews are *bonded* to the victims by an unbreakable bond. They fear that they and their descendants are exposed to the threat of its recurrence. So they will keep reminding us all of the Holocaust. I believe many Christians do and will feel some resentment toward present-day Jews for persistently recalling the Holocaust for us.

Remembering the Holocaust is actually of great benefit for Christians; for Christians are not bonded to the victims. If it were only up to Christians to keep the Holocaust from being forgotten by most people, it would be lost in oblivion, just as the millions of Armenians who were led on a death march in 1915 by the Turks are on the edge of being forgotten by non-Armenian Christians. It is because there are enough living Jews, who are bonded to the victims, that the Holocaust is not likely to be forgotten (even though its reality has been denied by some, just as the Armenian death march is denied by many present-day Turks). Christians ought even to be grateful to present-day Jews for calling the Holocaust to our minds, so that we have the opportunity to act redemptively, instead of suppressing its reality out of discomfort for being implicated in it in any way.

I can only call upon Christians to recognize that present-day Jews are our only assurance that, as the years go by, the Holocaust will not be forgotten. Likewise, I can only hope that Christians recognize the outrage suffered by Jews in the Holocaust, so that Christians can rise above their resentment. Otherwise our resentment toward the presentation of the Holocaust will keep us from facing the horror of the Holocaust and of our possible indirect responsibility for it, and certainly it will keep us from facing the anti-Semitic feelings many of us harbor. In such a case, not only will nothing redemptive happen, but the total event will be worse.

If we can rise above any sense of resentment, then we Christians and others can actually look at the past, see the horror of innocent people slaughtered, and recognize in ourselves the seeds of the kind of hatred and evil that did such things. It can lead us to a moral and spiritual renewal. Perhaps we can then pay our humble tribute to the Jews of today who have actually risen, again and again, above natural human reactions.

Consider this one news report that appeared in the *New York Times,* February 12, 1980, under the headline, "Three Nazis Convicted of Abetting Murder of 50,000 Jews." We read that Ida Greenspan, who was sent to Auschwitz at the age of fourteen in one of the boxcars that the defendants supervised, attended the trial. She said to a reporter afterward that she thought the sentences (six to twelve years) reasonable. In addition, she is quoted as saying,

> The three of them lived easy lives until now, and the sentences don't really mean much. Perhaps reliving all of this was harder for a person like me than for them. If I did hate them, that would mean in a way that their inhumanity had won.

This response to the outrage of the Holocaust is part of the total event. If both Jews and Christians respond as Ida Greenspan did, not only are we today moved toward deeper moral and spiritual renewal, but also, the meaning and significance of the victims of the Holocaust is affected. Instead of being victims of unmitigated horror, devoid of any redemptive feature, they become our honored dead, who help to redeem us from our bitterness, hatred, and prejudices. In them we can find the prophecy of Isaiah fulfilled in a new way, "Upon him was the chastisement that made us whole, and with his stripes we are healed" (53:5b RSV).

PART THREE
THE DIVINE SACRIFICES

Chapter 9

The Sacrifice in Creation

We cannot conceive of the power of God, except to say that it is unlimited and the source of all that exists. Even then, we cannot fully imagine the immense power that is needed to create a universe. For example, since the birth of Christ, light—traveling 186,000 miles a second—has only crossed a distance of about 2 percent of the length of our galaxy. Our galaxy consists of a hundred billion stars, and it is only one of billions of galaxies. Each galaxy not only has a vast number of stars, but they are so numerous that Allan Sandage, the astronomer, has said, "Galaxies are to astronomy what atoms are to physics."[1] It is not only the matter of size that gives us a glimpse of the immensity of God's power. The complexity of the universe, which has been unveiled by thousands of highly trained and gifted minds, adds to our wonder at God's power. Then too, there is the variety of living beings, which on our tiny planet is so great that we have not even named most of the species.

Yet it is not power alone that the creation reveals, for it takes more than sheer power to create. Dorothy Sayers and Iris Murdoch, both creative writers, claim that the creation of characters for a story requires some renunciation on the part of their creator. Writers must restrain their own personalities to create a personality that is not their own. In order that something may exist beyond and apart from themselves, good writers are required to hold back and to renounce something of their own selves. Good literature is not an extension of a writer's personality; instead, it requires an ethical act of self-renunciation so that something else might exist in its own right.

Writers do not make actual people, but in creating convincing characters they perform an act of ethical renunciation that imitates, whether they realize it or not, the self-limitation of God. When God creates, God brings into existence a universe that is not part of God. This requires an act of profound renunciation, not only because God creates real beings with their own active natures and not just imaginary ones as does a writer, but also because God renounces God's status as the only reality. God shares the status of being real by God's free creative action. Without the existence of anything else, God has a fully complete and rich existence in the divine life of love between Father, Son, and Holy Spirit. There was no need whatsoever to create anything: there was no lack in God's Trinitarian life, no instability to make God create something else, nor any external compulsion. Yet God, who filled all reality, chose out of love to pull Godself back, so to speak, to limit Godself, and to make from nothing realities that are not God or part of God. By allowing creatures to be themselves, active according to the natures God gives, God has limited Godself. For there to be free creatures, God must limit the way God exercises God's power or they cease to be free creatures. Similarly, God must limit Godself in the treatment of nonfree creatures so that they operate according to their created natures. So the creation of the universe means that God renounces God's status as the only one existent—God pulls Godself back, so to speak—in order to create utterly new beings. Since God lacks nothing and is not under any other compulsion, God's creative action is one of self-sacrificing love. The word "sacrifice" is made up of two Latin words, *sacer* and *facere*, which together mean "to make sacred or holy." So the creation is a holy or sacred action.

God's creative self-sacrificing or self-giving love in creation is the prototype of human moral action. It is the kind of love that should be at the root of all human action. This will take some time to explain. Consider how each of us is a conscious center, aware of how our body feels, and with an unreflective, automatic self-concern that is enormous. We usually perceive everything from the perspective of ourselves; in terms of how it affects us. When we have a *unique* concern for ourselves, we estimate the value and significance of all things in terms of their worth for us. Their value is *conditional;* our own is not. Since our unconditional concern is for ourselves and for other things only as they relate to ourselves, we experience ourselves as primary, with other beings in orbit around ourselves.

But this condition is a distortion, for each of us is but one item among many; each of us is not the center of the universe, but only one focus. Other items exist independently of us, and so their significance and value is not to be measured solely in terms of their relation to ourselves. But we usually fail fully to experience other people and things as independent of ourselves. We regard all things as if they are in orbit around ourselves. Such a position is unrealistic, since they are actually not in orbit around us.

This condition of ontological primacy is a particular kind of self, which I call a de facto person, in contrast to a moral person. This distinction parallels the distinction between illegitimate and legitimate governments, or de facto and de jure governments. To be a de facto person is to have a unique self-regard, and thereby to judge all things only as they relate to oneself. In that condition, we do not perceive or experience the most obvious truth, the utter independence of other things from us. One does not experience oneself as standing in the relationship with others but as one among others, one item among many. We even complain about others regarding us as one among others. We do not as de facto persons experience or have ontological humility. But what is it like to experience things as a moral person?

A moral person experiences all things with *perfect* love. All of us rightly believe that we know what it is to love. We have experienced it in one form or another. But most of us have experienced it only to a limited degree or in less than perfect form. Perfect love is a rare experience; we all crave to be loved properly, yet such a love eludes us. W. H. Auden gives a remarkable account of the experience of perfect love between people (which is similar to the love between the persons of the Trinity):

> One fine summer night in June 1933 I was sitting on a lawn after dinner with three colleagues, two women and one man. We liked each other well enough but we were certainly not intimate friends, nor had any one of us a sexual interest in another. Incidentally, we had not drunk any alcohol. We were talking casually about everyday matters when quite suddenly and unexpectedly, something happened. I felt myself invaded by a power which, though I consented to it, was irresistible and certainly not mine. For the first time in my life I knew exactly—because, thanks to the power, I was doing it—what it meant to love one's neighbor as oneself. I was also certain, though the conversation continued to be perfectly ordinary, that my three colleagues were having the same experience. (In the case of one of them, I was able later to confirm this.) My personal feelings towards them were unchanged—they were still colleagues, not intimate friends—but I felt their existence as themselves to be of infinite value and rejoiced in it.
>
> I recall with shame the many occasions on which I had been spiteful, snobbish, selfish, but the immediate joy was greater than the shame, for I knew that, so long as I was possessed by this spirit, it would be literally impossible for me deliberately to injure another human being. I also knew that the power would, of course, be withdrawn sooner or later and that, when it did, my greeds and self-regard would return. The experience lasted at its full intensity for about two hours when we said good-night to each other and went to bed. When I awoke the next morning, it was still present, though weaker, and it did not vanish completely for two days or so. The memory of the experience has not prevented me from making use of others, grossly and often, but it has made it much more difficult for me to

deceive myself about what I am up to when I do. And among the various factors which several years later brought me back to the Christian faith in which I had been brought up, the memory of this experience and asking myself what it could mean was one of the most crucial, though at the time it occurred, I thought I had done with Christianity for good.[2]

This is experiencing the death of the self as the one reality, the only reality one recognizes—the de facto person—with all else subordinate, orbiting around oneself, having significance and value assigned unrealistically because assigned primarily in terms of its relation to oneself.

Dante as a young man had the same experience. He saw a young girl walking down the street one day and said that he was so filled with love that for some days, if anyone had done him an injury, he could not have helped but to forgive them. He described this incident as a personal sacrament, or means of divine grace, and it became the guiding experience of his life. He decided that the goal of his life would be to feel always the way he felt for those few days.[3]

The act of perfect love can be experienced in aspects of one's life. For example, to study nature as a scientist, if it is done humbly, with the desire to understand it as a focus of value in its own right and not just for its utility, is a religious act. It is to participate (whether knowingly or not) to some degree in the kind of love God bestows on his creatures. Putting a child to bed with consideration, or being touched by the beauty of a landscape so that for a moment we lose our self-centered consciousness, are at least to touch the fringe of a love in which the entire universe is perpetually held by its Maker. The more we are able to recognize other things as irreducible particulars, worthy of regard for their own sakes, and free of our own orbit, the more we can understand God's creation as an act of perfect love and can participate in bestowing that kind of love ourselves. But as Auden observed, we can easily revert to our de facto selves, and most of us spend most of our lives in that condition, with only short periods of living as a moral person. But we can also become more free of self-deception, and we can also repent of it. We can improve and live more in the light of love and the truth. When we grasp even the idea of what a moral person is, we start developing the character and habits that can enable one to improve as a moral person.

God regards all things with perfect love, and the experiences I have cited are a way for us to understand the nature of God's perfect love. But God's situation is unlike our own. Once there was no created universe to love. So God's love not only recognizes and respects the reality of others, but in the first instance it makes something when before there was nothing. In Genesis 1, after various acts of creation, it is said, "And God saw that it was good." This means that it is good that the creatures are there, not because they are needed by God nor because they are part of God nor even good because God is their author (although all that God makes is good). God in creation respects the presence of what God has made simply because they are what they are. Though dependent on God utterly to be and to continue to be, God lets them exist as realities: they have power to act and some have power to be centers of consciousness. Though human beings can and have become bloated as mere or primarily de facto centers, they can also become moral centers of consciousness. For these reasons, the creation doctrine, with its view of God's completeness, freely creating all things from nothing, is a statement of the kind of love that God has for all things, and the kind of love we ought to have.

The second Genesis account of creation stresses a feature of God's love that is important to notice. In the story Adam is put into a paradise, a glorious garden, with animals to interest him, and with the presence of God to enjoy. Yet Adam is lonely; something is missing. God perceives this, and remarkably God is not resentful or jealous, but graciously creates a woman for him. Adam needs another that is like himself. Eve is made from Adam's own flesh (not from dust, as he was). Yet she is not completely like him, and partly because of their sexual differences, there can be the mutual enrichment of human love. So our fulfillment involves not only a right relationship with God, but also an intimate life with another. This fulfillment is explicitly endorsed by God's first commandment to be fruitful and to multiply.

The presence of God's Word as the agent of creation and the movement of the Holy Spirit over the chaotic waters are usual parts of the Christian doctrine of creation. But the doctrine of the Trinity as formulated in the early fourth century is often treated separately in doctrinal theology and is not explicitly connected to the creation of the universe. Yet as we briefly mentioned, it is God's fullness of life as Father, Son, and Spirit—a life in which there is mutual giving and receiving between each person of the Trinity—that enables God to be free of the need to create, and the need to gain anything for Godself by creating others. It is precisely because God does not need us, nor any other creature, that God's freely chosen creative action is an act of *perfect* love. Only because God's life is complete in the inner life of Father, Son, and Spirit is it possible for God's self-giving love in creating others to be an action that is wholly gracious. Other views of God and of reality, some of which have been used to state the Christian faith, are incapable of expressing this understanding of divine love in creating as a pure action of self-giving.[4]

This point is so important that we need to look at a brief but brilliant and intelligible statement of the *movement* in God's life: the begetting of the Son by the Father, and the giving of the Holy Spirit as the act of mutual love of the Father and the Son. It is this movement that enables us to gain some understanding of why God is Father, Son, and Holy Spirit, and of the completeness of the life of God. Only because of the fullness and completeness of God's life is God able freely to create, and to love with a pure or perfect love.

Of all the theologians who have written on the Trinity, seeking some, and I stress some, understanding of how God is three persons and one God, I believe Bonaventure (1217–74) in his *Disputed Questions on the Mystery of the Trinity* gives the most helpful and useful understanding of it. There is no question but that the New Testament affirms the reality of God as Father, Son, and Holy Spirit. But how God is three persons is not explained. In his account, Bonaventure creatively synthesizes several sources. According to Plato, good is by its nature self-diffusive. This was widely and fully accepted in the Christian church for centuries; by this principle, Bonaventure says that it is God's nature to communicate Godself. In addition, Bonaventure uses Anselm's understanding of God in which Anselm argues that because God is a perfect being, none greater or better can be conceived. (This is not a matter of the limitations of our minds to conceive, but it would be a logical contradiction from the very meaning of the notion of God to have a being greater or better than God.) Putting these together, Bonaventure says that God as the highest or perfect good is, therefore, the most self-diffusive, giving God's self fully. What can be the perfect or full self-diffusion of God? It cannot be the created universe, for it is a creature and thus limited. Because it is limited, even though marvelous and good, it is not sufficiently great or good to be the self-diffusion of God's very substance and nature. The universe is in no way coequal to God, than whom none greater or better can be conceived. The only possible self-diffusion or full expression of God is God. The self-diffusion of the divine goodness and greatness are the Son and the Spirit. God's diffusion of Godself by *nature* is the Son who, as the perfect diffusion of the Father, is himself God. Divine self-diffusion by *will* is God the Holy Spirit who, as the perfect diffusion of God the Father and Son, is also God. Since one diffusion is by nature and the other by will, the Son and the Spirit are distinct.

In addition, there is only one Son and one Spirit, and no other self-diffusions of the divine goodness and greatness. This is because, according to Aristotle, there are only three ways things can happen: by accident, by nature, and by will. God does not act by accident. God acts by God's nature, and since this act in the divine self-diffusion is perfect, there can be only one Son. God acts freely or by will, and since this in the divine self-diffusion is also perfect, there can be only one Holy Spirit. God is thus three persons and one God, since Son and Spirit are the self-diffusion of the Father, and they in turn, as divine goodness and greatness, return themselves fully to the Father.

This eternal and never-ending self-diffusion and return is the divine life; this is the living God. The eternal and never-ending self-diffusion and return in the divine life was actually worked out in the fourth century and in different language than used by Bonaventure. For example, the distinction between the Son and Spirit was made by saying that the procession of the Spirit is *out of* the Father and *through* the Son, so that the Son is an agent in the procession of the Spirit from the Father. In the latter half of the fourth century, the eternal giving and receiving of the divine life was worked out in its classic form by the three Cappadocian fathers: Basil the Great; Gregory of Nyssa, his brother; and their friend Gregory of Nazianzus. It is usually referred to as the "co-inherence" or "perichoresis" of the divine persons.

> Everything that the Father is, that is seen in the Son, and everything that is
> the Son belongs to the Father. The Son in his entirety abides in the Father,
> and in return the Son possesses the Father in entirety in himself. Thus the
> hypostasis [person] of the Son is, so to speak, the form and presentation by

which the Father is known, and the Father's hypostasis [person] is recognized in the form of the Son.[5]

The same is said of the Spirit. Certainly the unity of God is beyond any unity we know in the created universe, including ourselves, who are in the image of God. The formulations of the divine Trinity given by the Cappadocians and Bonaventure do not pretend to make the divine life fully intelligible. But they do claim to show us why we are able to speak of God as one God and three persons. It took a long generation of controversy before the Trinity first formulated at the Council of Nicaea in 325 was reaffirmed at the Council of Constantinople in 381.

This account of Bonaventure is offered to help us gain some understanding of how, with the notion of divine self-diffusion or communication, it is intelligible to say that God is one God in three persons. We can see why the Nicene Creed says, "We believe in one Lord, Jesus Christ, the only Son of God, eternally begotten of the Father, God from God, Light from Light, true God from true God, begotten, not made [not a creature], of one Being with the Father." Likewise by Bonaventure's stress on the fullness or perfection of God's action, he well captures the completeness of God's life within Godself. God lacks nothing within God's life because there is an eternal giving of the Father fully to the Son and Spirit; as God, Son and Spirit likewise return all that they are and have to each other and to the Father. This life of God we cannot fully grasp, but we can see that it is a sound way to speak of God. And we can see that God's creation of the universe is a fully free and gracious act of love because God is a Trinity with a fullness of life within Godself. In addition, although we cannot imagine the eternal life of God as Father, Son, and Spirit, it is that eternal life, as we will see later, that God seeks to share with human beings, and that we can to a degree receive and experience in this life. Because of our sin and evil, we can participate in the life of God through the Holy Spirit's bringing us into full unity with the crucified, incarnate Son.

As we mentioned, other views of God or ultimate reality, some of which have been used to state the nature of Christianity, are incapable of expressing this understanding of divine love as a pure action of self-giving love in creation and redemption. For example, the greatest intellectual alternative to Christianity in the early third century was the philosophy of Plotinus (205–270). Plotinus's ability to portray nonmaterial reality so impressed Augustine, as he was making his journey toward Christianity, that Augustine acknowledged the help of "the Platonist" (as Plotinus and others like him were called; now called Neoplatonist) as critical in that journey. Yet Augustine and other Christian theologians pointed out that the One or the Good (the ultimate reality) from which, according to Plotinus, all things flow or spill over is inadequate to express the Christian view of creation, and so the divine love. This is because Plotinus claimed that all that exists flows from the One by *necessity:* there *has* to be a universe. The One, lacking stability and completeness, *needs* a universe in order to be. The

One, so to speak, eternally spills itself out, and at the same time draws back into itself all that it spills out, in a never-ceasing flow. This ceaseless flow in some ways parallels the eternal life of the Trinity; yet the going out from the One and the returning to the One simply makes the universe part of the divine. There is no fundamental distinction between God and the universe, as in Christianity. There is no creation of the universe by a God who is the full, complete, and perfect reality. The doctrine that God is Trinity, though requiring abstract ability to discuss, is the foundation for an understanding of the profoundness of God's love in creation.

In modern times, process theology, favored by some who study the relation of theology and science, has inadequacies similar to those in Plotinus. In process theology, God is not full or complete in Godself, but God needs a universe in order to increase and grow in value. God profits from the value produced by others. In addition, God is not a transcendent, holy being. Although the greatest, God is a being among other beings. God is a member of the universe. For all its sophistication, in process theology we have returned to a pagan view of the divine. All these features of the divine mean that it is not possible to characterize the divine generosity that we find in God as Father, Son, and Spirit. It is God's fullness that enables God freely to be generous in creating a universe, and indeed to share God's life.with those who are made in God's image. If these convictions matter, the doctrine of the Trinity matters.

The freedom of God graciously to create a universe and to bless us with eternal life is paralleled by Jesus' freedom in his earthly ministry. Jesus can serve and elevate us because his status as Son is not dependent on us. As we will see in chapter 14, precisely because Jesus does not need us in order for him to be the Son, he is able to be our servant. I observe this here, without explanation, because the Son's status is secured by the Son's life in the divine Trinity, and because God is able to establish a bond of pure love with us without seeking any gain.

It is often said that the doctrine of the Trinity is not in the Bible. This is true. As I have mentioned, the doctrine of the Trinity was not formulated until the Council of Nicaea in 325, in order to repudiate the Arian heresy. But one can see how the development of our understanding of God proceeded on this matter fairly easily. Mark in his Gospel makes it clear that Jesus was God's Son at the very beginning of his ministry. He did not become God's Son through the resurrection, nor will Jesus become God's Son with his return. This still leaves open a question: Was Jesus the Son of God before his baptism, when the Holy Spirit descended on him? There is no reason to think that Mark believed Jesus was adopted as God's Son at that moment. But his silence on this matter before the baptism leaves an ambiguity. It is removed by both Matthew and Luke, who with their prebirth narratives make it clear that Jesus was God's Son before his ministry and baptism. The opening of John's Gospel identifies Jesus with the Word of God at the creation. So Jesus has always been God's Son. But Arius raised the possibility that before the creation, there was a time when the Son had not yet come into being. This was firmly denied by the Council of Nicaea.

It was made clear that the Son is an eternal Son, and that for God to be Father, Son, and Holy Spirit, as the New Testament abundantly teaches, the doctrine of the Trinity needed to be formulated. This pattern is quite general in the development of Christian doctrines. Some new questions arise, positions are formulated, and finally a decision is reached as to which position best protects and expresses the biblical testimony.

Now let us consider how creation and incarnation are connected to the creation of the universe as sacrifices of self-limitation.

Chapter 10

Incarnation as a Sacrifice

The Father's self-limitation or love is also performed by the Son. Not only is the Son present (with the Spirit) at the creation, and active in it as God's Word that brings all things into existence; the Son is also the agent of the redemption of the human race from sin, evil, and death. In chapter 12, I will discuss how God redeems us by the cross. Here I want to concentrate on the Son's sacrificial love by his self-limitation in becoming incarnate.

We may not realize that to become a human being is degrading for God. It means changing from one level of being to another, far inferior level. We may imagine it to a degree by thinking of those situations in which we are badly treated, and we indignantly say, "I was treated like a dog." It is perfectly all right to be a dog, but for a human being to be treated as a dog is a deep insult. Likewise, it is perfectly all right to be a human being, but for God to become a human being is a deep reduction in God's status. It is actually an infinite step downward. God's being is infinite, and for God to become a human being is for God to become limited as a human being. In creation, God limits God's self to allow creatures to exist and operate according to their nature. So God surrenders God's status as the only existing being and adapts God's will to allow creatures to operate according to their natures. But it is only by God's power that all creatures remain in existence and act, and God the Father is not subject to the operations of nature. In the incarnation, by becoming a human being, God the Son is subject to the laws of nature. God incarnate must eat, get tired, sleep, and be vulnerable to injury and death.

Paul stresses the voluntary character of this unique act of self-limitation in his Letter to the Philippians (2:5–11):

> Let the same mind be in you that you have in Christ Jesus,
>
> who, though he was in the form of God [preexistent and divine],
>   did not regard equality with God
>   as something to be exploited [never relinquished],
> but emptied himself [the extreme limit of self-denial],
>   taking the form of a slave,
>   being born in human likeness.
> And being found in human form,
>   he humbled himself
>   and became obedient to the point of death—
>   even death on a cross.
>
> Therefore God also highly exalted him [at the resurrection]
>   and gave him the name
>   that is above every name,
> so that at the name of Jesus
>   every knee should bend,
>   in heaven and on earth and under the earth,
> and every tongue should confess
>   that Jesus Christ is Lord [the title of Israel's covenant God,
>   is applied by Christians to the risen and glorified Jesus],
>   to the glory of God the Father.[1]

Throughout Jewish history there is a yearning for God to be near and present. But in the wilderness, only Moses was allowed to approach God on Mount Horeb, or Sinai, because of the awesomeness of the Lord God. Moses acted as a mediator between God and the people. For example, Moses had a tent far off, outside the camp. When Moses entered the tent, the pillar of cloud (God's presence) would descend and stand at the entrance of the tent, and so God would commune with Moses, and then, through Moses, let God's will be known. By God's command, the tent was replaced by the ark of the covenant, in which the scrolls of the covenant and the Law were kept; the Israelites carried this ark with them from the holy mountain as they made their way to the promised land. We have already seen how the holy presence of God made the ark too dangerous to touch. In the promised land, David made a temple of stone to house the wooden ark. In time the king became an earthly symbol of the presence of God, who was the true king of Israel. It was during an annual celebration of the enthronement of the king that Isaiah had a vision of the glory or presence of God in the temple. The temple was the place that symbolized the presence of God, and the place par excellence to meet God or to be in God's presence. N. T. Wright tells us that "the Temple was, so to speak, an incarnation symbol—they really did believe that the Creator of the universe had promised to come and make his home in this building."[2]

In the wilderness on Mount Sinai, Moses received the covenant that bound Israel to God, and also the Ten Commandments, which the people were to obey as their response to the covenant. The commandments and the rest of the Law are viewed as life-giving. They work within one like an immanent force, "reviving the soul" (Ps. 19:7b), and so are a way God is present. This brings us to the celebration of the wisdom of God in which humans may share and thereby learn how to live well and fruitfully. Likewise, God is near through his word. The word of God uttered at creation changes the chaos into a wonderfully ordered cosmos, suitable for human habitation and joy. God's word is present in and through the order of the cosmos, in which God's power, wisdom, and goodness, indeed glory (or presence) can be perceived and enjoyed. It is also by God's word that the prophets are called, and it is God's word that they speak.

There was also the expectation that God would act to defeat all of Israel's enemies and restore the nation. The expected savior was called the Messiah, meaning the anointed one (oil was used to anoint kings at their coronation ceremonies). The awaited king, the earthly representative of the Lord God, king of the universe, was expected to be of the royal line of David, since David had been Israel's most successful fighting king.

Jesus spoke and acted in such a way as to fulfill the yearnings for nearness expressed in all these notions of word, wisdom, Spirit, law, temple, and messianic king. But the surprise is that the nearness of God is Jesus himself; for Jesus is the incarnation or embodiment of God. As John put it so powerfully,

> In the beginning was the Word, and the Word was with God, and the Word was God. . . . All things came into being through him, and without him not one thing came into being. . . . And the Word became flesh and lived among us, and we have seen his glory, the glory as of a father's only son, full of grace and truth. (John 1:1, 3, 14)

In Luke the wisdom of God is exhibited by Jesus as a boy. Jesus was found by his parents in the temple, "sitting among the teachers, listening to them and asking them questions. And all who heard him were amazed at his understanding and his answers" (Luke 2:46b–47). As an adult, people were amazed at his authority (not needing to cite others for what he said) and the wisdom of his teachings.

At Jesus' baptism, "as he was coming up out of the water, he saw the heavens torn apart and the Spirit descending like a dove on him. And a voice came from heaven, 'You are my Son, the Beloved [chosen]; with you I am well pleased'" (Mark 1:10–11). Unlike the visitations of the Spirit in the Old Testament, in Jesus' case the Spirit dwells with him permanently, and throughout the Gospels Jesus is described as the Spirit-giver, especially in one of the resurrection appearances in which Jesus breathes his Spirit into the disciples, thereby giving them authority and power to be his witness to all peoples (John 20:22–23).

After his baptism, Jesus is driven by the Spirit into the wilderness to be tempted by Satan for forty days and forty nights. There Jesus firmly holds to his view of the nature of the Messiah. Then in Matthew, after Jesus calls his first disciples, he teaches the Sermon on the Mount. Like Moses, he is on a mountain, and he gives his radical (and to the Jewish leaders, unacceptable) interpretation of the law.

After his temptation in Luke, Jesus returns to Galilee to teach in the synagogues. In Nazareth, his hometown, he reads the following passage from Isaiah:

> The Spirit of the Lord is upon me,
>> because he has anointed me to bring good news to the poor.
> He has sent me to proclaim release to the captives
>> and recovery of sight to the blind,
>> to let the oppressed go free,
> to proclaim the year of the Lord's favor.
>
> (Luke 4:18–19)

He claims to be the fulfillment of this passage and to be the kind of Messiah it describes (4:21). The transformation of the notion of "Messiah" from that of a warrior to this understanding of the kingdom is graphically symbolized at the time of the Passover feast by his humble entry into Jerusalem on the back of a donkey (Matt. 21:1–9; Zech. 9:9).

Perhaps the most provocative action is when a paralytic is brought to him. Jesus tells the paralytic that his sins are forgiven. This causes the scribes to think, "Why does this fellow speak in this way? It is blasphemy! Who can forgive sins but God alone?" (Mark 2:7). Jesus responds,

> "So that you may know that the Son of Man has authority on earth to forgive sins"—he said to the paralytic—"I say to you, stand up, take your mat and go to your home." And he stood up, and immediately took the mat and went out before all of them; so that they were all amazed and glorified God, saying, "We have never seen anything like this!" (Mark 2:10–12)

The claim to forgive sins, which is wholly the prerogative of God, is to make a claim far greater than the claim to be the Messiah. It is so central that John indirectly implies that it lies at the center of Jesus' dispute in the temple. John takes the story of Jesus' driving the money changers from the temple during the Passover festival and places it near the beginning of Jesus' ministry, rather than near the end (as in the other Gospels). When Jesus is challenged, "What sign can you show us for doing this?" (2:18), Jesus answers in a cryptic way, "Destroy this temple, and in three days I will raise it up" (2:19). His hearers misunderstand him, thinking that he refers to the temple, but Jesus is referring to himself as a temple. Jesus has replaced the temple as the dwelling place of God. His death will be for the forgiveness of the sins of the whole world, and God the Father will vindicate him by raising him from the dead. In other words, the sacrifices of the temple for the sins of the people will now be replaced by Jesus' own sacrificial death and victory over sin, evil, and death. John finishes the passage by pointing out that his disciples remember this incident after he is raised from the dead (2:22).

The order of events given in the other three Gospels is significant. Jesus goes to the temple and casts out the money changers after he has entered Jerusalem in triumph on a donkey, with some in the crowds cheering him as king of the house of David. But Jesus does not confront the Romans. As Messiah or Savior, he is a king who is at odds not with Rome, but with the leaders of Israel—the opposite of messianic expectations.

At the time of their occurrence, however, not all of these and other sayings and actions of Jesus are understood properly even by his disciples. Consider Peter's confession on the road to Caesarea Philippi that Jesus is the Christ (Messiah). As soon as Jesus explains that he must suffer, be rejected by the Jewish leaders, and be raised after three days, Peter firmly denies that Jesus will be rejected and killed. Such is not part of the common expectation of the Messiah (Mark 8:27–33). Only after Jesus' resurrection do the disciples begin to understand much more clearly who Jesus is and what Jesus has done. They then see all of his previous actions in a new way, and this is reflected in the way the four Gospels are like double exposures. Scholars and even sharp-eyed ordinary readers can often tell that a story of an incident has been overlaid by the understanding of it given by the resurrection. As Paul put it so well, "Even though we once knew Christ from a human point of view, we know him no longer in that way" (2 Cor. 5:16b). Jesus' resurrection has changed everything. They now understand Jesus as Word, wisdom, Spirit, law, temple, and king. This is wonderfully summarized in the birth narrative of Jesus by Matthew's quotation of the passage from Isaiah, "Look, the virgin shall conceive and bear a son, and they shall name him Emmanuel" (1:23; cf. Isa. 7:14). "Emmanuel" means "God is with us." Israel's yearning for God's presence and nearness is fulfilled by the Son of God becoming a human being.

Living so long after the time of the incarnation, with a knowledge of the resurrection, and so accustomed to the church's teaching that Jesus is the Son of God, we often do not think of Jesus in terms of his full humanity or realize what is involved in the incarnation. We usually think of Jesus as divine, able to perform miracles, aware of his status as the Son of God as he undergoes his capture and trial and crucifixion, serenely confident of his resurrection. His humanity seems to consist only of his having a body, somewhat like Greek gods. But this is not the incarnation to which the Gospels testify. A simple story inserted by Kierkegaard in his difficult book *Philosophical Fragments* has helped me more than anything to realize what it is for God the Son to become a human being.

Kierkegaard tells a story of a king who fell in love with a humble maiden. He playfully makes fun of the use of a childish romantic tale to discuss such a profound notion as incarnation. He freely grants that we no longer live in a time when we take kings seriously. Nonetheless, Kierkegaard begs the reader's indulgence because for all its artlessness and fairy-tale quality, the situation contains a serious problem for an author writing on this theme. We can see the difficulty if we imagine that we have a very unusual king, one who wishes in no way to embarrass or offend the humble maiden. If the king goes to her cottage to announce his love in all his kingly glory, with magnificent garments and a large retinue, he would utterly overwhelm the girl. If the maid, however, manages to rise to the occasion and responds to his love, it will never be wholly clear to the king whether it is he whom she loves or the external glory of his power and majesty. One solution to his problem might be for the king to disguise himself as a beggar. But a new problem would then arise. Suppose the king actually succeeds in winning the girl's love while disguised as a beggar. Then she would not really love him. He is a king, but she would love a beggar. No solution can be found in reversing the procedure: Rather than lowering the king, elevate the maiden. For this would suggest that as a humble maiden, she is not good enough to be loved by the king, whereas it is precisely as humble maiden that the king loves her. After exploring every feasible maneuver, the writer might be driven to the only solution possible if a happy love between the king and the maiden is ever to be achieved. It is for the king actually to *become a beggar,* and not merely pretend to be such, and as a beggar to seek to win the maiden's love.[3]

This allegory, for all its apparent simplicity, shows powerfully that the Christian belief in the incarnation is a belief that God became a human being, actually *became* something that God had not been before. God was not just in the shape or appearance of a human, disguised as one, but actually became one; and from the ascension of Jesus to the right hand of the Father, we learn that the Son remains a human forever.

Yet the Son of God incarnate continues to be what the Son has always been: God; only now the Son of God has become human. Jesus is of two natures, divine and human, but he is one person. So *everything* that Jesus says and does is *simultaneously* both a human and a divine action. Thus it does not work to point to something that Jesus did, such as a miracle, and say, "Oh, that is the divine side of him showing," as if he were only a *disguised* beggar whose robe parted slightly, revealing his royal vestments underneath. Nor can we point to something else, such as Jesus weeping over Jerusalem or becoming angry at the money changers in the temple, and say, "Oh, that is the human side of him showing." *All* of his actions are both human and divine at the same time. Jesus is what God the Son became when he became man. But although he is a man, Jesus is not *merely* a man. As we just read in Paul's powerful statement of God self-limitation in Philippians 2, the Son of God incarnate continues to be the Son of God. So all that Jesus says and does are divine actions, including eating and sleeping. Jesus is the divine doing things in a human way.

One way for us to understand how Jesus can be both fully divine and fully human is by a simple analogy from plane geometry. Imagine a flat surface, which a geometer would call a plane, and assume that everything we can experience is on that plane—the human plane, so to speak. Now if there is a divine reality, we could have no experience of it unless its plane touched or intersected our own. In that case most of it would still not be on our plane, but only that small part of it that crossed the human plane. Most of the divine reality would remain outside and still be unknown. With the idea of intersecting planes, we can gather some understanding of how Jesus is both fully human and fully divine. In plane geometry the place of intersection of two planes is a straight line: that straight line is *simultaneously* part of *both* planes, and it is a *single* line. The Son of God is more than what is visible to us on the human plane when the Son becomes incarnate. The Son of God is also part of the entire divine plane. So Jesus, as the Son incarnate, is both on the human plane and part of it, but also on the divine plane and part of the divine plane, extending to all infinity. God in God's fullness is still hidden in his essence because the Son of God even in incarnation extends far into another dimension inaccessible to us.

Because there is no precedent for an incarnation, we have to look at the life of Jesus to see what is involved in the Son's self-limitation. We will do so first in relation to miracles and then in relation to temptations.

For centuries, Jesus' miracles (which the New Testament calls "signs and wonders," "deeds of power," "mighty works") were thought to establish his authority. For example, the eighteenth-century philosopher John Locke claimed that if a man purports to come from God, and performs miracles, he is to be believed. But with the rise of modern science, there developed among the intelligentsia an ideology that all phenomena, without exception, must be explained without reference to any divine action in nature and in the course of history. Much of their assault was against the occult and magical, and biblical miracles were regarded by many as magic. By the nineteenth century, miracles had become an embarrassment to liberal theologians and laypeople. Instead of being a witness to the gospel, they became something that had to be defended.

Let us begin by noticing an apparent dilemma. On the one hand, if miracles were scientifically impossible, as some people held, then Jesus did not perform them. As David F. Strauss put it in the introduction of his *Life of Jesus* (1835), "We may summarily reject all miracles, prophecies, narratives of angels and demons, and the like, as simply impossible and irreconcilable with the known and universal laws which govern the course of events."[4] Before Strauss, David Hume developed a more subtle position, arguing from his experience as a historian. In effect, Hume said that as historians we cannot claim that miracles are impossible. But we should not believe reports about their occurrence in ancient times. We must judge what most likely happened in the past by what now happens, and miracles most likely do not now happen. Fraud and gullibility are always more plausible as a hypothesis than that a reported miracle did occur.

On the other hand, if miracles are possible, then Jesus may have performed them. But the history of religions is full of miracle stories, and so Jesus is not unique. The power to work miracles might give Jesus some authority, but not unique authority. This then is the form of the dilemma we face with miracles: either none, following a supposedly modern and enlightened point of view, or too many claims of miracles performed by other people to establish Jesus' authority as divine Lord.

Neither of the horns of the dilemma is as strong as they may seem to some. Our present view of science does not give us a closed universe, however much the popular eighteenth- and nineteenth-centuries view lingers in many people's minds. And Hume, for all his subtleness, actually relies on what he called "the normal course of nature," which functions in an equivalent way to Strauss's supposedly "iron laws of nature," and so also results in a universe closed to God's actions. The way to deal with the other horn of the dilemma—too many claims to miracles—is to look at the way Jesus' powers were regarded in the New Testament.

In the New Testament miraculous powers are not unique to Jesus; he is not the only person who is thought to have been able to perform wonders. Also, the ability to perform miracles does not mean a person is from God. It means that a person is either from God or from Satan; either one can convey unusual powers on a person. We even have a warning in Mark 13:22 against diabolical wonder-working: "False messiahs [christs] and false prophets will appear and produce signs and omens, to lead astray, if possible, the elect."

The way to tell whether a person performing wonders is from God or Satan is whether the person lives a godly life or not. In Jesus' day it was perfectly clear to many of the religious leaders that Jesus was not a godly person, for he repeatedly broke the Jewish law as it was interpreted by the religious leaders. The Gospels are replete with instances of Jesus' controversies with the Pharisees and the scribes over his actions and teachings in relation to the law. For example, Jesus claims to be Lord of the Sabbath, to have authority over the law. Perhaps his strongest claim in this regard is saying, "Before Abraham was, I am." Jesus thus claims to take precedence over the covenant established with Abraham, which precedes even the law itself (John 8:58). We find similar claims of authority after a series of clashes over the law with the Pharisees and scribes (Luke 6:1–19). In the so-called Sermon on the Plain, Jesus pronounces a series of blessings on his followers (6:20–23) and gives a series of parables (6:39–49), including one about using a blind person as a guide (6:39), and one that includes the assertion "No good tree bears bad fruit, nor again does a bad tree bear good fruit" (6:43). He concludes with the claim that to follow his teachings is to be like a man who builds his house on a firm foundation of rock in contrast to a man who builds on the ground: the house built on the rock is able to withstand floods, but the house built on the ground collapses (Luke 6:46–49).

Since Jesus breaks the law as it is understood by the Pharisees and scribes, the acceptance of him as an authority from God cannot be established by his miracles. But his disciples do accept his authority. How do they come to accept his authority? Apparently the disciples judge Jesus to be a godly person from his compassion for those in need, from the purity of his life, from his teachings, despite the fact that according to the religious authorities of the day he sometimes breaks the law. But all this does not make him divine or unique.

It only shows that he is not from the devil; rather, he is a saintly person and a revealer of God's will, as were the prophets of old.

Although miracles by themselves cannot establish Jesus' authority as one from God, if one judges him to be a godly person, then miracles can show the *extent* of his authority or of his power. This interpretation is suggested by the disciples' remarks, when Jesus saves their ship from sinking in a storm: "Even the wind and the sea obey him" (Mark 4:41). They have already learned that he has power over demons (and/or illness). He has used his power to heal to show that his authority also extends over sin (when he heals a paralytic and is challenged over his authority to forgive sins; Mark 2:1–12). Now they learn that his power or authority extends over the wind and the sea. (The chaos of the waters of a storm, and Jesus' power to still the waters, both strongly allude to the power of God's Word at creation, in which the primal watery chaos is ordered.) Eventually they come to learn that he has power or authority even over death. The progressive unveiling of the extent of his authority culminates in their confession of him as "Lord," a title hitherto reserved for God alone.

If we interpret the cryptic remarks concerning the destruction and rebuilding of the temple in three days in John 2 as a claim of authority over the sacrifices for sin that occur there, we see that his miracles can be construed as *part* of a revelation or unveiling of the extent of his authority. Miracles thus are not isolated phenomena in his ministry, but *one fashion* in which the extent of his authority or power is revealed. With his resurrection and appearance in his glorified body, it is an unveiling that is to be completed with his return, when all things shall be seen to be put "under his feet" (1 Cor. 15:24–28). So I suggest that the miraculous in the New Testament accounts of Jesus is not used to establish that he is from God—as did John Locke following a long apologetic tradition—but one fashion in which he exhibits the extent of his authority.

The miracles also have another vital function. They exhibit or reveal the nature of the kingdom of God, or the rule of God. This is encapsulated in the following passages:

> When John [the Baptist] heard in prison what the Messiah was doing, he sent word by his disciples and said to him, "Are you the one who is to come, or are we to wait for another?" (Matt. 11:2–3)

Even though when Jesus approaches John to be baptized, John recognizes Jesus as the promised Messiah, who is to bring the kingdom of God, now some time later in prison, John is troubled. Apparently things have not gone as he has expected. The kingdom of God is not evident to him. Jesus answers John's disciples by saying:

> Go and tell John what you hear and see: the blind receive their sight, the lame walk, the lepers are cleansed, the deaf hear, the dead are raised, and the poor have good news brought to them. And blessed is anyone who takes no offense at me. (Matt. 11:4–6)

Jesus' reply is to point to his healing miracles and particular concern for the poor as indications of the kind of work that the Messiah or Christ is to do, and the nature of the kingdom he is inaugurating. These actions are part of the introduction of the kingdom of God. This is not what is expected of the Messiah, and so apparently the reason John is confused at Jesus' ministry. In his response to John's disciples, Jesus deliberately alludes to Isaiah 29:18–19; 35:5–6; and in particular 61:1—which have been neglected in people's understanding of what the Messiah will do. Jesus invites John to answer his own question, basing his decision on what he hears of Jesus' activities in light of Isaiah's prophecies.

In his reply to John, Jesus indicates that his claim to be the Messiah and his understanding of what it is to be the Messiah can be a cause of offense or rejection. After his baptism by John, Jesus begins his ministry. As we have seen, when he comes to Nazareth where he has been brought up, he goes to the synagogue on the Sabbath day and teaches, as he customarily does. He unrolls the scroll of Isaiah and reads a passage (61:1–2; 58:6) that he takes to contain many of the marks of the Messiah.

> The Spirit of the Lord is upon me,
>   because he has anointed me to bring good news to the poor.
> He has sent me to proclaim release to the captives
>   and recovery of sight to the blind,
>   to let the oppressed go free,
> to proclaim the year of the Lord's favor.
>
> (Luke 4:18–19)

Jesus then tells the congregation that this Scripture has been fulfilled in their hearing. As what he says begins to sink in, they become increasingly hostile. After an exchange in which Jesus points out how prophets are never accepted in their own hometowns, the people are enraged and lead him to the brow of a hill, so they might throw him off the cliff. But they lose their nerve. So he walks through the midst of them and goes on his way, to teach elsewhere.

The approach I am using toward miracles has now become common among biblical scholars.[5] The rejection of miracles in the name of science by F. D. Strauss and more recently in the mid-twentieth century by Rudolf Bultmann in his "demythologizing" program is no longer followed. Rather, scholars are concerned to determine the role a miracle plays in an incident or in the overall story of a Gospel or other scriptural document. Scholars ask, "What does the extraordinary event mean? What is the divine message imparted through the event?" (They do this with ordinary events as well, especially with what the Gospels call "signs.") Thus we view the puzzling story of the healing of the man born blind, who according to Jesus is not guilty of anything, nor are his parents, so that he should have been born blind; John interprets this event in part as a sign of the blindness of traditional Jewish piety toward Jesus' works.

By approaching miracles from the point of view of their role in the biblical story, we can rightly reject ancient and contemporary revivals of magic, astrology, witchcraft, spiritualism, and the like as irrelevant to theology. They play no role for us in discerning God's purposes or will in the signs and wonders that are part of the biblical accounts. Likewise, even if we obtain impeccable evidence of psychokinesis (the power to affect objects by one's thought) and telepathy and clairvoyance, they have no relevance in our determination of the purposes or will of God revealed in both ordinary and extraordinary events in the biblical accounts.

Although the Son of God has greatly limited himself in becoming incarnate, the Gospel stories show that the incarnate Logos still has great powers. To understand the incarnation still better, we need to explore the self-limitation revealed in his temptations, particularly on the cross. All four Gospels stress that Jesus is subject to temptations, and their reality is briefly indicated by saying that he is subject to temptations just as we are (Heb. 4:15). Matthew and Luke give detail in describing the three great temptations Jesus endures in the wilderness right after his baptism by John, and before he begins his public ministry. In the next chapter we will examine Matthew's account (4:1–11) of these temptations before we turn to the last and greatest temptation, the crucifixion.

Chapter 11

The Temptations
in the Wilderness

As a human being, the Son of God must face the same temptations as we face if he is to lead us from where we are onto a path that leads into his Father's kingdom. So we find that right after his baptism by John, Jesus is led by the Spirit into the wilderness, where he is tempted for forty days and nights. That God's Spirit leads him means that his Father subjects him to these temptations, and also that he obeys the prompting of the Spirit. The time span is symbolic and important. In Noah's time, it rained forty days and forty nights, which acted as a kind of baptism. Moses fasted forty days and nights on the mountain of God before he received the law. The people took forty years to reach the promised land and were tested or tempted in the wilderness. So Jesus is like Noah as a righteous person who is saved alive from the floodwaters; he is a new Moses, who after his forty-day fast begins to lead a new people into the kingdom and to give them the law they are to follow in his Sermon on the Mount. He is the new Israel, since he overcomes the same temptations in the wilderness to which they succumbed centuries earlier.

Each of these Old Testament stories marks a major turning point, a major change in humankind's relationship to God. The flood (Gen. 6–8) washed away all evil and gave humanity a new start. God gave Moses the law as one of the conditions of the covenant (Exod. 19–24). The exodus from Egypt was what made Israel a nation. Forty, then, is a sign or symbol of a *decisive* change. Jesus' temptations, just before the beginning of his ministry, are a struggle in which a new path to the Father is being created for us to follow. Forty is a symbol to mark this event as the hinge on which a turn is made into a new future for us all. So we need not worry about whether a person can do without food for forty days or not.

And yet Jesus does fast. There is no food, and he grows hungry. It is then that the temptations start. When he has grown weak, when it becomes hard to see straight in that sun-drenched land, it is then that the temptations come. Exposed to terrible hunger, with his body giving him no rest, perhaps he is looking at the smooth stones that lie at his feet, and notices how they look something like the smooth loaves just out of a baker's oven, and then it strikes him: "Turn these stones into bread" (Matt. 4:3).

It is a temptation to use his powers to bring comfort to his body, to use his unique relationship to his Father as a magic wand to care for his earthly needs. That is a personal temptation he faces: to avoid the pains of a bodily life. More broadly, it is to avoid being subject to one of the common human conditions we face. It is a temptation to reject a condition set by his Father, that we are to seek him as beings who must eat, who are vulnerable to starvation, as beings who are made to desire material goods and who can therefore become greedy, covetous, envious. To use his powers to provide food in a miraculous way when he is in trouble would mean rejecting one of the conditions his Father sets for us. He then can hardly pioneer a new way *for us* to the Father if he rejects one of the conditions to which we are subject in our pilgrimage. He must have a kinship with us; he must share our situation, if he is to lead us from where we are to the Father. As Hebrews 2:18 puts it, "For because he himself has suffered and been tempted, he is able to help those who are tempted" (RSV).

But for him it is also a temptation that concerns the welfare of others. He can make his mission to the world an attempt to satisfy people's bodily needs. He can try to see to it that everyone has food, clothing, and shelter; to see that everyone's physical needs and desires are fully satisfied.

His Father faced that decision when he made the universe; he could have protected us from all shortages, from being vulnerable to starvation. But clearly we are vulnerable and we are not fully protected. Whatever the reason for this situation, it is where we are. Now Jesus faces the decision the Father made at creation to allow this. He has to ratify or to reject his Father's decision by deciding what his mission is to be.

This is for him a temptation, a terrible temptation. For are not we all, as Jesus was, frequently moved by compassion at the suffering of people, their terrible suffering? Not all people are being fed. At the same time do not we all know that people do not live by bread alone? None of us is hungry. We have foods for our breakfast that even a king could not have five hundred years ago. Orange juice, for example, was not available to lands of the north, far from the warmth of Spain or Africa. We drive cars that have more power than an entire factory had in the eighteenth century. And yet are we happy? The human capacity for unhappiness is so enormous that the entire world cannot fill it.

The attempt to deal with this enormous capacity is the theme of the legend of Faust. In a pact with the devil, Faust is allowed to have every delightful experience and enchantment imaginable. All the sweetness the earth can offer is his. But the moment he becomes bored, he will forfeit his life to the devil. Sure enough, Faust has a ball; sure enough, in time he becomes bored. All that the world has to offer cannot satisfy him except for a time. There is about us an indefinable craving that the whole world cannot fill. It may take a person a long time to find this out, for we are also animals and take animal delight in what we consume. And we should, for it is needed and it is good. But that is precisely the temptation: our need and its goodness. We consume and consume and consume, and we learn the hard way, if we learn at all, that we cannot be satisfied this way. We find here that we are tempted into evil, to following the wrong path, not by something that is evil, but by something that is good. So we are faced each day with the terrible temptation, the powerful pull of two forces: our need and enjoyment of the goods that are of this world, and our need for the good that is not. We need *both*. For we cannot live by bread alone; we do not live without it either. How can we face this temptation?

Jesus faces it by quoting the Old Testament: "One does not live by bread alone, but by every word that comes from the mouth of God" (Matt. 4:4; cf. Deut. 8:3). We shall live by listening to all that God tells us. The danger is that we shall not notice that the world cannot satisfy us, or notice it and forget it again and again. We overlook the craving that material goods do not satisfy. When we do thus forget, we miss the gateway into the kingdom of God. Sometimes in the very name of Jesus, Christianity is used in order to obtain material goods. Some popular religious movements are led by people who tell us that Jesus has helped to make them a success. They claim that we too can reach our goals through following their example. Yet in the wilderness, Jesus rejects the use of his special powers to gain bread, much less wealth.

Later in his ministry, Jesus tells us that if we seek his Father's kingdom first, then the food, drink, and housing that his Father recognizes that we need will be obtained. He knows that his Father does not govern the world or overrule people's actions so that there is no hunger. Jesus apparently is teaching us that people who seek the kingdom will not necessarily starve *because* they are seeking the kingdom. They may starve for other reasons, but not because they seek the kingdom. In spite of the terrible suffering of people who lack food, clothing, shelter, and proper medical care, and his great compassion for them, Jesus never loses sight of the fact that we do not live by bread alone. It is the powerful pull of both these facts, their suffering and his compassion, that constitutes his temptation. To reject either in favor of the other would destroy his mission.

In the second temptation Jesus faces in the wilderness, we see another way the Son of God limits himself when he becomes incarnate. The devil takes Jesus to Jerusalem and sets him on the pinnacle of the temple (perhaps by means of a vision). He introduces the temptation by quoting Scripture (imitating Jesus' response to the first temptation). He tells him, "If you are the Son of God, throw yourself down; for it is written, 'He will command his angels concerning you,' and 'On their hands they will bear you up, so that you will not dash your foot against a stone'" (Matt. 4:6; cf. Ps. 91:11–12).

What is the temptation? Is it to test Jesus' confidence in his mission and the care of his Father so that he can accomplish it? Possibly. In the wilderness the strong sense of assurance he has felt at his baptism might be beginning to ebb. He can gain reassurance by testing God and putting all doubt to rest. Such a method seems perfectly correct, given the scriptural passages Satan quotes. Maybe this is the nature of the temptation: a surge of self-doubt brought on by the devil challenging him to jump from such a great height. But if it is, this is not all that is involved.

When Satan says, "If you are the Son of God, then do this or that," he implies that such acts are what a Son of God would do. He does not argue that they are so; he just speaks as if it were so as matter of course that this would be Jesus' behavior. Perhaps his frontal attack is to sow doubt, or at least to try to do so. But concealed in that more obvious attempt is the subtle, casual presumption of what the Son's behavior would be—as if this is not at all the issue.

In response to this presumption, Jesus in effect replies, "Precisely because I am the Son of God, I will *not* do these things." Such deeds would be contrary to the very essence of his sonship. Instead of showing that he is the Son of God, to do them would prove that he is not. As we saw in the first temptation, to turn stones into bread would remove him from the vulnerability to starvation that all people face. Jesus could try to make himself immune from that threat by making use of his special relationship to his Father. He then cannot himself blaze a trail for us to follow to the Father, since he would not be starting from where we are. Precisely because he is the Son, he will not turn stones into bread. Precisely because he is the Son, he will not use his special relation, his special powers, to avoid being where we are—vulnerable to starvation. He hazards starvation. He trusts his Father's care, as he seeks to open the kingdom for us to enter.

Likewise, Jesus will not jump from the temple, not because he doubts his sonship, but precisely because of his sonship. Jesus is faced with the task of convincing other people who he is. He has to do something or give us something that we can recognize as coming from God. There was a tradition that the Messiah, when he comes, will appear on a pinnacle of the temple. If Jesus chooses to make such an appearance, it might have the character of a sign. When the New Testament speaks of "signs," it often means deeds that reveal God to people who have spiritual discernment. Without spiritual discernment, the significance cannot be recognized and understood. So an appearance on the pinnacle of the temple, if performed as a sign, might be a perfectly permissible act. It would be a way of making the claim that he is the Messiah, a symbolic way of saying, "I am the Christ."

But the temptation is not merely to *appear* on the pinnacle. It is to *jump* from it with the expectation that he will be miraculously saved. Such an act would *not* be a sign; it would require no spiritual insight to be understood. It would satisfy a common expectation concerning what God does for us: God protects us from danger. Jesus could display his special relation to the Father by a spectacular act of divine protection. By jumping and being miraculously saved, Jesus could say, "Follow me, for God's special care is on me; I have jumped from the temple and been protected. I will see to it that protection is extended to you as well." He would overcome the difficulty of convincing people who he is by a miraculous display in which something that they expect God to give to people—miraculous protection—has indeed been conferred.

There is a strong connection in our minds, as well as among the people in Jesus' time, between faith in God and being protected from harm. Faith in God's goodness and love, indeed, faith in God's very existence, is deeply bound up with the idea of God's care. We certainly are upset when we see a good person, who has been a wonderful neighbor and a fine parent, suddenly struck down by a terrible disease or accident. We saw this with the man with whose letter we began, when as a boy he was deeply troubled by the death of a young, innocent child. So then, how can we believe in God as a loving Father?

When God made the world, God faced this problem: whether there were to be creatures who were not only spirits—able to choose their destiny—but who were also to be spiritual animals, creatures liable to harm and destruction. And moreover, given that there were to be spiritual animals liable to injury, God had to choose whether God would intervene and suspend both nature's destructiveness and the harmful effects of freely chosen evil. We know the choice God made: God decided that our situation would be one in which we would have to find God, learn to trust God and love God, while we are exposed to injury and destruction.

This choice that the Father made now comes to Jesus as a temptation. Jesus has great compassion for those who suffer, and he is faced with the temptation of asking that the Father protect us from all harm—perhaps even to demand that the Father protect us. And why not? Doesn't God love us? Isn't God master of heaven and earth? Doesn't God know when even a sparrow falls? Then why not expect such care? Why not look to God to show God's love and care and concern for us? Otherwise, how can we trust God? How can we believe or have faith in God?

Once again we discover that we are not tempted by something that is in itself evil, but by something that is good. For we are fragile. We can easily be hurt and even destroyed. A slip off a ladder while doing simple home maintenance, a momentary lapse of attention while driving, a virus or an unexpected strain on the heart—and our life is gone. People we dearly love, whose lives are so inter-twined with ours that we cannot distinguish between their welfare and our own, can in a moment be seriously injured or utterly destroyed. Quite naturally we seek whatever protection and security we can find. We constantly try for better safety measures on our highways, protection in our factories and mines, and advances in medical knowledge. All of us go as far as we can to protect ourselves and those we love. We certainly know that our own power and knowledge are limited. Yet we long to be completely safe, to have an assurance and a confidence that we and those we care for are safe.Is it wrong to turn to God for help and protection? We have been taught by secular thought that crying for help retards the development of personal maturity. To suppose we can make ourselves fully secure by calling on God is to indulge in wishful thinking. It reflects an incapacity to face our inevitable and ultimate vulnerability. True maturity is to face the fact that there is no complete security, we hear.

This secular view contains a grain of truth. In a distorted way it reflects a truth of Scripture: some human misery is inevitable. Without realizing it, it endorses the scriptural truth: Rain falls "on the just and on the unjust" alike (Matt. 5:45b RSV). However, in rejecting the idea that God will protect us, the secularists are actually rejecting only a false, misguided religion. This misguided religion, just like its secular opponent, assumes that God is *supposed* to give special protection to those who call on him. The two views merely disagree over whether God in fact does or does not protect us. Both views ignore the scriptural text that rain falls "on the righteous and on the unrighteous" alike.

We can see something of the falsity of their assumption, as far as scriptural religion is concerned, by the way Israel once succumbed to the second temptation. Israel thought that Jerusalem could never be conquered because the temple of God was there. Israel assumed that because the nation had a special relationship with God, it would be saved from its enemies in its various wars. Otherwise God could not carry out God's purposes. And indeed, there were times when, though destruction seemed imminent, the city was spared. But eventually it was captured by foreigners and the temple itself destroyed. The Israelites learned that their special relation to God did not give them special immunity.

Jesus does not call on his Father to get him out of dangers. He tells us, when he is arrested, that he has the power to summon legions of angels to save him. And when he is on the cross, his enemies wait to see if God will rescue him, and they taunt him when no help comes. The assumption is that God can and does protect his own. In the Garden of Gethsemane, Jesus does ask his Father to deliver him from an ordeal, but then, throughout his life, he recognizes that he cannot be immune from all danger and suffering, and in particular from the ordeal of the cross, so in the garden he adds, "Nevertheless, thy will be done" (cf. Luke 22:42). His trust in God is shown to be complete by his confidence in his Father's love even when undergoing suffering.

It is perfectly natural to want to be secure. But whether we like it or not, we do not have immunity from all harm. Yet so much of religion in our land is a religion of "God protects us from the ordinary dangers of life," so that "our foot will not be dashed against a stone." Sometimes it is explicit, as it was among the Jews when they expected their temple to make Jerusalem impregnable. Sometimes it is a quietly made assumption out of which we operate. Yet Jesus explicitly turns from this temptation. Our Father does not let himself be found out so easily. After all, are we so stupid that we would not turn to God—or to anything, for that matter—if it is found to pay off? Suppose all we need to do is to say, "OK, I'll pray to you if I can expect no disastrous illnesses, no accidents, a long prosperous life, and everything going well with the kids." If this were the case, we would not be able to build churches fast enough! But God is not a means to our ends—even good ends such as these.

As we saw in William Temple's assessment of Job's trials, to know God is to grasp a felicity that is beyond pain and compensation for losses. To deal with God is to find a reality who is *incommensurate* with all the world. God is not on the same scale of measure or on the same balance as anything else; and what God wants to give us is Godself.

Let us look more closely at this felicity or joy that we receive when God gives himself to us. The small craving, that one desire that exists buried amid our multitude of desires, of which I have already spoken, is one of the major places where God touches us, indeed enters us. It is the feeding of *that* hunger that makes us realize that the nourishment received there is incommensurate with all else that we can receive: it is without price. It gives us a joy that is different from the satisfaction or frustration of all the other desires we have.

As is well known, Beethoven's Ninth Symphony has a choral section in the last movement. Out of a sea of sound, a voice thrusts itself like a massive cliff, repeatedly singing, "Joy!" followed by a chorus. To anyone who knows the felicity of God's presence, even to a degree, that choral outburst suggests the same reality. Paul frequently alludes to it at the beginning of his letters: "Grace and peace to you from God our Father and our Lord Jesus Christ." The experience of God's presence, which feeds our hunger, is an experience of grace, peace, and joy—a felicity the world cannot give. This is not esoteric mysticism. We can receive it in such prosaic ways as hearing a hymn sung, or thinking of some of the words of Jesus, or in a Communion service. We find in them and through them a nourishment for our hunger, a nourishment that nothing else gives us. The Christian faith is not based on the projections of immature people.

It should now be apparent how we can legitimately pray for God's help and protection without injury to our spiritual welfare. It is because the felicity that we receive from God is outside the network of worldly satisfaction, beyond loss, pain, and compensation. In this life we can and do receive much consolation and help from God without harm to our spiritual welfare, without its being destructive to our love for him. By God's providence we can also receive protection from many ills and dangers without harm to our spiritual well-being. For in both cases we love God: we recognize God's reality and experience the joy of knowing God because God nourishes a hunger, a longing that is a desire *only for God*. We are not in danger of trying to turn him into a *means* to our ends.

In the third temptation, ironically, the Son of God is offered rule over the kingdoms of this world, though it is actually by and through the Son that all things were made. This offer can only be made because the Son of God has limited himself in the incarnation. Since he has renounced power and glory, he might be tempted to reclaim them, because he rightly has a claim to them. But the power and glory of nations that he is being offered are not the same as the power and glory of God. All power comes from God as creator, but the power he gives becomes increasingly demonic and corrupt when used without any reference to God.

When Satan shows Jesus the kingdoms of this world and their glory, he offers him success and the prestige that goes with success. He is offering the highest social recognition possible: Jesus is to be Lord of all the earthly kingdoms and to enjoy prestige, deference, and acclaim. Such would certainly be more in line with the kind of Messiah expected.

Perhaps Jesus' lack of sufficient status to gain acceptance by the Jewish leaders and large parts of the population is reflected in the comments of his detractors who said, "'Is not this the carpenter, the son of Mary and brother of James and Joses and Judas and Simon, and are not his sisters here with us?' And they took offense at him" (Mark 6:3). Jesus apparently feels the lowliness of his position when he says, "Foxes have holes, and birds of the air have nests; but the Son of Man has nowhere to lay his head" (Matt. 8:20).

The attractiveness of social prestige may have its pull on Jesus. Nonetheless, the main attractiveness of Satan's offer is not the prestige that goes with success, but success itself. Jesus' mission is to enable people to find the kingdom of God. But how is that to be achieved? How is he to win people over? How is he to save us?

When the Father created the universe and decided to make spirits who could be like himself—creative, with imagination, capable of moral insight, and of spontaneous devotion—God faced a dilemma. God faced the problem of allowing people freedom or using God's power in such a way as to compel them to recognize God's sovereignty. The greatest and first commandment of the universe is that only God is to be worshiped; only God is the foundation and fountain of life. But how is that commandment to be kept? By force? By punishment when we do not turn to God, so that it becomes obvious that it pays to worship God? (Would that even be devotion? Wholehearted attachment?) Or by God's restricting Godself, by pulling back on the exercise of his power, by limiting Godself, and letting us seek God because of our hunger, because we have learned to love God? This is a terrible choice because it means exposing creatures to awful suffering—to all the ills and torments and ravages that our history and life are full of. It is to expose us to evil, to rampant and hidden evil that can destroy us utterly. We know what our Father chose to do.

Jesus in the wilderness faces this temptation: to accept or to deny his Father's choice. He is faced with accepting the suffering, the brutality, the evil of people—or to refuse to accept it and to *impose* himself on people. He could use the devil's way: maximization of power—use all you have to get your own way, no matter how you do it. And that is a temptation because the end is good: to stop people's suffering, to stop their wandering in darkness, to end the terrible beastliness and destruction that plagues us.

It is not an easy choice. It is so hard that later in his life Jesus weeps over Jerusalem, "O Jerusalem, Jerusalem, killing the prophets and stoning those who are sent to you! How often would I have gathered your children together as a hen gathers her brood under her wings, and you would not!" (Matt. 23:37 RSV).

Jesus painfully and faithfully shows the same kind of compassion and restraint as his Father does. He does not try to use force any more than his Father does in order to get his way. And Jesus suffers the consequences of his renunciation in at least three ways. First, he suffers in sorrow at the failure of many to follow the path he opens up, as we saw in the passage about his weeping over Jerusalem. Second, by his renunciation of might, he renounces the social prestige that goes with its successful use. We see echoes of the pain this causes in his comment about having no place to lay his head. He has to bear the contempt of his detractors who jeer at him as the son of a carpenter. The third consequence only becomes apparent near the end of his life. His lack of social position and renunciation of physical might make it possible for others to use force against him. So he not only rejects might as the basis of his life's work; he is also willing to become its victim on the cross.

How beautiful it is that Jesus chooses to live in the realm of justice, the realm of forgiveness, and the realm of reconciliation. He will not use might. He teaches and heals. In his acts of forgiveness and compassion, he shows us what is good; and he asks us to hear of God's mercy as good news. But he never imposes himself on anyone. On the contrary, he not only rejects force as a means, but as we have said, he suffers and endures the effects of force applied against himself.

Jesus did not have earthly or carnal greatness, as do those who lead great armies, or who have immense wealth. A person who sees such greatness as the only kind of greatness is blind to the greatness of the mind. Pascal observes:

> The greatness of intellectual people is not visible to kings, rich men, captains who are all great in a carnal sense. Great geniuses have their power, their splendor, their greatness, their victory and their luster, and do not need carnal greatness, which has no relevance for them. They are recognized not with the eyes but with the mind, and that is enough.[1]

Both those who are enclosed in a carnal understanding of greatness and those who prize only the greatness of the human mind cannot recognize the greatness of Jesus' teachings and his holiness with their categories. Pascal writes:

> Jesus without wealth or an outward show of knowledge has his own order [domain] of holiness. He made no discoveries; he did not reign, but he was humble, patient, thrice holy to God [his victory over the three temptations in the wilderness], terrible to devils, and without sin. With what great pomp and marvelously magnificent array he came in the eyes of the heart, which perceive wisdom![2]

So although Jesus was Lord, his lordship was not based on force, like that of most earthly rulers, but on justice, mercy, and humility before the Father. Justice, mercy, and humility create and promote community. They enrich us all by giving us access to each other across the barriers of social position. They heal the withering effects of force. We see them in operation throughout Jesus' life. He was oblivious to the barriers created by social status. He made some who were lowly, like fishermen, and even social outcasts, like Matthew the tax collector, into his disciples. He ate with publicans and sinners and showed compassion for the poor and lepers. He was bringing a different kind of kingdom to us. By his renunciations in the wilderness, Jesus pioneered a way to the Father, telling us, "Those who love their life lose it, and those who hate their life in this world will keep it for eternal life" (John 12:25).

The self-limitations of Jesus exhibit the same kind of love as exhibited by his Father in the creation of the world. The Father, by his self-limitation, creates genuine realities that are not part of himself, and gives them the scope to operate according to their natures. So God respects the freedom bestowed on human beings not only to turn from him, but also in his efforts to redeem them. These features of God's love and actions as Father and Son exhibit another feature of the divine holiness. Not only does God's nature transcend all other realities, so that even in God's manifestations to Moses and Isaiah, for example, God remains "hidden" in God's inmost nature—but also in God's actions, God also voluntarily holds back a great deal of God's power. His Son incarnate respects our person, inviting and calling us to eternal life in the kingdom, rather than imposing his rule. No wonder God seems so elusive. Yet God is present to us all the time in sustaining all things and our very own existence, and God can be available to us by our sincerely responding to God's goodness in our creation, preservation, and redemption, a response that includes our community worship, personal prayers, and loving service of others.

But now we need to turn to the greatest temptation Jesus faced and so too his greatest self-renunciation: the cross.

Chapter 12

The Sacrifice of the Cross

Jesus in his temptations in the wilderness, and then in his subsequent teachings and actions, pioneered a path from where we are to the Father. To open access for us to the Father, Jesus endured a final and decisive trial or temptation on the cross. There he experienced the full force of the effects of sin and evil without losing confidence in the love of his Father. Jesus' endurance on the cross is the victory over the power of sin, evil, and death, and it forms the core of the Christian faith.

That Jesus is our Savior is never a matter of dispute among theologians in the history of the church, but there are several theological accounts of *how* Jesus' death on the cross makes our salvation possible. They are called "atonement theories." "Atonement" or "at-one-ment" means how sinful human beings can be made one (be united) in fellowship with God, or united to God, who is holy. But the church has never designated any theological theory as definitive, or the orthodox doctrine, or dogma, as with the doctrine of the Trinity or the nature of Jesus as both human and divine.

In the early church one line of thought—largely based on Mark 10:45, which speaks of the Son of Man giving his life as a ransom for many—explored the idea that Jesus' death was a ransom paid to the devil, under whose power we had fallen by sin and evil. But it was never satisfactorily explained how Satan had a right to possess us, and so how he was owed a ransom for our release, nor how the ransom was paid. Another line of thought that we call a theory of recapitulation was developed on the basis of Paul's contrast between Adam as the old Adam and Christ as the new Adam. Adam had failed to live the life God intended, and it resulted in our being sinful and subject to death. But Jesus is the new Adam, who by his incarnation passed though all the stages of life from birth to death, and thereby sanctified or made them holy. Jesus as the new Adam generates a new humanity. Our solidarity with Christ renders us holy. The theory of recapitulation usually relied on a Platonic concept of forms in its working out, and so it is limited in its appeal today.

In the high Middle Ages, Anselm with his *Cur Deus homo* (*Why God Became Man,* 1097) fathered what is now called "satisfaction theories" or "substitutionary theories." In the Western church this line of thinking became the most widely used way to discuss our redemption by Christ. In this line of thought, we have incurred a debt to God by our sin that we cannot repay. Only God can pay it, and the Son of God does pay our debt by becoming both God and man in the incarnation and by suffering death on our behalf. Jesus by his death renders satisfaction to his Father. Sometimes the Father's just wrath is a major part of the theory, and that wrath is satisfied by the suffering of Jesus, who dies in our place. But this approach has serious problems. As John Habgood puts it,

> The essence of the doctrine, intended to explain why Christ had to die for sinners, is that he died as our substitute, and through his suffering and death received the fullness of God's wrath as penalty for our sins, thus making it possible for God [the Father] to forgive us.
> The reason for questioning the theory is that it raises profound moral problems. Where is the justice of substituting a sinless victim for a sinful one, as the means of dealing with the latter's sin? And what are we to make of the depiction of God as fundamentally wrathful [toward us] and determined [even required by justice] to exact punishment?[1]

A rival line of thought, originally put forward by Abelard (d. 1142), claims that Christ saves us by inspiring us to live in accord to God's will by his example. This theory has had its defenders over the years, but the vast majority of theologians have considered that, in spite of its element of truth, it is not by itself able to do full justice to the biblical witness.

Most theologians who discuss the atonement do so in terms of these theories. But since no theory has been made definitive for Christian belief, instead of discussing these theories themselves, I will instead look at the biblical account itself and see if we cannot increase our understanding of the significance of the cross in that way. In addition, since it is God—Father, Son, and Spirit—who saves us, we will begin with a brief review of the relation of the Father and the Son as the overarching framework to understanding as much as we can the significance of the crucifixion of Jesus.

As we have seen, the Father, Son, and Spirit are one God through their love for one another before the foundation of the world. The Son is the full and perfect expression of the Father's being and, as the full and perfect expression of the Father, the Son is also divine. The Holy Spirit is the full and perfect expression of the Father and Son and, as their full and perfect expression, the Holy Spirit is divine. We have already seen some distinction in their activities, with the Father as the creator and the others participating in the creation as Word and Spirit. Now we will see their distinctive activities in our redemption.

The Son, when he became incarnate, became separated by a distance from the Father. "Distance" is a metaphor. As we mentioned earlier, its concrete meaning is to designate what is subject to the power of created forces in contrast to what is not. The incarnate Son is subject to the power of created forces and so is *in* the world; the Father is not subject to them and so is *not in* the world. *Through* the Father, Jesus can command nature, for example, when he stilled the stormy sea and walked on water. But of himself, in the New Testament accounts up to Jesus' resurrection, Jesus is subject to the forces of gravity, to the need to eat, and to death. So the Father and incarnate Son are separated by the "distance" of the created world.[2] Although separated from the Father in the sense of being subject to the forces of creation, the incarnate Son is still in communion with the Father.

The crucifixion introduces another way the Father and the Son are separated. On the cross the Son incarnate is not only separated from the Father by being in the world, subject to its forces, but the Son incarnate is also afflicted so that communion between the Son and the Father is threatened. To understand this threat is to understand how the cross is a temptation and a victory. Let us examine this threat and the victory of the cross.

Affliction is a particular kind of suffering, involving physical pain, social humiliation, and despair.[3] It can utterly destroy a person. Jesus perhaps alludes to this when he says, "do not fear those who kill the body but cannot kill the soul; rather fear him who can destroy both soul and body" (Matt. 10:28).

Although social degradation and despair are the principal ingredients in affliction, physical pain is a necessary ingredient; without it we do not have affliction. This is because we can obtain temporary relief from the wretchedness that arises from social humiliation and despair by turning our attention to other things for a time. But physical pain prevents this by keeping our attention focused on our wretchedness.

Even though physical pain is a necessary ingredient in affliction, the primary ingredients in affliction are social and psychological. In affliction, people are socially uprooted so that they have little to no social value, as are lepers in the Gospel stories, who are socially ostracized. Social standing affects Jesus, as we saw earlier in examining the temptations in the wilderness. Jesus feels the effect of failing to gain acceptance of the Jewish leaders and their cutting remarks about him being no more than a carpenter and from a socially inferior family. The social rejection becomes even more devastating when at his execution as a blasphemer and a criminal, he is flanked by two thieves.

Before his execution, Jesus is mocked by the soldiers. They strip him and put a scarlet robe on him; after putting a crown of thorns on his head, they kneel before him and mock him: "Hail, King of the Jews!" Then they spit on him, take the reed they have put in his hands, and strike him on the head. After they finish mocking him, they strip him of the robe, put his own clothes on him, and lead him away to crucify him (Matt. 27:28–31). This social degradation continues most cruelly while he hangs on the cross:

> Those who passed by derided him, shaking their heads and saying, "You who would destroy the temple and build it in three days, save yourself! If you are the Son of God, come down from the cross." In the same way the chief priests also, along with the scribes and elders, were mocking him, saying, "He saved others; he cannot save himself. He is the King of Israel; let him come down from the cross now, and we will believe in him. He trusts in God; let God deliver him now, if he wants to; for he said, 'I am God's Son.'" (Matt. 27:39–43)

Social degradation leads a person to feel inwardly the contempt and disgust that others express toward one who is socially of no account, as refugees, displaced persons, the disabled, and people of various races often do. An afflicted person feels self-contempt and disgust, and even guilt and defilement; yet often, like a leper in the Scripture stories, they are innocent of any evil. Thus they are led in the direction of despair, to be without hope. This means experiencing death of the body and the soul, as Dante realized when he put an inscription over the entrance to hell: ABANDON HOPE, ALL YE WHO ENTER HERE.

Jesus realizes that to be a Messiah, he must suffer. He deliberately takes upon himself the figure of the Suffering Servant.

> He was despised and rejected by others;
>   a man of suffering and acquainted with infirmity;
> and as one from whom others hide their faces
>   he was despised, and we held him of no account.
>
> Surely he has borne our infirmities
>   and carried our diseases;
> yet we accounted him stricken,
>   struck down by God, and afflicted.
> But he was wounded for our transgressions,
>   crushed for our iniquities;
> upon him was the punishment that made us whole,
>   and by his bruises we are healed.
> All we like sheep have gone astray;
>   we have all turned to our own way,
> and the LORD has laid on him the iniquity of us all.
>
> He was oppressed, and he was afflicted,
>   yet he did not open his mouth;

> like a lamb that is led to the slaughter,
>   and like a sheep that before its shearers is silent,
>   so he did not open his mouth.
> By a perversion of justice he was taken away.
> . . . .
> They made his grave with the wicked
>   and his tomb with the rich,
> although he had done no violence,
>   and there was no deceit in his mouth.
>
> Yet it was the will of the LORD to crush him with pain.
> . . . .
> The righteous one, my servant, shall make many righteous,
>   and he shall bear their iniquities.
>   (Isa. 53:3–8a, 9–10a, 11b)

Isaiah does not tell us who the Suffering Servant is, and certainly does not identify the Suffering Servant as the Messiah. It is Jesus who connects the two for perhaps the first time in Jewish history.

The Gospels refer to Jesus' death as a passion. Though now archaic, the word "passion" then meant the condition of being acted upon. It is to be passive; to endure the effects of forces on oneself. So the events of Jesus' death are referred to as a passion to signify that Jesus is being acted upon. He is not in charge of events. He does not avoid them but willingly exposes himself to them because he recognizes the cross and the events surrounding it as something that he should endure because it is his Father's will. This is stressed well before the events of the passion story of Jesus' last days of ministry in the chronology of John's Gospel:

> [Jesus said,] "I am the good shepherd. The good shepherd lays down his life
> for the sheep. The hired hand, who is not the shepherd and does not own
> the sheep, sees the wolf coming and leaves the sheep and runs away. . . . No
> one takes it [my life] from me, but I lay it down of my own accord. . . . I
> have received this command from my Father." (10:11–12b, 18a and c)

We saw the same emphasis as we quoted Paul: "He humbled himself / and became obedient to the point of death— / even death on a cross" (Phil. 2:8).

The voluntary character of his passion, and hence the self-limitations of the Son of God incarnate, and the struggle it caused him—all are evident immediately after the Last Supper. Jesus leads his disciples to an olive grove called Gethsemane. His disciples tell us he is in terrible agony, agitated and trembling. Even to their sleepy eyes, his distress is evident. At the time they do not know what to make of it. But Jesus' prayer gives us some indication: "My Father, if it is possible, let this cup pass from me" (Matt. 26:39b).

Jesus is beginning to experience the full force of sin and evil, the full separation from his Father, which will come to him on the cross. He is beginning to experience that terrible emptiness that later leads him on the cross to cry out, "My God, my God, why have you forsaken me?" (Matt. 27:46b). Apparently Jesus normally feels God's presence; he has an openness that allows God's Spirit to be fully present. He always looks to his heavenly Father, and because he does, the Father is nearly always present to him. But in the garden a dread is upon him—a separation begins to be felt. God's presence is not there as it usually has been. Jesus begins to sense what lies before him: Perhaps God is going to withdraw from him *fully*—he is to be abandoned; the space within him that God has occupied is to be left void, empty. He is to be at the farthest distance of all from God.

That is the dread that is upon him, so that his sweat is "like great drops of blood" (Luke 22:44). And he prays that this trial, this cup, this terrible complete absence of God's Spirit, will not happen. Death on the cross is a physical death—a terrible way to die. But that death will have to be endured while the presence of God is being withdrawn. In the garden he begins to sense that withdrawal: He becomes aware of the possibility that God will completely withdraw and he will be left alone—left to suffer the complete absence of God while he hangs on a cross, exposed to the humiliation of penal execution and the mockery of those who hate him. He will descend to hell, for that is what the full absence of God means.

On the cross Jesus knows that he is forsaken, but before that, in the garden he has already begun to feel it. He prays that it might not happen. But it does. And when it does, he does not understand why. He cries out, "My God, my God, why have you forsaken me?" (Mark 15:34). People have often tried to soften the shock that these words arouse by pointing out that Jesus is quoting from the beginning of Psalm 22. He is, but that does not change the fact that he chooses those words to quote and that he feels forsaken.

In the garden we see how hard it is for Jesus, the very image of God, to follow his Father's will. Yet in the garden we also find him consenting to God's will: "Let this cup pass from me; yet not what I want but what you want" (Matt. 26:39a). When the dreaded thing has come to pass, his last words on the cross are "Father, into your hands I commend my spirit" (Luke 23:46b). He consents to endure this dreadful death; he gives himself up to it, a death of body and a death more terrible than any bodily death, the death a person knows when forsaken by God. The one who has known no sin, who has always been open to the Father's presence and has known him, now is left empty of that spirit. Yet he loves and longs for the Father. When the poetic figure Job was afflicted in various ways, he was tempted to "curse God and die" (cf. Job 2:9). Jesus, when he is utterly forsaken, overcomes the temptation to "curse God and die."

What happens is later explained by Paul, as far as it can be explained: "He made him to be sin who knew no sin" (2 Cor. 5:21). Holiness and sin are infinitely distant from one another. As we have seen, holiness refers to God's transcendence, and holiness in God is seen to be God's purity, justice, and concern to redeem. Sin is to live a life apart from God, not oriented on God, from which specific sins result, taking us further and further into evil and further from God's holiness.

Following Paul's interpretation, Christ becomes the focus of all the sins of the world, so in suffering the crucifixion, Jesus is the farthest removed from the Father's presence that it is possible to be, even though in his life he is always oriented toward the Father and has not committed any specific sins. He who is one with the Father, whose heart, mind, and soul love and long for God, and who knows the rich and glorious presence of his Father, is put at the greatest distance anyone can be from God. And Jesus endures it. He dies in an agony that no one else has ever experienced, in an agony no one else can endure, an agony no one can comprehend. He has not expected to be forsaken. To die, yes, but not to be forsaken. He apparently has had no hint of it until that night in the garden. But as Paul puts it in Philippians 2:8, he is obedient unto death. He still looks to the Father, trusts him, and loves him, even though he has been forsaken and does not know why.

Let us explore these understandings for our faith today. Christ endures the Father's complete absence. This is to endure the effect of evil; for evil destroys communion, and the full effect of evil is to destroy all communion. Evil at bottom is the refusal to recognize the reality of others, to refuse to restrain ourselves, so that another does not have room to live and develop freely. We have not made enough room for each other; our appetite for our own worth and significance has not left enough room for others. Most of the time we do not know each other very well, nor our Father, nor ourselves, because we cannot limit the boundless horizon that is our own overexpanded self and let another person appear independently of our interests. Yet the Father does not allow our evil to have its full effects. Our Father does not allow it to drive his Spirit away from us completely. God does not leave us to experience the full absence of the Spirit. To some extent, God sustains all of us, even when we are utterly unaware of God. Only Jesus endures the complete absence of the Father; only he bears the full effects of the destroyed communion that results from sin and evil.

The distance between the Father and the Son when Jesus is on the cross is also an exact measure of their love. Although separated by an infinite distance, the love of the Son for the Father and the Father for the Son is able to span the infinite distance between holiness and sin. At each extreme of the infinite distance, there is love. Sin and evil are unable to destroy the bond of love—God the Holy Spirit—that unites them. Because the Father loves the crucified Jesus, and because Jesus, in his faithful endurance of the effects of sin, continues to love the Father, our sins are received into the very divine life of God—Father, Son, and Holy Spirit. Because our sins are received into God's divine life, we have the opportunity to receive remission of our sins and deliverance from the power of evil and death. So Paul writes, "We know that a person is reckoned as righteous not by the works of the law but by the faith of Jesus Christ. . . . And the life I now live in the flesh I live by the faith of Jesus Christ, who loved me and gave himself for me" (Gal. 2:16a, 20 AT).[4]

The dual nature of the cross—as the infinite separation of Father and Son caused by sin and also at the same time an expression of the infinite love between the Father and the Son—is powerfully presented in George Herbert's poem "The Agony":

> Philosophers have measure'd mountains,
> Fathom'd the depths of seas, of states, and kings,
> Walk'd with a staff to heav'n, and traced fountains:
> But there are two vast, spacious things,
> The which to measure it doth more behove:
> Yet few there are that sound them—Sin and Love.
>
> Who would know Sin, let him repair
> Unto Mount Olivet; there shall he see
> A man so wrung with pains, that all his hair,
> His skin, his garments bloody be.
> Sin is that press and vice, which forceth pain
> To hunt his cruel food through ev'ry vein.
>
> Who knows not Love, let him assay
> And taste that juice, which on the cross a pike
> Did set again abroach; then let him say
> If ever he did taste the like.
> Love is that liquor sweet and most divine,
> Which my God feels as blood, but I as wine.[5]

The Son, then, is afflicted by the Father for our sakes: the Son enters the world, accepting the limitations of being subject to it, and he is crucified in obedience to the Father's desire to save us from sin, evil, and death. This has happened because of the Father's loving will. The Son's great victory is to yield to what happens to him as the will of his Father. Thus they are united over the great span of distance between holiness and sin, since there is love at both ends. Their distance from one another thus becomes a measure of the extent of their love; the extent of their love is expressed by the very medium of their separation. Christ's pain is real; his affliction is horrible; the experience of being forsaken is beyond endurance for anyone but the Son. Hence only God can redeem us from sin and evil by the separation between God the Father and God the Son, and yet we see their continuing and unbreakable love for one another. Jesus responds to the pain and suffering as the result of the Father's will and paradoxically to the separation itself as a medium of contact with his Father.

Our joy and the foundation of our hope is that sin and the greatest depths of evil that kill him cannot overwhelm him. They do not overwhelm him or overcome him; for he does not "curse God and die." He dies enduring the effects of sin and evil, enduring the greatest distance from God, still longing for that presence. That is the victory over sin and evil: to endure it and not know why; to endure it and to trust the Father. We see that evil, for all its power, is not all-powerful, for it cannot destroy Jesus' love and trust. Jesus' goodness is greater than evil; evil is able to break his body but not his will. It cannot change the direction toward which he looks and in which he is pointed.

Our opportunity to find our true life has been made possible by Jesus' death. No matter how far we have walked into evil, the love of God surrounds us, stretching the infinite distance from the Father to the Son, from holiness to sin, and so God's love can reach people at any *intermediate* distance, within the infinite distance of the Father and Son's mutual love. *Neither before Jesus' coming nor after it* has anyone had to bear the full effects of evil. That was his destiny. His greatness, his glory, is that he was able to accept it and endure it. God's forgiveness and graciousness to God's people in the Old Testament is validated by Christ's suffering and death. This is indirectly suggested by such events as the near sacrifice of Isaac by Abraham, in the way the Last Supper was celebrated during the Jewish Passover festival, and in Jesus' claims of superiority to the temple. This was realized after Jesus' resurrection; both the ancient Passover event in Egypt during the time of Moses and even earlier the near sacrifice of Isaac by Abraham are interpreted by New Testament writers as events that foreshadow the crucifixion of Jesus. Although only a poetic figure, Job is seen as a foreshadowing of the suffering of Christ. They drew their force or virtue from his sacrifice. The power of the cross extends not only backward in time, but also to the future, including people who never learn of the cross, as we pointed out in our examination of the parable of the sheep and the goats in Matthew 25:31–46. On the cross, God the Son incarnate is the sacrifice for the sins of the world.

Because we have wrestled with temptation and suffered from evil and know their power—their destructiveness of community—we are able to participate in the cross. We know in our own bodies and minds and hearts the kind of conflict that took place on the cross between Christ and the full force of evil. The wisdom we have gained from our suffering from evil enables us in some degree to enter into the depth of the divine wisdom of the cross. There we see most fully in the death of the Son, in the suffering he endured, that there is no life apart from God. At the greatest distance from the Father, Jesus experienced the kind of death that results from the total absence of God. Our struggle with evil—a struggle through which our true life is beginning to emerge—is only possible because we are spared the full effects of evil. We are spared being placed at the greatest distance from God. God has not allowed us to experience the complete absence of God's Spirit. We can make a journey from evil toward God because we have been spared an exposure to the consequences of our thoughts and actions and inactions that would completely destroy us. We could not bear what only the Son could bear. We may find life because the Father loves us enough to send the Son; we may find life because the Son loves us enough to be able to endure the full effect of the absence of the Father's Spirit.

In the cross we see most fully the wisdom of God. God does not use force to bring us into submission, nor does God seek to annihilate us, nor does God use arguments. Rather, God takes the consequences of sin and evil into God, displays the effects of sin and evil on the Son, and hopes to win us over by this great love. George Herbert describes this self-restraint in his great poem "The Sacrifice." Jesus from the cross says, "They use that power against me, which I gave: / Was ever grief like mine?"[6] All the power we have comes from God, and we not only misuse it but we also use it against God as God is seeking to redeem us. And yet God does not strike out at us, but instead, as Herbert puts it, "I answer nothing, but with patience prove, / If stony hearts will melt with gentle love."[7] God calls us to see the wisdom of this restraint, the wisdom of what we may find by pulling back ourselves and recognizing the reality of communion we may have with God and the life that it brings. Herbert then tells us that God uses God's power to transform the murder of Jesus into a holy act, a sacrifice by which we are redeemed: "I, who am Truth, turn into truth their deeds."[8] God's power and love make the rejection of Jesus and his crucifixion into the entrance way into God's kingdom, God's way of ruling. Of itself, the crucifixion is but a judicial murder. Only God's power and love make it a holy and saving sacrifice. We are asked to see and confess that Jesus' crucifixion is the wisdom of God.

Jesus' passion reveals a division between two categories of suffering. One category includes all the suffering that springs from selfishness, ruthless ambition, envy, greed, the desire to be superior to others, and other misuses of our freedom. We move so easily from a moment of contentment to misery by hearing about the achievement of our contemporaries. Reading a class letter in an alumni/ae magazine is usually enough to stir up a host of resentments and regrets. Because of our self-preoccupation, every day and nearly every hour are marked with suffering. Christ came to save us from the suffering that is avoidable and the consequences of our own sins. The other category is innocent suffering. It includes the suffering that we undergo as a result of other people's actions, and the suffering that results from natural causes. Because Jesus was utterly free of all envy, self-seeking ambition, and hatred, he never acted unjustly and never suffered from self-inflicted injury. Whatever he suffered, he endured in complete innocence. His suffering was caused either by people's injustices or by natural processes. His life opens our eyes to the possibility that all our suffering may become like his, wholly innocent suffering. Because of Jesus, we can seek to be just to others always, and to suffer only as the result of injustices committed by others and the effects of natural processes. To follow Christ is to *desire* to be like him and to *strive* to become like him. The more a Christian succeeds in becoming like Christ, the less suffering one inflicts on self and others.

We can accept our own innocent suffering only as Jesus accepted his in the Garden of Gethsemane: with dread, with the desire that it not happen, and yet with trust in God. With fear and trembling, we are to desire that all our suffering be the result only of the inevitable consequences of being a creature, rooted in the workings of the natural world, and that none of our suffering be self-inflicted or the result of our own injustices. With trust in our Father's power to redeem all creatures from unrighteousness and death, we bear what we cannot change at a particular instant of time. When Jesus had done all he could do, his innocence and trust enabled him to say, as we have seen, "Father, into your hands I commend my spirit!" (Luke 23:46). May we, when we have done all that we can do, also offer ourselves into God's care. If we seek to follow Christ—to allow our suffering to become like his, free of self-seeking and malice—then it will cease to be pointless suffering. It will be like his own: innocent and borne for the sake of God's redemption of the world.

Life under God is strenuous but not grim. We have the power to improve things; we may enjoy the beauty of the world; we are to enjoy the glories of this life; and we have Christ, our blessed Lord. Without him we would simply suffer without hope.

How very distant now is the description of God merely as omnipotent, omniscient, and all-good with which we began this book. The biblical view of God's power, wisdom, and goodness that we gain from studying the way God uses his power, wisdom, and goodness is quite different from what could be deduced by logic from those abstractions, as is evident from the absence of any treatment of God's holiness, redemptive purposes, incarnation, and the crucifixion of Jesus. These are generally set aside by philosophers of religion as inadmissible because they are "revealed" and so are not in the domain of philosophy, which deals only with what is accessible to reason. But what we are actually dealing with are God's actions in seeking us. The biblical witness to those actions does call for the response of faith. But faith, as we pointed out, is not primarily the acceptance of biblical beliefs because they have been revealed outside of and overriding human reason and good sense, and so in that sense are imposed on us without proper understanding. Faith is not a blind faith in the inspiration of seers. What happened to Moses or Isaiah was indeed a revelation, but we believe what they say about God because of the understanding of God and our condition that they teach. So too with Jesus. It is the account that we give of him based on the Bible and its effects on us that leads to faith. Because we cannot gain this response from the limited abstractions that philosophy considers does not make faith irrational nor an unreasonable act. God reveals or shows us a unique love, and this revelation is sufficient for many to respond. The response comes because love yields itself to love. Atonement is the restoration of the human capacity to know, love, and obey God—the restoration of the image that God bestowed in the first creation. According to Paul, it is so significant as to amount to "a new creation" (2 Cor. 5:17).

PART FOUR
THE NEW LIFE IN GOD

Chapter 13

The Resurrection of Jesus and Eternal Life

A few years ago there was quite a flurry in the media when some biologists were able to extend the life of some fruit flies, mice, and that sort of creature by some 30 to 50 percent. They extrapolated from that success to the claim that aging should be treated as a disease. Just as we have cured many diseases, we should also seek to eliminate the disease of aging and biological death for human beings. The goal was to extend human life indefinitely, maybe even forever. The Templeton Foundation sponsored a conference titled "Extended Life, Eternal Life," which was held at the University of Pennsylvania. After the scientists had presented their views on extended life and their hopes of defeating aging, I as a theologian was asked to speak on the conference theme itself, "Extended Life, Eternal Life."[1]

It was not difficult to clear up the confusion between the two. Extended life is just that, an extension of our present life. No matter how long the extension, even if were forever, it would still be just that, an extension of this life. Eternal life, on the other hand, is the life that is lived by God. In the Bible, eternity can be applied properly only to God, who is not subject to time. (As we saw earlier, time, like space, is created by God.) Eternal life is the holy life of God that is shared by the Father, Son, and Holy Spirit. To take the meaning of "eternal life" to be the same as "to last forever" is woefully inadequate.

We are invited to share in the divine life. Through Jesus, a relationship, indeed an intimacy and participation in the life of God, is possible for us. This relationship is the result of the "righteousness that comes through the grace of Jesus Christ" (Rom. 5:21 AT). We are made righteous or just by God's forgiveness because of Jesus' sacrifice of himself on the cross. By his death, Jesus opens for us the possibility of a new relationship with God. To share in the divine life is a gift, something that cannot be earned or deserved.

Our present life is a wonderful gift, and it is full of glories, but it is also very seriously marred. Eternal life is a life utterly free of the burdens we now bear. It is free of failure, guilt, and sorrow; it is free of rivalry, gossip, and boasting; it is free of envy, jealousy, and strife; it is free of boredom, depression, and addiction; it is free of aggression, rudeness, ruthlessness, anger, heartlessness, and treachery; it is free of unfaithfulness, deceit, and fraud; it is free of foolishness, violence, destruction, and war. Eternal life is a life filled with the love, peace, and joy that come from above.

As we saw in Auden and Dante (see chap. 9, above), an experience of God's Spirit filled them with an amazingly liberating gratitude for the existence of others. And as we also saw in them, these moments of being full of perfect love do not presently wholly remove us from sin and evil. But a new reality, the Holy Spirit, does enter our lives. This does not always prevent us, as Auden put it, "from making use of others, grossly and often"; but as he pointed out, in his own life "it has made it much more difficult for me to deceive myself about what I am up to when I do." For Dante, such a moment of the powerful presence of God's Spirit revealed to him the goal of his life: to become always the way he had been for a few days when struck by the beauty of a young girl. This goal cannot be achieved even with a lifetime of serious and wholehearted dedication. Our resistance to God's Spirit, even when powerfully experienced, is extremely deep. At our best moments, we are aware of another kind of life that inspires and attracts us, and often within ourselves we are aware of a conflict indicating that God's Spirit is at work, seeking to draw us more fully into the Spirit's life.

Extended life is biological life, based on the Greek word *bios*. It is to exist. John in his Gospel uses the Greek word *zōē* to refer to eternal life. (John uses the noun 36 times and the verb 18 times.) *Zōē* is the life of God that God shares with us. Just to extend our lives indefinitely does not bring us one inch closer to eternal life, to live in the Spirit of God.

At the conference I thought I had done a rather good job of distinguishing extended life from eternal life. But as soon as I had finished speaking, a man in the audience (not one of the scientists) rushed up to me and in a gleeful, aggressive voice shouted, "You religious people are going to be put out of business! We don't need your promises of life after death. Science will eliminate death, and we will live forever!"

Alas, I realized once again how right my old speech teacher was. I was saying, "Blue, blue, blue," and this listener was thinking, "Yellow, yellow, yellow," and what was heard was "Green, green, green." The man had disdain for religion, and all he cared about was longevity. He could not hear the difference between two quite different kinds of life.

Nearly two thousand years have passed since Jesus rose from the dead, and people still scramble the message of eternal life. For example, more than once I have been asked to describe what heaven is like. The questioners want a description that is so appealing and so convincing that they might consider believing in such a place and making an effort to get there. But the biblical witnesses to Jesus' resurrection are not interested in describing a place. So if we do not listen carefully to what they are saying, we too will miss the whole point of their witness to the glorious news that Christ has risen.

Jesus returned from the dead to reestablish the broken relationship with the disciples, for Peter had denied him three times, and the rest of them had fled when he had been arrested. But the risen Jesus seeks them out. For example, in one of the resurrection appearances, Peter and a half a dozen of the disciples go fishing (John 21:1–19). After fishing all night and failing to catch anything, just after daybreak Jesus appears on the shore and tells them to cast their nets to the right side of the boat. Their net becomes so full that they cannot haul it in. Realizing that it is the Lord, Peter leaps into the water and swims ashore, while the others come in the boat, dragging the net full of fish. Jesus has prepared breakfast and invites them to eat. None of them dares to ask him who he is because though they know who he is, as resurrected Lord, he looks different. After they have eaten, Jesus asks Peter three times (with slight variations), "Simon, do you love me?" Each time, Peter replies, "Yes, Lord; you know that I love you." After each reply, Jesus tells Peter to feed his lambs and tend his sheep. This will show the genuineness of Peter's love. The three questions parallel the three times Peter has denied Jesus. By his reply Peter is restored to fellowship with Jesus, and he is now given responsibility for the care of Jesus' followers.

With his resurrection appearances, Jesus establishes a new kind of relationship with his disciples and followers. Jesus is no longer simply a teacher (they have often referred to him as master, rabbi), nor even simply the Messiah or Christ. With his resurrection, Jesus is now seen to be Lord, the expression used to refer to God only. The first confession of the primitive church was "Jesus is Lord" (1 Cor. 12:3). As Paul puts this new relationship, "Even though we once knew Christ from a human point of view, we know him no longer in that way" (2 Cor. 5:16b). The resurrection has so transformed the situation that all four Gospels are written from the point of view of the resurrection. All Jesus' sayings and the events of his life are seen from that new, extraordinary perspective. The sayings and events are reconsidered carefully, and what was concealed or not plain in them at the time is now, in the light of the resurrection, seen to contain new and deeper import. The glory of God now becomes increasingly evident. The accounts in the four Gospels are like double exposures: there is a story line—the way things seemed at the time—but superimposed on the story line is the way things are now understood because of the resurrection. It is rather like reading about events in a story in which the reader is told things by the author that the people in the story do not know at the time.

Consider only one example in which what the reader knows about Jesus and what the people who see and hear Jesus is very different. Mark opens with a proclamation of who Jesus is, "The beginning of the good news of Jesus Christ, the Son of God" (Mark 1:1), yet throughout the Gospel, until the entry into Jerusalem, this truth is kept hidden from the people who see and hear him. In Mark, the demons recognize Jesus, but Jesus does not let them speak: "He cured many who were sick with various diseases, and cast out many demons; and he would not permit the demons to speak, because they knew him" (Mark 1:34). Mark believes that it is necessary to keep the fact that Jesus is the Christ a secret because to announce it during his ministry would lead to complete misunderstanding of who he is. Then Mark makes this explicit when he reports that Peter, who first declares that Jesus is the Christ, is severely rebuked by Jesus because Peter rejects Jesus' explanation that he will be rejected by the Jewish leaders, suffer, be killed, but rise again. If the Jewish leaders reject him, and his leading disciple utterly misunderstands him, what can be expected of the populace?

Matthew and Luke do not cast their entire presentation as one in which the identity of Jesus is kept a secret from those in the story. Rather, at certain points the glory of God in Jesus shows itself to individuals and to the crowds in Jesus' ministry, to make specific points. John has the glory of God show right from the start and throughout Jesus' entire life. But even so, John stresses the Jewish leaders and people's constant misunderstanding of Jesus. For example, Nicodemus, a Jewish leader, misunderstands Jesus' explanation that a person must be "born from above" or "born again" (the Greek means both; John 3:3–7). Nicodemus thinks that Jesus means that he must somehow perform the impossible task of entering his mother's womb to be born a second time. Likewise, the woman at the well misunderstands Jesus' explanation that he is the water of life to mean that she will no longer need to come to the well to draw water. So at one extreme, Mark keeps who Jesus is a complete secret from those in the story because what Jesus offers would be misunderstood. At the other extreme, John proclaims Jesus' identity openly to all who appear in the story; indeed, what Jesus has to offer is misunderstood. Throughout Mark's Gospel, people are mystified; and throughout John's Gospel, Jesus and his hearers are at cross-purposes. In different ways, they make the same point: something utterly new—which cannot be fully understood with current ideas, expectations, images, and concepts—has come into the world with Jesus. Jesus' life, ministry, and death could not be properly understood until after his resurrection, and then only with a considerable expansion of one's horizon.

Understanding who Jesus was and what Jesus said and did in the light of his resurrection did not happen all at once, in a flash. The resurrection of Jesus was an unprecedented event, and what it meant for our relationship to God took time for them to absorb. Luke stresses, and John implies, that the resurrected Jesus himself has to teach the disciples before he ascends to his Father;

even before that, Jesus has promised them that, with the coming of the Holy Spirit, what he has taught them will become more clear (John 14:25–26). So over a period of time—no doubt with a great deal of discussion, prayer, and reflection—the early disciples were able to bring into focus and to present the story of the salvation brought by God through Jesus. The oral traditions of the earliest church then became the basis of the four Gospels, each of which presents the significance of Jesus' ministry, death, and resurrection.

It became evident to the disciples that the fundamental significance of Jesus' resurrection was that Jesus' teachings, life, and death had been validated by God. When God raised Jesus from the dead, Jesus was vindicated against all the charges made against him and all the misunderstandings of his mission. He was shown to be God's Son incarnate, with the power to bring us salvation from sin, evil, and death. He was to be listened to, obeyed, and followed. He was indeed the one who can bring the divine life into our lives; for in him the Spirit of God lives. Jesus could and did confer God's Spirit into those who open themselves to him.

For example, this vindication of Jesus is the reason Peter explains to a crowd, who has witnessed his power to heal a lame man, that the power he exhibits has come from Jesus (Acts 3). Peter boldly tells them that God has "glorified his servant Jesus," whom they, the people of Israel, have rejected and handed over to Pilate to be killed. But since they and their leaders have acted in ignorance, they now have the opportunity to repent. The raised Jesus has been ordained by God to be the judge of the living and the dead. As judge, Jesus does not look at people's record of good and evil and then decide on that basis whom he will and will not allow into his Father's kingdom; nor does he act in an arbitrary or utterly inexplicable way. Rather, Jesus opens for all of us the possibility of life in God (Acts 3:25–26). As Paul put it later in a letter, "The saying is sure and worthy of full acceptance, that Christ Jesus came into the world to save sinners" (1 Tim. 1:15). We enter into God's kingdom or, by our refusal, we exclude ourselves.

Jesus' resurrection means that the community Jesus has created, the community that follows his way of life, cannot be destroyed by hostility or death. Nothing has the power to eliminate what God has begun with Jesus. So a community marked by a life of repentance and mutual forgiveness, a community marked by service, a community that shows the fruits of the Holy Spirit (which Paul summarizes in Gal. 5:22 as "love, joy, peace, patience, kindness, generosity, faithfulness, gentleness, and self-control")—that community will continue in spite of the continuing power of sin, evil, and even death. By Jesus' resurrection, God's kingdom is shown to be invincible against all negative forces. And our life with God cannot be severed by our own failures, for we can return again and again for forgiveness and restoration. Our life with God cannot be severed and defeated by our physical death because God has shown in Jesus' resurrection that God's will is to raise us from the dead. Nothing can defeat the love of God that dwells in those who receive it.

According to N. T. Wright, Jesus' resurrection from the dead has ample, not to say overwhelming, historical support. Wright has powerfully and convincingly argued that the best and only viable hypothesis that fits the data is that Jesus was indeed raised from the dead. This is quite encouraging, but it should not distract us. Jesus himself, in the parable he told about a rich man and Lazarus, made it clear that the mere fact of resurrection does not turn people into believers. Earlier we examined this parable as an example of Jesus' rejection of the deeply held view that earthly prosperity means that one is favored by God, and poverty means that one is rejected by God. Yet in the parable the question of the resurrection also comes up. In his suffering in Hades, the rich man begs that Lazarus be sent to his father's house to warn his brothers and the other members of the household of what has happened to him, so that they would not also come to the place of torment (Luke 16:27–28). But according to the parable,

> Abraham replied, "They have Moses and the prophets; they should listen to them." He said, "No, father Abraham; but if someone goes to them from the dead, they will repent." He said to him, "If they do not listen to Moses and the prophets, neither will they be convinced even if someone rises from the dead." (Luke 16:29–31)

This brings us to where we are today. We actually have strong and sure testimony that Jesus returned from the dead. Indeed, he more than just returned: he was resurrected to an utterly new kind of life. But unless people have been engaged with what Jesus taught and did, wrestled with their own sin and evil, and found themselves moved to admire and love the kind of life he lived and invited them to enter into—then Jesus' resurrection does not signify for them his divine nature, nor what his death accomplished, nor does it bring God's Spirit into their lives. His resurrection is isolated from all to which it gives meaning and significance. It is what Jesus' life and death mean in the light of his resurrection that is the good news we are called to receive. Just as in the parable, if one is not engaged with Moses and the prophets, the mere return of Lazarus from the dead would not turn a person toward God.

The issue at the forefront for us, what we need to do, is to follow the way of life that Jesus has revealed to us. The resurrection of Jesus is near the end of the story of Jesus' earthly ministry. If we have not paid attention to the story of his life and teaching, and sought to follow him, it is unlikely that we will find the last part of the story convincing. The resurrection, all by itself in isolation, has nothing to validate, nothing to vindicate. But if we have come to love him and to follow his way with all our heart, then his resurrection is part of a story that leads us into his Father's kingdom, a kingdom against which sin, evil, death, and hell cannot prevail. That life—eternal life—was so fully present in Jesus and is what God vindicates by God's resurrection of Jesus. What is at issue is not whether we say "Yes" or "No" to what historians tell us is the best available hypothesis. Rather, it is whether we repent of our way of life and seek to follow him.[2]

The resurrection of Jesus not only vindicates Jesus' life, teachings, and death; his resurrection appearances also have additional significance. As we saw in our brief examination of one of those appearances to Peter and some of the disciples when they are fishing, Peter, who has shamefully failed to keep his pledge to support Jesus to the death, is both restored to fellowship with Jesus and given the task of caring for the church. We will not be able to explore all the resurrection appearances, but before examining one of them at length, I want to indicate a few important items present in the resurrection stories.[3]

All four of the Gospels tell us that the tomb of Jesus is first visited by women. It was a custom to visit the tomb of a beloved one. But given the patriarchal biases of the day, it is surprising that their visit is stressed, much less mentioned, in all four Gospels, especially since the testimony of women was not considered to be credible in lawcourts or in general. If a writer is trying to convince people in the ancient world that Jesus was raised from the dead, this is not the way to go about it. The retention and prominence given to the story of the women's visit in all four Gospels is a solid ground for trusting their authenticity. This is especially the case since there is a subtle criticism of the disciples for their failure to believe the women who are the first to learn that Jesus is alive.

In addition, among the women, Mary Magdalene is always given primacy. Mary has been a notorious person. It is said that Jesus cast seven demons out of Mary. In ancient Israel, "seven" implied totality, fullness, or wholeness, as we find in the opening of Genesis, where it is said that God created the heavens and earth in seven days. In the case of demonic possession, "seven" signifies total, complete, or maximal possession. Thus Mary has reached a point where no one can help her. To be possessed by seven demons indicates the completeness of her corruption; to cast out seven demons indicates the completeness of her restoration. In the Gospels, Jesus is portrayed as able to restore to wholesomeness those who have become corrupt. (This contrasts sharply with Plato's account of his hero, Socrates, who though the wisest man in Athens, was unable to restore from corruption his former and most promising pupil, Alcibiades.) Jesus' parable of the Prodigal Son, who is restored to a place of honor by his father's power and love, is not just a story; it describes something that Jesus himself can do, and something that people can see that he has done in the case of Mary Magdalene. Her restoration is also one of the greatest witnesses to Jesus' goodness, and it counters the claim of his detractors and opponents who say that Jesus is not from God but from the devil. Nonetheless, it is surprising that such a person as Mary Magdalene is featured in the story of Jesus' first appearance.

All the appearance stories indicate that there is some difficulty in recognizing the raised Lord because he looks significantly different. Again, this is not something one would stress when trying to convince others that Jesus is raised from the dead. The difference in his appearance also suggests that in the general resurrection from the dead, we too will not be precisely like we now are. This is clearly implied in Paul's comparison of our resurrected bodies and our present bodies to the difference between a plant and its seed. So though there is difference, there is continuity as between a seed and a plant. It is stressed that Jesus is not a disembodied spirit by the fact that he is touched by Mary Magdalene, invites the disciples to put their hands on his wounds, and eats with them (Luke 24:39–43; cf. John 21:9, 13). Yet,

Jesus exhibits some unusual qualities, such as being able to appear and disappear suddenly in a locked room. I do not think that this should necessarily be taken to apply to our resurrected bodies, however. But if you are trying to convince others that Jesus was not just a spirit, ghost, or even a hallucination, you would not stress the unusual qualities of his body. Once again, the traditions drawn upon by the Gospels bear the distinct marks of authenticity.

Finally, in all the appearance stories, the risen Lord commissions the disciples, now called apostles (messengers), to go into all the world to proclaim Jesus. The details vary, but generally it is to make disciples and to baptize them in the name of the Father, Son, and Holy Spirit. It is from him that the apostles receive the authority to do this, but it is not until they receive power from the Holy Spirit that they embark on the mission. All this makes it clear that the founding of the church is not their idea, but that it is based on the authority and power of God. In addition, we find that the Gospels' stress on the commission given to the disciples follows from the vindication of Jesus' claims, by his resurrection, about who he is and what he was doing. At this juncture there is no attention given to *our* resurrection from the dead. So although salvation from death by Christ's resurrection is a major theme in Paul's teachings, it is not among the first reactions of the first disciples to Jesus' resurrection. They were not focused on Jesus' resurrection because they were concerned about their own mortality and hoped to escape it. It strongly suggests that the vindication of Jesus, rather than overcoming our fear of death, was the foundation and start of the church.

> I have stressed that the significance of the resurrection initially focused on it as a vindication of Jesus. This was largely because, as I have already pointed out, the Messiah was not supposed to be a victim, but was expected to lead the Jewish people to military victory over their enemies. This was so widely and deeply held that, as we saw, after Peter confessed that Jesus was the Christ, he immediately rebuked Jesus when Jesus explained that the Messiah must suffer and be killed because of the rejection of the Jewish leaders (Mark 8:31). In addition, hanging on a cross put Jesus among those who were cursed. In that day, a curse was believed to be a living entity which generated a poisonous atmosphere all around its victims. Among the most horrible curses was that which rested upon a criminal whose body, after execution by some other mode of capital punishment, was hung on a tree for special retribution. . . . According to the law, the death of Jesus upon a cross delivered him into the sphere and power of God's special curse.[4]

So it was not only his death that made Jesus' claim to be the Messiah null and void in the eyes of the Jewish people, but also the fact that he hung from a cross. Paul wrote, "We proclaim Christ crucified, a stumbling block to Jews and foolishness to Gentiles, but to those who are the called, both Jews and Greeks, Christ the power of God and the wisdom of God" (1 Cor. 1:23–24). For the disciples, it took Jesus' resurrection to transform Jesus' death on a cross into a victory over sin and death.

The discrepancies in details in the appearance stories—such as how many and which women went to the tomb, whether one or two angels were at the tomb—indicate that the Gospel writers were not copying from each other, but were relying on oral testimony from the very earliest church. In addition, the stories in the Gospels are in fundamental harmony with the oldest account of the resurrection. It is cited by Paul in his letter to the Corinthians, describing what was handed down to him.

> For I handed on to you as of first importance what I in turn had received: that Christ died for our sins in accordance with the scriptures [Old Testament], and that he was buried, and that he was raised on the third day in accordance with the scriptures, and that he appeared to Cephas [Peter], then to the twelve. Then he appeared to more than five hundred brothers and sisters at one time, most of whom are still alive, though some have died. Then he appeared to James, then to all the apostles. Last of all, as to one untimely born, he appeared also to me. (1 Cor. 15:3–8)

So we should not be troubled by variations in some of the details as we study the appearance stories to see what they teach us. In addition, we should approach the stories as we approach paintings of the resurrection. The great paintings of the resurrection are all quite original in their composition and thus render quite different scenes. A child looking at the various paintings of Jesus' resurrection might ask, "Which one is true? Which one shows us how it actually looked that morning? Is that what Jesus looked like?" As adults, we know that all artists use their imagination. Each great depiction has a distinctive way of conveying to us a message about the significance of the resurrection of Jesus. If we know how to understand art at all, we can enjoy every great, or at least most of the great, depictions and learn something important from each one of them.

The same is true of the four Gospels, which depict the resurrection of Jesus. Even though the four Gospels use words instead of paint to tell a story, the Gospels are works of art. To call them works of art does not mean that they are not telling the truth. But it means that we must learn how to read them as works of art if we are properly to understand what they are saying. If the four Gospels were biographies, we would read them for information. Factual accuracy, proper sequence of events, and the like would be expected and necessary. We would be scandalized by the fact that the four do not tell the story of Jesus in the same way. We would ask, "Which one is telling the tale correctly?" But the Gospels are not biographies. They are Gospels, a unique form of writing, without precedent. They proclaim the significance of what Jesus is and did. They are certainly about an actual person and about what he said and did, yet they are especially concerned to tell us about the saving significance of who Jesus is and what he has done. Jesus is unique and what he did is unique, so it is no wonder that the Gospels are a unique form of writing. This means that we have to learn how to read this unique form of writing.

I remember all too well as an eighteen-year-old taking a summer school course. It happened on a blistering hot summer day, before air conditioning had been installed in our benighted university's buildings. A wonderful scholar of

Middle English literature, with perspiration on his face and with a weary voice, walked around the room, returning our papers to each of us. Like a priest distributing the elements, he said to each of us, "You must learn how to read, you must learn how to read." Then he returned to his desk and gave us the homily of the day: "To learn to read better means hard work. I have to keep working at it. You will have to work at it too." I wondered if any of us understood him at the time. But it did have some effect. It stayed in my mind, and slowly I came to learn that reading is not just calling the words off a page, or repeating what the story said. It was especially to learn how a story, with events and people, conveys meaning. In subtle ways a story communicates the significance of an event or the character of a person. It took me a lot of time and practice to learn that something is a symbol, how images work, and how the arrangement of a story itself communicates.

We can see something of what my professor meant by considering another one of John's appearance stories. After John tells the story of the women's visit to the tomb and Jesus' appearance to Mary Magdalene, Jesus appears to the disciples.

> When it was evening on that day [when he appeared to Mary Magdalene], the first day of the week, and the doors of the house where the disciples had met were locked for fear of the Jews, Jesus came and stood among them and said, "Peace be with you." After he said this, he showed them his hands and his side. Then the disciples rejoiced when they saw the Lord. Jesus said to them again, "Peace be with you. As the Father has sent me, so I send you." When he had said this, he breathed on them and said to them, "Receive the Holy Spirit. If you forgive the sins of any, they are forgiven them; if you retain the sins of any, they are retained." (John 20:19–23)

Consider the part of the story in which Jesus gives the apostles the Holy Spirit by breathing on them. This act recalls the scene in Genesis when the Lord God formed the first human of dust from the ground and breathed into his nostrils the breath of life, and man became a living being. But the gift of natural life is not the same as the gift of the Holy Spirit. No one in the Old Testament ever received the Holy Spirit as a permanent possession. The Spirit filled people episodically. The Spirit came and went as the task for which the Spirit was given was achieved. In the Bible story, Jesus is the first person who possesses the Spirit of God permanently. Jesus is the bearer of the Spirit, and in this brief scene, Jesus conveys the Holy Spirit to others permanently, thereby creating a new kind of human being. When the disciples baptize people, the Holy Spirit is given to them and also dwells with them permanently. So Paul reminds his converts that they are a temple in which God dwells: "Do you not know that you are God's temple and that God's Spirit dwells in you?" (1 Cor. 3:16). The great promise of God to Israel to be present among them is now realized with the gift of the Holy Spirit. "For we are the temple of the living God; as God said, 'I will live in them and walk among them, and I will be their God, and they shall be my people'" (2 Cor. 6:16b).

The fact that Jesus gave his disciples the Holy Spirit in a fashion that recalls the creation of the first human enables us to realize something of the significance of Jesus' resurrection. With his resurrection, a new creation has begun. He is "the firstborn from the dead" (Col. 1:18), and with the gift of the Holy Spirit, Jesus creates a new kind of person, one filled with the divine life. By breathing the Holy Spirit into the disciples, Jesus also gives them the authority to start a new mission, to spread the Breath or Spirit of God to all people. They are to go into all the world, conveying that new life by telling people about the resurrected Lord. "As the Father has sent me, so I send you" (John 20:21b). The conveying of the Spirit includes the authority to proclaim the remission of sins to those who are repentant, and to warn those who are impenitent that they are forfeiting the mercy of God and the life-giving Spirit who is offered. The apostles' authority is emphasized: "If you forgive the sins of any, they are forgiven; if you retain the sins of any, they are retained" (John 20:23).

In Genesis what is inert mud is given life by God's breath; now the risen Lord gives a life that cannot die, a life that is eternal, a life that loves and obeys God, a life that is given a task and purpose. It is like the first life given in its intimacy and dependence on God, but it is also a higher, different kind of life. As we stressed at the beginning of the chapter, it is eternal life. It is a life that is to be received by receiving the testimony of the apostles, who have been empowered to tell the story of God's saving love; through living into that story, its hearers may receive the Spirit of Christ.

Now, besides what I have said so far, if we think for a bit, we can see that the very location in which the story of the gift of the Holy Spirit is placed tells us something more. Jesus' breathing into the disciples is an event that occurs when the apostles are in great fear of their fellow Jews, a fear that has caused them to lock the doors of the room. Even though Mary Magdalene has told them that she has seen and touched the risen Lord; even though John, the beloved disciple, has visited the empty tomb with Peter and (from the way the grave clothes are lying there in their regular folds as if the body of Jesus has simply evaporated out of them) has become convinced that Jesus is alive—the disciples nonetheless are in a locked house, gripped by fear. Are they also to be apprehended and killed? At this precise moment, Jesus comes to them and breathes into them the new life of the Holy Spirit. This visit and the gift of the Spirit turns them from a fearful and confused band of disciples into apostles, apostles who in time will boldly and fearlessly proclaim the good new of Christ's victory over death. That is what the gift of the Spirit does. With the Spirit of Jesus, they have the assurance that he will always be with them, that when two or three gathered in his name, he will be in their midst (Matt. 18:20). When John's Gospel was written, the author already knew of the great event of Pentecost, when the Spirit swept over the disciples and gave them the voice to proclaim Jesus to the crowd and to found the church. John's story makes it clear that the apostles are what they are because of the Spirit of God given to them by Jesus. The Holy Spirit is never to be separated from Jesus, a separation that we find in the early church in Corinth and sometimes in our own day.

These observations ought to be enough to make the point that the Gospels are works of art and that we must read them as works of art to discover the significance of Jesus. They ought also to remove any worry, for example, about the apparent discrepancy in the way the keys of the kingdom, or the power to remit or retain people's sins, are conveyed. In Matthew's Gospel, Jesus conveys the keys of the kingdom to Peter as they were on the road to Caesarea Philippi, immediately after Peter recognized that Jesus was the Messiah (Matt. 16:19; cf. 18:18, with plural "you"). In John, the keys are conveyed to all the apostles, presumably so that no one should think that only Peter is the guardian of the authenticity of the gospel message. And John has this authority granted right after Jesus breathes the Holy Spirit into the disciples, presumably so that the gospel message is not regarded to be mere words and facts, but especially a message that conveys life in the Spirit of God. The two scenes are like two different paintings, each bringing out different aspects of the great truths that Jesus has enacted. If we take the trouble to read with our imagination, as we do in looking at great paintings, then instead of wondering whether it was on the road to Caesarea Philippi or in the upper room that the keys of the kingdom were granted, we will find the rich and wonderful reality of the salvation of God brought to us in Christ.

But let us continue with the way the story goes in John. There are two scenes in the story. The climax of the first scene is when Jesus appears to the disciples and gives them the Holy Spirit. With this gift they are enabled to spread the gospel with authority and power. The gospel message itself is symbolized by the keys of forgiveness. "The Church, having received the Spirit, embodies Christ's mission of forgiveness."[5]

Now the climax of this first scene is connected to the climax of the second scene. In the second scene, Thomas turns up. He has been absent when Jesus has appeared to the other disciples, so he has missed seeing the risen Lord. Thomas is quite adamant that he will not believe the other disciples until he himself sees the marks of the nails in Jesus' hands and has put his finger in the mark of the nails and his hand in Jesus' wounded side (John 20:24–25). The testimony of the other disciples is not good enough for him. From the emphatic way Thomas speaks and the uncompromising line he takes—flat-out refusal—we can guess that the conversation must have been quite heated. You can almost hear the disciples, who have seen Jesus, say, "You mean you don't believe us?" And the firm, blunt, reply, "No, I don't!" Nothing will do for Thomas but his own eyes and hands. No one's testimony will do.

Although the doors are again shut, Jesus suddenly stands among them (a detail found in both scenes and, as I pointed out earlier, one telling us that Jesus' resurrected body is unusual; 20:26–29). Jesus once again says to them, "Peace be with you." This greeting cannot be the mere conventional greeting widely used among Jews, since the sudden appearance of a person in a locked room is quite a shock. The greeting is to calm them down and overcome their fears. The earlier visit of the resurrected Lord is hardly enough to make them sanguine over another spectacular visit. After his greeting, Jesus gets right down to business.

He lets Thomas know that he knows what has been going on without need-ing to ask. He bluntly says, "Thomas, put your finger here and see my hands. Reach out your hand and put it in my side" (cf. 20:27). Naturally Thomas is overwhelmed. He cries out, "My Lord and my God!" This is the theme of the entire Gospel of John, and ironically it is uttered by "doubting Thomas," as we tend to call him.

In spite of his initial disbelief, Thomas's heart has been in the right place. He has followed the Lord, and indeed earlier on, when he realized that Jesus is determined to go to Jerusalem, Thomas said, "Let us also go, that we may die with him" (John 11:16). When the arrest of Jesus occurred, Thomas lacked the courage to go through with his earlier declaration, but at least he knowingly exposed himself to the danger of going to Jerusalem with Jesus, and even now he and the others have not fled from Jerusalem, even though they believe that they are in great danger. Thomas does care; he cares a lot. But he wants to be sure that the claim that the Lord has risen is indeed true. Nothing will satisfy him but his own eyes and hand.

This brings us to the climax of the second story. It is in Jesus' response to Thomas. His reply is the last blessing that Jesus pronounced in his earthly life. "Have you believed because you have seen me? Blessed are those who have not seen and yet have come to believe" (20:29).

The climaxes of the two scenes are connected. In the first scene the disciples receive the Holy Spirit and are given the mission of taking the forgiveness of Jesus and his Spirit into the world. Jesus expects people to receive the gospel on the basis of the apostles' testimony. The apostles have authority, the authority of having seen the glory of the risen Lord, and the authority and power of the Holy Spirit. In the first chapter of John we read, "We have seen his glory" (1:14), and in the opening of his First Letter, John writes, "That which was from the begin-ning, which we have heard, which we have seen with our eyes, . . . that which we have seen and heard we proclaim also to you, so that you may have fellowship with us [be part of the church]" (1 John 1:1–3 RSV). Their authority is what they have witnessed and also the presence of the Holy Spirit. Their authority is in the message they bear. Their power is the power of the Holy Spirit at work in them, who can give conviction to those who will listen to the them.

But Thomas does not recognize their authority. He does not respond to the Spirit they bear. Ironically, the very first person to whom the apostles speak is a disciple, and that disciple does not respond. For whatever reason, Thomas has partly withdrawn himself from their fellowship and only turns up a week after Jesus has appeared to the group. When he does turn up, he is not in a receptive mood. So even though Thomas, when he has seen the risen Lord for himself and has responded with the fundamental message of the gospel by confessing, "My Lord and my God!" he is not praised by Jesus. In effect, Jesus says in rebuke, "You believe in me only on your own terms. Thomas, that is not the way it is going to be for others. How fortunate, how blessed are those who have not seen, who yet are receptive to the apostles' testimony, who thus come to believe and by believing become part of the fellowship." Faith rests on the apostles' testimony or witness and the power of the Spirit at work in us. Jesus makes an exception in the case of Thomas and uses that occasion to teach us that the church is to be spread by the divine Word carried in earthen vessels and by the hidden power of the Spirit. And what Jesus has said is what has happened. All over the world, in every age and on every continent, people who have not seen him yet have believed and have become part of the fellowship.

How is it that we come to believe the testimony of the apostles? People have come to believe in many different ways, each finding their own way to God, as I pointed out in the preface. Many people's journeys may fall into some general type or class, but each probably has unique features for each person. Each of us would likely have a different story to tell. But in every one of our stories, whether we realize it or not, there is the presence and the help of God's Spirit. However gently and silently, it is God's Spirit who moves our hearts, illumines our minds, guides our steps, and provides opportunity after opportunity for us to respond to the glorious hope held out to us in the gospel.

In chapter 7, on "Life beyond Death," I argued that the love of justice or righteousness gives us a basis to believe in a life beyond death. But now we can see clearly that in Christianity, it is not a belief in immortality—the continuation of life. It is a life that is given with our resurrection from the dead, a life that is received by those who respond to God's desire to share in God's life. It is eternal life. Its coming in fullness is to be hoped for because of Jesus' resurrection from the dead.

As I pointed out in chapter 7, love of justice can strengthen a person's reasons to believe in the resurrection. But there is also another range of motives or reasons to be open to the testimony of the apostles and the stirring of the Spirit. It is the sheer horror of death, of insignificance, of the retention of our evil. Paul bluntly describes to the immature Christians in Corinth some of the consequences they and we would have to face if Jesus has not been raised from the dead.

> If Christ has not been raised, your faith is futile and you are still in your sins. Then those also who have died in Christ have perished. If for this life only we have hoped in Christ, we are of all people most to be pitied.
> But in fact Christ has been raised from the dead, the first fruits of those who have died. (1 Cor. 15:17–20)

Ludwig Wittgenstein forcefully describes some of the needs that open a person to belief in the resurrection. His reflections on Jesus' resurrection were found in one of his private notebooks, which was published more than forty years after his death. This entry is in the year 1937:

> What inclines even me to believe in Christ's resurrection? . . .
> If he did not rise from the dead, then he decomposed in the grave like any other man. *He is dead and decomposed.* In that case he is a teacher like any other and can no longer *help*; and once again we are orphaned and alone. So we have to content ourselves with wisdom and speculation. We

are in a sort of hell where we can do nothing but dream, roofed in, as it were, and cut off from heaven. But if I am to be REALLY saved,—what I need is *certainty*—not wisdom, dreams or speculation—and this certainty is faith. And faith is faith in what is needed by my *heart*, my *soul*, not my speculative intelligence. For it is my soul with its passions, as it were with its flesh and blood, that has to be saved, not my abstract mind. Perhaps we can say: Only *love* can believe the Resurrection; Or: it is love that believes even in the Resurrection; holds fast even to the Resurrection. What combats doubt is, as it were, *redemption*. Hold fast to *this* must be holding fast to that belief. . . . So this can come about only if you no longer rest your weight on the earth but suspend yourself from heaven. Then *everything* will be different and it will be "no wonder" if you can do things that you cannot do now. (A man who is suspended looks the same as one who is standing, but the interplay of forces within him is nevertheless quite different, so that he can act quite differently than can a standing man.)[6]

This testimony is all the more remarkable because it comes from perhaps the greatest philosopher of the twentieth century and, though committed to rigorous intellectual standards in his philosophical work, at the same time he shows a deep and profound understanding of the spiritual life. He sees that we are to respond with *love* to the love of God that is exhibited above all in the life and death of Jesus, and that is what gives one the certainty of salvation. One is, so to speak, lifted or suspended from above by that divine love.

So often it is faith that is spoken of as the primary relation we are to have toward the testimony or witness of the apostles and the church. But it is *love* that leads the way; it is love that responds to divine love that is primary. Faith or certainty is the *consequence* of love. Yet almost always, whenever Christianity (or religion in general) is described in relation to science, philosophy, or other fields of inquiry, Christianity is said to be a matter of faith, in contrast to the reliance on reason. This makes religion look unworthy of serious consideration by thinking people. But Wittgenstein has the matter absolutely right. It is not an unsupported, blind faith that we rely on in relation to revelation. Wittgenstein knows that it is a love responding to love that issues in conviction, in the certainty that is faith.

Wittgenstein would also understand the approach I have taken to the Gospels. His friend, the eminent psychiatrist Maurice O'Connor Drury, reports:

We had a discussion about the difficulty of reconciling the discourses and history of the Fourth Gospel with the other three. Then he suddenly said: "But if you can accept the miracle that God became a man, all these difficulties are nothing, for then I couldn't possibly say what form the record of such an event would take."[7]

The incarnation is not like the of stories of the Greek gods, for example, who take human form but do not become human beings. The Son of God becoming a human being is a unique idea and claim. We have no precedent to draw upon to portray it. We have to look at Jesus to learn what is involved, especially the self-limitation we have stressed. Wittgenstein had the intelligence and spiritual humility to recognize that we have no template by which to measure the way this claim should be presented. So he saw that in the four Gospels we have, as in paintings, attempts to convey the unparalleled claim that God became a human being, and the significance of that action. Each writer of the Gospels found a distinctive way to present to us the salvation and life Jesus brings. And Wittgenstein put the issue before us very clearly: Do we stand on our own feet, or are we suspended from above, attached to the living Lord? Once we understand the resurrection to some degree, we are no longer to regard Jesus as merely human. Similarly, we are to have a new understanding of ourselves as a people who draw their energy and inspiration from God.

Chapter 14

Jesus as Lord
and Jesus as Servant

At the core of the Christian life is the fact that people have a Lord, someone to whom they belong and to whom they are obedient. But today it is commonly said, especially by those who endorse a postmodern creed, that all values and meaning are human or cultural projections. This means, in turn, that all social hierarchies are based on domination by the most powerful groups in various societies. This claim is also made about religious institutions and teachings. How can people be free if they have a master? How can people be free if they have someone they must obey?

Like so many in our culture who want to be in personal control of their lives, Jean-Paul Sartre (1905–80), the French philosopher, claimed that the two notions—freedom and God—contradict each other. To be human is to be free, to be autonomous. So the very idea of God reduces people to slavery and is essentially antihuman.

You do not need to endorse Sartre's claim to recognize the resentment we would feel at having a boss, a ruler, or anyone else telling us what to do all the time. How would that be human fulfillment? How could that be self-fulfillment? How could that be happiness? The Christian gospel claims that the spiritual life is one of fullness of life and blessedness. How can that develop from a relationship with one who has unquestionable authority over us, especially if we think that blessedness includes a significant degree of self-direction?

So at its center the spiritual life has a question: "How can we be free when we are ruled by a master?" To answer this question is another way to vindicate Jesus' life, teachings, and death in addition to the vindication of them by his resurrection. It is especially necessary to address the question of our freedom since I stressed that in his resurrection Jesus reestablished his relation to his disciples as their Lord God. I will approach this question by examining Georg W. F. Hegel's (1770–1831) analysis of the relationship between master and slave in his *Phenomenology of Spirit*,[1] and then by comparing that relationship to Jesus' treatment of his disciples.

Hegel tells us that in human life there is a conflict, with each person seeking to get one's own way. One resolution of this conflict is the master-slave relation. One person dominates the other completely. From the point of view of one of the people—the master—this is the optimal resolution, for that person's will is obeyed and hence his personhood is fully realized.

But there is an irony in the situation. The master cannot be truly independent or free. To assert one's independence or mastery, one must have something that is not oneself. One must have something other than self to pay deference to oneself, something to subordinate to oneself. One has status as master only as long as one has a slave. Thus one does not have perfect independence.

The master tries to keep this truth hidden, to suppress it, by making his control more and more arbitrary, so that there is no recourse beyond his will as to how one treats the slave. The more arbitrary the master's control, the stronger the slave's dependence, and hence the greater the master's sense of independence. But clearly this approach is self-defeating; for this consciousness of independence requires the existence of something to subordinate and something that can recognize the master's dominance.

Another feature of the master-slave relation is the master's contempt for the slave. By becoming subservient to the master, the slave is debased and so is odious. The slave is debased and odious because the slave is really a person, just like the master. They are essentially the same. If the slave were not a person, there would be no contempt. Why be contemptuous of a river that yields to a dam? Nor do we hold dogs in contempt because they obey us. To call a person a "dog" shows that we have contempt for such obedience when it is exhibited by a person. So the master's very contempt is an implicit recognition that the slave is a person and that the relation is an improper one.

The relation is also marked by resentment. The master resents the slave because the master needs the slave in order to have the status of master. The slave resents the master because the slave must obey the master. Finally, there is envy. Slaves wish that they would have power like the master. The slaves envy and secretly admire what the master can do and want to do it as well. Each slave wants to be a master himself or herself.

In the four Gospels it is quite clear that the relation of Jesus to his disciples, though one of dominance and subordination, is very different from the one Hegel describes. Jesus does not gain or hold subordinates by force. He calls disciples: thus there is an element of choice on their part in becoming subordinate to him. Jesus seeks to confer benefits on them by teaching them. He even performs an act of a servant or slave (it is the same word in the New Testament) when he washes their feet. We perceive no resentment or contempt in his treatment of his disciples. Why is this so? What enables Jesus to be a different kind of lord?

Let us approach this by looking at a relation I have lived with for most of my adult life: the relation of teacher to students. In the classroom, teachers are in the role of superiors. Within certain limits, we tell our students what to do. What keeps this relation from being that of a Hegelian master with slaves? How can we be the boss and the student not feel or be degraded, or feel resentful? How can we operate on the basis of being boss and not feel contempt for students as underlings?

The relation of superior-subordinate is justified if there are genuine grounds for one to be dominant and the other to be subordinate. If there is some basis for the teacher to command, to lead, and for the student to follow, then there is no violation of personality.

One ground of justification for a teacher's superiority is that a teacher knows something the pupil does not know. The teacher has some skills, some means of getting answers, and some experience that the pupil lacks. The relation is thus based on a difference.

But this is not enough to justify the relation of superior and subordinate. The goal of the teacher must be to enable the pupil to become independent of the teacher. Many of us teach in such a way that the pupil depends on lecture notes and never masters the principles and skills of a field. Some teachers not only fail to do these things but even take a secret delight in their pupils' remaining dependent, in remaining in this respect essentially inferior to themselves forever.

Each type of relation differs. Doctor-patient, lawyer-client, pastor-congregant, parent-child, society toward the individual, the state toward the citizen. We need to look at each relationship in terms of its own particularity. One cannot simply transfer what is true of the teacher-pupil relation to others, or vice versa. There may be similarities; there may be great differences. I only want to make one point: For a relation of superior and subordinate to be different from Hegel's master-slave relation, there must be some genuine basis for the two roles. There is none in Hegel's; there is only brute, raw power.

Now what is the basis of Jesus' lordship? On what does it rest, so that he can indeed be our Lord, can command us, have us depend on him always, without this being destructive of our personality? What makes him a different kind of lord than Hegel's master?

The foundation of Jesus' relation to his disciples and to us is that he does not need us. This may sound harsh and false at first, but it is really the basis of his ability to serve us and elevate us. He does not need us in this sense: Jesus is Lord because of who he is, not because he has followers. He is Lord by his inherent reality. He is Lord because he is the Son of God. It is not because of us that he is the Son of God. Hegel's master is a master only if he has slaves. His status depends on his having subordinates. He cannot afford to have them come to any sense of fullness, for any degree of independence threatens his status.

But whether we like it or not, Jesus is the Son of the Father. His position, his status, his authority do not spring from anything human. They do not depend even on our acknowledgment. Without a single disciple, he is still the Son of God.

Precisely because Jesus does not need us, precisely because his status does not rest on us, he can serve us. He can wash his disciples' feet and not thereby cease to be the Son. Jesus can free people of demons and from other ailments, and this improvement in their condition does not threaten his status. He can be free to let people voluntarily choose to respond to his call to follow him; for whether they reject or accept him, he is still the Son of the Father. Jesus can even be slain for us, bearing the awful catastrophe of human evil, without ceasing to be Lord. Precisely because he differs from us in kind, his lordship does not need to reduce our reality. Because his lordship rests on the Father, he is free to enhance us.

Because Hegel's master does not really differ in kind from that of the slaves, since both are equally creatures, his lordship is destructive. Hegel's master must deny the personality of the slaves. The master must seek to absorb their reality by making them an extension of his will: "Do this, do that. Give me the product of your labor." The master does everything for his own sake, in order to be a lord, in order to have the status of a master.

How different orders and commands are when they are from one who seeks not to deny our personhood but to enhance it. By his commands and authority, Jesus does not seek to deny our persons but to free us. He seeks to free us of the need to have our own person established by domination over others. Jesus seeks to free us of the need to gain recognition at the expense of others. The basis of our freedom is that he gives us our status as people destined to share in the life of God, now and always. That is who we are, that is what we are: creatures destined for an eternal happiness. That status is conferred on us. It is not a gift of this world, for it cannot be grasped by an employment of all our talent, ingenuity, power, or status over others. We therefore do not have to compete with each other in order to become ourselves; for what we are to become is not to be gained in the realm of earthly dominance, founded on the standards of earthly success. We can be free precisely because Jesus is free. His lordship is not based on anything earthly. So he can serve us. It is by following Jesus that we can enter the kingdom in which we can serve each other.

In chapter 9, where we considered the doctrine of creation in relation to the doctrine of the Trinity, we pointed out that it is because God's life as Father, Son, and Holy Spirit is full and complete that God's creation of the universe is an act of utter graciousness, done freely, done with perfect love, since God has no need of anything but Godself to be fully realized. We mentioned that it is likewise because the Son of God's status is fully secured by the Son's life in the divine Trinity that the incarnate Son does not depend on us for his status. Jesus' freedom to serve and elevate us has its ground in the divine life of God. Because of God's own fullness, God is able to establish a bond of pure love with us.

Another aspect of Jesus' power is evident in the way he met his death at the hands of those with authority. In the face of a threat to public order, those with authority and the responsibility of maintaining peace—even if they did care about justice, as Pilate did—are sometimes under pressure to sacrifice justice, and with it, to sacrifice all pretense of determining whose views are correct when it comes to life's big questions. In spite of the faith of the eighteenth- and nineteenth-century political reformers such as Voltaire and Marx in the "verdict of history," the arena of political decisions is not likely to be a place where the big issues of life are discussed or decided solely or even primarily on the basis of truth and justice.

So when Pilate washes his hands in public to indicate his personal disagreement with the charges against Jesus, he makes it clear that the truth of the matter in the controversy between Jesus and his adversaries has not been settled (Matt. 27:24). His enemies succeed in having Jesus condemned to death, but Pilate indicates that what they are doing is unjust and does not settle the matter of who is right. Ironically, Pilate has tried to get around the controversy by letting Jesus go and yet is the one who orders his execution (27:26). But at least he makes it clear that Jesus is executed not for political sedition but because of what he claims to be (27:11, 23, 37).

In spite of the sentence passed on Jesus and in spite of his execution, the question still remains: Is what Jesus claims actually true? Pilate—who is not a Jew and perhaps is somewhat cynical, as evidenced by his rhetorical question "What is truth?" (John 18:38)—nonetheless allows the question of the truth of what Jesus claims to remain in the forefront. In all the confusion of arrest and accusation, in the smell, dust, heat, and noise of the crowd, this crucial matter does not get lost. God's purpose is achieved: Is what Jesus claims actually true?

Jesus' refusal to resist arrest and to have his disciples fight to save him enables Pilate to realize that the truth of what Jesus claims is the real issue between Jesus and his accusers—not sedition or treason. Jesus' behavior does not allow the threat of a cruel death by crucifixion to deflect the focus of attention. In all the confusion of history and the noise of life around us, this question still comes through today: Is what Jesus claims actually true?

Jesus, then, was a particular kind of victim of injustice. To keep the crucial issue in the forefront by a commitment to God was an active role, not a passive one. He faced death and died in such a way that people are forced to face the important questions of life. We are so familiar with Jesus' trial and death that we frequently miss this feature. We might see it better by recalling the death of Socrates.

Socrates was accused of three things: atheism, leading young people astray, and endangering the security of Athens. Those who brought the charges demanded the death penalty. This punishment was ridiculously severe. The jury of five hundred citizens would have been happy to close the whole affair by imposing a minor fine. According to Athenian law, the jury had to choose between the alternatives proposed by the plaintiff and those of the defendant. Socrates' friends begged him to propose a fine and even offered to pay it for him. But Socrates refused. He had obeyed a divine call to awaken his city to its ignorance and its need to search for a truer way to live. Socrates said that he surely was only a minor person in the great city of Athens, no more than a gadfly, stinging a large beast in order to make it take notice of the way it was stumbling along, heedless of its direction. To carry out this mission, he had neglected his own business affairs. Now, as an old man, he was poor. He therefore proposed that the city provide him with a pension in recognition of his services.

The jury had to decide between the death penalty and a pension for services. The majority was so outraged with Socrates for making the situation so awkward that it voted for the death penalty. Everyone expected that, while in prison, Socrates would come to his senses and admit that he was wrong. The city officials tried to arrange for Socrates to escape, but he refused to cooperate: "Either I have been a benefactor and should receive a pension," he said, "or my accusers are right."

The jury had not reckoned on the seriousness of this little citizen; it was amazed at his passionate love of truth and his deep commitment to the well-being of his fellow citizens. Through his refusal to back down, even in the face of death, Socrates forced his fellow citizens to face a vital issue. Is the basis of life to go unexamined? Are we just to stumble along? Will the gods allow this to go unpunished? If he had accepted a minor fine, or when he saw that the authorities meant business, had escaped from prison, then people would have been able to slide over these questions and continue to live untroubled but superficial lives.

By accepting a grossly unjust death, Socrates did not allow the people of his city to continue to live the way they wanted scot-free; they could live that way only at the price of the death of a wise, generous citizen who had devoted his life to their betterment. To be his kind of victim is not something that just happens. Socrates' and Jesus' deaths differed from those of countless victims of injustice because of the way they conducted themselves. Each of them suffered from injustice in such a way that each caused people to face the questions that each life raised.

But the question "Is what Jesus claims actually true?" can be and has been somewhat deflected by much of nineteenth- and early twentieth-century biblical scholarship. Biblical scholars quite commonly have argued that there is a difference between what Jesus thought and taught about himself, on the one hand, and what the apostles and the early church proclaimed him to be, on the other hand. They have contrasted the Jesus of history to the Christ of faith. To pose the issue *today*, "Is what Jesus claims actually true?" we must determine what Jesus actually did claim, and whether it is the same as what the apostles and early church proclaimed about him: Jesus is the Messiah, or Christ, and the Son of God.

As I have emphasized, on historical grounds there is no doubt that the four Gospels are written in light of belief in Jesus' resurrection. All scholars agree on this. Should this make us skeptical about the content of the four Gospels? Not if we understand the nature of history. Take our own lives and consider the way we regard events as they happened to us at, say, age 10 or 15. Then consider how we regard these same events at the age of 25, 35, or 45. We see them quite differently. Our way of understanding their significance when we are older is often more sound than the way we regarded them as they were experienced at the time.

In the same way, after Jesus' resurrection, the disciples understood what was taking place in Jesus' ministry far better than they did at the time of Jesus' public ministry. The Gospels themselves indicate this by describing the way the disciples were frequently confused and puzzled by what Jesus was saying and doing, not to mention the others who heard Jesus.

The crucial issue in New Testament studies of the Gospels is *not* whether the four Gospels were written in light of what came later. This is true of all history because time is needed for us to realize the significance of events. We cannot see the pattern they fit into, and so we come to better understanding of their meaning after more things happen, and we see a larger pattern of events. Thus after the resurrection, the disciples were in a much better position to understand who Jesus was, what he had done, and what he had taught.

The crucial issue is whether there is *essential continuity,* explicit or implicit, between what Jesus said, did, and thought of himself and the way the writers of the Gospels present him. Is there essential continuity in the development of the disciples' and church's understanding of Jesus, Jesus' message, and what Jesus himself thought and taught about himself, or is there an essential discontinuity in the development?

Scholars divide into two major types on this crucial issue in scholarly study of the Gospels today. The first group argues that there is an *essential continuity* between what Jesus taught and thought of himself and the accounts given of him in the Gospels. The continuity is either explicit or implicit. For example, in John's Gospel we find that Jesus says, "Whoever has seen me has seen the Father" (John 14:9b). In this example, Jesus himself explicitly claims that he is divine. In some fashion (as in his will) he is one with the Father. Explicit claims are a feature of John's Gospel. Now consider an example of an implicit continuity between who Jesus claimed he was and what the Gospels say he was: Jesus says to a paralytic, "Son, your sins are forgiven" (Mark 2:5b). Some of the scribes who hear this recognize it as an implicit claim to some kind of equality with God. "Why does this fellow speak in this way? It is blasphemy! Who can forgive sins but God alone?" (2:7). Jesus takes up the challenge and demonstrates that he has the authority to forgive sin by healing the man (2:10–12). Jesus also forgives the sins of a well-known prostitute at a meal in the home of a Pharisee. The woman has bathed his feet with her tears, wiped his feet with her hair, continued to kiss them, and anointed them. Jesus emphatically contrasts this woman's loving behavior to the gross neglect by his host. Those who hear him forgive the woman's sins know what it implies: "Who is this who even forgives sins?" (Luke 7:49b). To forgive is a divine prerogative. Jesus does not explicitly say he is divine, but he acts as if, at least in this respect, he is.

A more subtle type of reason than the examples I have given is a consideration of the following kind. It is most implausible that Jesus ever denied that he was the Messiah; otherwise, his followers would have said he had been executed on a totally false charge.[2] So in either case, explicitly or implicitly, these scholars believe that there is an essential continuity between Jesus' claims about himself and what the apostles taught and the early church believed about Jesus.

The second type of scholarly reader claims that there is discontinuity between what Jesus taught and thought of himself and the accounts of the four Gospels. These scholars have the task of explaining how Christianity arose, since (in this view) Jesus did not claim to be Messiah or divine and did not rise from the dead. Every account that has been given over the centuries, including those that received a great deal of publicity when they first appeared, has failed, and indeed failed *by the standards of historical-critical scholarship itself.* Some of these attempts have been of a sufficient standard of scholarship to warrant careful consideration, and some have contributed to a better understanding of the New Testament period, but in their main effort they have failed. But as long as there are scholars who do not believe the Gospels, there will be further attempts to give an alternative explanation of the historical phenomenon of Christianity.

According to Raymond E. Brown, the overwhelming majority of biblical scholars of the Gospels today believe that there is an essential continuity between what Jesus taught and thought of himself and what the apostles, the early church, and the four Gospels say of him—in spite of what media publicity may suggest to the contrary by the amount of attention it gives to those who believe that there is a discontinuity. Brown is considered to be a very careful, moderate, and accurate reporter of scholarly views. We may therefore say that biblical scholarship on the Gospels cannot rightly be used to undermine the issue put before us by the way Jesus met his death: Is what Jesus claimed actually true? The claim that there is an essential discontinuity between the Jesus of history and the Christ of faith has been put to rest. He did put himself forward as Messiah and Son of God, reinterpreting these titles to suit his self-understanding as one who must suffer for our salvation. One other old objection also needs to be put to rest: the claim that there were many would-be messiahs in Palestine. "In fact, there is no evidence that any Jew claimed or was said to be the Messiah before Jesus of Nazareth. . . . Thus one must offer an explanation for the unanimity attested in the New Testament that Jesus was the Christ."[3]

We now need to consider what we are to say about our response to Jesus' claim.

Chapter 15

Revelation and Faith

Science distinguishes itself from religion by its study of the physical world and by making its claims on the basis of reproducible observations, controlled experiments, and theoretical reasoning that in the final analysis connects with observations and experiments. All this involves independent verification of any claim that is made. In contrast to science, Western religions depend on revealed truth and faith.

As far as it goes, these remarks about religion, and its differences from science, are true. But often they are only half-truths. Without any explanation of this brief characterization, revelation is often taken to be a method of special delivery, so to speak, of some truths that one supposedly is simply to accept: "The Bible says 'x,' and therefore 'x' is true."

The philosophers who are unsympathetic or even hostile to religion are especially prone to this distorted characterization in their contrast of science and religion. In addition, they also rather gleefully point out that philosophy relies solely on human reason, in contrast to religion, which relies on an acceptance of revelation, implying that reason is not used in religion at all. Frequently they crown their distortions by saying that religious people, in contrast to scientists and philosophers, rely on their emotions, not reason and evidence. Anyone who cares about intellectual inquiry, including religious people, cannot help but unfavorably regard religion so characterized.

How should we understand revelation and faith? God's love for us is not something that we are to seek to determine by controlled experiment because it would be a violation of our relationship, just as experiment would be a violation of the relationship of friendship or marriage. So it is not scientific procedures that we are to use in relation to the love revealed to us in Jesus. But scientific procedures are not the only way our rational powers are properly used. Earlier, in the case of Anselm, we saw how subtle the relation of reason to revealed truth can be. He improved his understanding of God's nature by thinking out what is implied in the very notion of God. He came to realize that God is a necessary being, in contrast to all other beings. This truth is something that can be grasped by our minds. It is not something that is simply a truth to be blindly accepted, with no understanding.

Quite clearly in the last chapter, where we considered the question of whether there is an essential continuity between what Jesus claimed about himself and what the apostles and church taught, the question was not decided by an appeal to revelation and faith, and certainly not to emotions. It was determined by historical inquiry, an inquiry that depends on evidence and reason and that can be conducted by anyone with the requisite training to be an historian. A negative answer to the question would have seriously affected, indeed probably undermined, the claim that Jesus' life, death, and resurrection reveal to us the extent of God's love. It would at the very least seriously raise the question of the propriety of the apostles' and early church's claims about Jesus. A favorable answer by historical inquiry to the question of the continuity between who Jesus was and the claims by the apostles and early church is perfectly compatible with the Christian religion being a matter of God's revelation of God's love to us in the life, death, and resurrection of Jesus because a favorable determination of the question still leaves it up to us to respond or not respond to that love.

In general, we may say that in Christianity the relation of revelation and faith to evidence and reason follows that pattern. Our reason is integrally related to revelation and faith. Without the intellect involved, there is no revelation; and without some understanding of what is revealed, there can be no faith. Unlike the Koran—which is said to have been dictated by God in Arabic to Muhammad, who simply acted as a scribe—in Christianity our understanding of what God is showing us and what God is doing involves our response. Just as friendship is a relationship involving mutual participation, or just as in teaching the teacher needs a response from the pupils, so too the Bible involves a long period of interaction between God and various people, interaction that involves some early understanding and misunderstanding, and an improving and growing understanding of God's purposes. We saw this in the misunderstanding of God's relation to human prosperity and adversity, which the book of Job and Jesus corrected; we also saw it in Jesus' difficulty in communicating to his disciples and others, such as the Samaritan woman at the well and Nicodemus, the

nature of the kingdom of God and of his own role in it. To come into a relationship with the holy God, we who rely on the Bible and the testimony of the
church must have misconceptions corrected, so that we in time may grow and
develop in our understanding of God, just as did those who initially responded
to God and, in time, wrote and edited and reedited the Bible. We are not simply
to say, as some unfortunately do, "The Bible says 'x,' and therefore I believe 'x.'"
To grow into a proper relationship with God, one specified by the witness of the
Bible itself, requires us to use our whole being, including our mind.

In theology, in contrast to what some misguided individuals and church
groups may do, it has never been a question of revelation and faith *or* reason.
Rather, it has always been a question of determining the precise relation of revelation and reason. Since they are so intertwined, to describe the precise relation
of reason and revelation would require us to go to a very advanced level in theology. In addition, there are several schools of thoughts on the issue, and these
different views have different theological implications. All agree that although
God, as transcendent, is above our powers to comprehend, we can have some
grasp of God's intentions for us, some intimate relation with God through Jesus
and the Holy Spirit, and that some use of the intellect in relation to God is
appropriate and needed. But we do not need to go into the sophisticated issue
of the relation of reason and revelation in order to deal with the question that
concerns this chapter: Is what Jesus claimed actually true?

My approach to this question is that we use theology like a flashlight. We are
to use it to cast light into the darkness. So we do not look at Christian beliefs in
isolation and ask, "Are they believable? Are they true?" That would be like looking at the bulb of a flashlight instead of using its light. We are to use Christian
beliefs to gain understanding that otherwise we would not have. The illumination that the beliefs give us helps to convince our minds of their truth. We use
this approach because God's being is above the power of the intellect to comprehend. But what Jesus is and taught casts a light on our self-understanding, our
behavior, our society, our natural world, and gives us an understanding of them
that otherwise we would not have.

As I pointed out at the start of this book, people are motivated to become
Christians for many different reasons. The illumination of our intellect is the
primary motivation for only some people. But even though people's motives
vary, everyone has to have at least some understanding of the Christian faith to
be moved to believe it. So the points I will be making concern the way anyone's
mind may be illumined.

We have already given some important instances of the light cast by the
teachings and actions of Jesus. For example, in the introduction we considered
the parables of the Prodigal Son, the Lost Coin, and the Lost Sheep, the one out
of a hundred. The stories claim that each of us is lost and that God so cares for
each one of us, so that God seeks to find us and welcome us into God's glorious
kingdom. God takes each of us more seriously than we take ourselves, more seriously than any theory about people takes us. This view of each of us as of equal

and inalienable value has so taken hold in Western civilization that our legal system, our understanding of human rights, and the emancipation of women and slaves is inspired by such simple parables as a Lost Son, Lost Coin, and Lost Sheep, especially when combined with God's actions in sending Jesus to save us. We also pointed out that nothing can give us the value and worth that underlies our civilization's convictions concerning human rights, which is spreading to the rest of the world, except the love of God. This understanding of people is revealed by Jesus. It is something that can be documented by historical study. Again, it is something that requires one's own response.

In chapter 2, we illustrated with the parable of the Good Samaritan that Jesus opened people's eyes for the first time to the depths of harm that human beings often endure, harm that cannot be conceptually articulated without an understanding of the absolute value of human beings (Luke 10:29–37). In the parable, the stricken man's relative value is taken away, because he is simply a battered piece of flesh, but he retains absolute value, as the action of the good Samaritan shows. The Samaritan recognizes that it is an outrage to allow such brokenness to lie unnoticed and unattended.

The parable was given in answer to the question "Who is my neighbor?" Before Jesus, love of neighbor had not been understood in Judaism to apply to any and every human being. We now take that for granted. So it is good to be reminded that Plato, in all of his brilliant writings on love, never broached the notion of love of neighbor. As I mentioned earlier, nine out of ten people in ancient Greece were slaves, and Aristotle argued that, as long as they were not Greeks, it was their nature to be slaves. Love of neighbor is not an ethical principle that we may adopt without any religious or metaphysical backup, so to speak, as modern philosophers once widely argued. God is not an extra here, so that we can keep the principle and dismiss God. Without the love of God revealed in and by Jesus, we do not have absolute value. Only because of God's love do we have absolute value. Our perception of people as neighbors whom we are to help in all cases of distress, especially great distress, is the result of our minds and hearts having been illumined by this and other parables.

We have already covered these instances of the use of reason and historical evidence. In the case of Anselm, we have an example of philosophic reasoning; in the cases of Raymond Brown and N. T. Wright, we have instances of the use of historical evidence and reasoning. From the parables and actions of Jesus, we have illumination concerning ourselves as of irreplaceable and absolute value and illumination concerning proper motivation for our action in relation to others. Now we want to turn our attention first to paradoxes concerning our human nature that Christian belief illumines, then to the way the Christian doctrine of creation has affected our perception and scientific study of the physical world.

Blaise Pascal (1623–62) is the master of the paradoxes in human nature that can open us to the illumination of our condition and nature as given by Christian beliefs. He was a mathematical prodigy and a pioneer in the scientific revolution. Pascal realized that to think about God requires a different approach. He said that he found his mathematical and scientific work easy in comparison with his examination of life apart from God and life lived by God's grace. Although Pascal had a powerful religious experience, he never told anyone about it (we learned of it only after his death from a record he made of it). Nor did he use it in his apology for Christianity. So for his authority he does not refer to an experience of the holiness of God, as did Moses or Isaiah. Rather, he wrote an apology of Christianity: in the Greek meaning of *apologia,* this is a *reasoned defense* of Christianity. That there are such things as apologies for Christianity ought by itself and for no other reason alert people who characterize religious faith as a blind belief and show that they are mistaken. Why would anyone write an apology if reason does not matter? Even if every reasoned case for Christianity should prove to be inadequate, the fact that believers try to offer reasons for belief should long since have undermined claims that Christianity is a blind faith.

Pascal seems to have worked in great haste, writing down his thoughts on many slips of paper. In 1659 he began classifying the nearly nine hundred fragments under twenty-eight headings, organizing nearly half of them in this way. But Pascal died before he could finish his classification, much less compose the projected book, and we have a great deal of difficulty determining precisely what Pascal's views were on many matters. But the pattern of his argument is clear and is summarized in a fragment that he placed in the first bundle of his papers.

> F 12 Order. Men despise religion. They hate it and are afraid it may be true. The cure for this is to show that religion is not contrary to reason, but worthy of reverence and respect.
>
> - Next make it attractive, make good men wish it were true, and then show that it is.
> - Worthy of reverence because it really understands human nature.
> - Attractive because it promises true good.[1]

This was written soon after Europe had been through the devastation of the Thirty Years' War (1618–48), largely a religious war between Catholics and Protestants. In the eyes of many educated people, this bitter conflict discredited both creeds. Pascal needed to break through the crust of their indifference and turn them into seekers after truth, so that they would not only become interested in religion but also come to respect it.

We will begin with the first part of Pascal's apology, in which he says that Christianity deserves respect if for no other reason than its understanding of human nature. By "respect" Pascal means for people to be so concerned for truth as to "put themselves out" (F 80). People will not be able to continue to follow their customary and habitual way of life. He presents a series of paradoxes showing that we are a riddle to ourselves and do not understand what we are, but Christianity illumines the paradoxes. In a series of paradoxes he shows that we have reason and can achieve remarkable things, but in making judgments, our reason is thrown off by the most irrelevant and insignificant factors.

> Would you not say that this magistrate, whose venerable age commands
> universal respect, is ruled by pure, sublime reason, and judges all things
> as they really are, without paying heed to the trivial circumstances which
> offend only the imagination of weaker men? See him go to hear a sermon in
> a spirit of pious zeal. If when the preacher appears, it turns out that nature
> has given him a hoarse voice and an odd sort of face, that his barber has
> shaved him badly and he happens not to be too clean either, then I wager
> that our senator will not be able to keep a straight face. (F 44)

More significantly jarring is the paradox that we who have such greatness
can be utterly destroyed by the slightest imbalance in our bodies, or crushed as
easily as an egg:

> Man is only a reed, the weakest in nature, but he is a thinking reed. There
> is no need for the whole universe to take up arms to crush him: a vapour, a
> drop of water is enough to kill him. But even if the universe were to crush
> him, man would still be nobler than his slayer, because he knows that he
> is dying and the advantage the universe has over him. The universe knows
> nothing of this. (F 200)

Thus we are both great and insignificant, and our greatness and insignificance
do not fit together. They are disparate truths that no philosophical or psychological theory has been able to render compatible. One or the other extreme is
stressed to the neglect of the other.

With Plato and Descartes, reason becomes our defining characteristic, so that
we are not subject to nature; with Freud, on the other hand, our affective, irrational, animal side becomes our defining characteristic. The first theory stresses
our greatness, the second our insignificance; yet neither theory can be sustained.
For when we try to affirm our greatness, our lower selves and the vastness of
the universe pull us from our lofty heights. When our insignificance is stressed,
our distinctiveness from the rest of nature resists this evaluation. However small
and irrational we may be, we are also able to become aware of our smallness and
irrationality, so that our uniqueness cannot be utterly undermined by the vastness of space or the irrationality of our passions. But we cannot conclude that
we are immensely significant because of the very smallness and irrationality of
which we are aware.

Our nature has both these extreme features and, since they are incompatible,
the inadequacy of philosophical or psychological theories that tend to go to
extremes is not accidental. These extremes push us in opposite directions, so that
as soon as we go in one direction, we are driven back toward the other. We cannot find a compromise by saying that we are neither great nor insignificant, but
something in between, because we indeed are both great and insignificant, and
these cannot be blended any more than can oil and water. Thus no philosophical
or psychological theory can tell us what we are: great or insignificant.

But by its recognition of two levels of reality, the natural and the supernatural,
Christianity can make sense of these extremes. According to Christianity, we are
natural beings with a supernatural destiny. As natural beings we are limited and

vulnerable, however much we exceed other creatures. Because of our limitations and mortality, we cannot base our greatness or significance on our *natural* endowments, but a greatness based on our *supernatural* destiny is not affected by natural endowments. They do not affect our irreplaceable and absolute value. When we try to base our greatness on our natural powers, nature's size and majesty mock us. When our greatness is based on God's gift of eternal life in God's kingdom, it is not affected by nature or our natural limitations. As the basis of our greatness, God's gift introduces a supernatural level into our understanding of human beings. It enables us to see how we are easily deflated insofar as we are natural beings, and yet how our greatness is secure insofar as we have a supernatural destiny.

As long as we stay on one level, the natural, we cannot find a resting place. We cannot know what we are or understand ourselves. But as soon as a supernatural level is introduced, we can understand the incompatible aspects of human nature. We can cease the vain attempt to determine what we are by staying on one level and being forced to go back and forth between two extremes. Our true nature includes a supernatural destiny, a greatness beyond the ceaseless seesaw, because its basis is another level of reality (F 131).

Christianity also explains *why* we have the natural and conflicting features of greatness and insignificance. Our limitations and vulnerability constitute the basis of our insignificance; our reason constitutes the basis of our natural greatness; all these are accounted for when viewed from a supernatural perspective. As mere creatures we are limited and vulnerable, as are all creatures in their different ways. But we are creatures made in God's image. We are able to reason and to relate to others on a personal basis. Our natural greatness is seen as part of God's image, and that natural greatness has been conferred on us to enable us to achieve our supernatural destiny: to be related to God and to obey God freely.

We tend, however, to use our natural abilities for self-elevation, ignoring the fact that we are great only because we are made in God's image. So our natural greatness leads us to pride, to an attempt to base our status on our own powers without reference to God. Our natural powers thus blind us to our true greatness, and God's good gift of natural powers becomes a powerful barrier between us and God. We therefore need to realize and constantly to be reminded that our natural greatness is the result of our *supernatural* origin and destiny. Our natural greatness, because it can fill us with pride, must be tempered by an awareness of our limitations and vulnerability. It must be tempered by a knowledge of our insignificance in an infinite universe, the fallibility of our judgment, and our susceptibility to microbes and viruses. Yet our insignificance cannot be allowed to take over completely, or we sink into despair. We are to use the disparate features of our nature to counter each other so that we neither become blinded by pride nor sunk in despair. Ultimately, the incompatibility of our greatness and insignificance is so great as to baffle us and open us to a supernatural understanding of ourselves.

The incompatibility that prevents us from understanding ourselves as natural beings has its source in God. God makes creatures who can be related to Godself.

If we were merely animals, we would not feel insignificant before the vastness of the universe. Because we are animals made in God's image, with a supernatural goal, it follows that we are a puzzle to ourselves, a puzzle no philosophical nor psychological theory can explain, as we have seen. Once Christianity has told us what we really are, however, we make sense to ourselves. We see why we have divergent aspects, and how we can make good use of the disparate features of our nature to keep ourselves from both pride and despair. For though we can learn much about ourselves from philosophy and psychology, neither one can resolve the riddle of our nature.

Christianity thus deserves respect. It should cause us to "put ourselves out," to seek God, if for no other reason than its understanding of human nature, which presents such puzzling features. If we believe that various philosophies and psychologies are intellectually respectable and important because of the insights they give us about human beings, then in all fairness we ought to give serious attention to Christianity as well. On a strictly academic basis, it provides an illuminating explanation of the paradoxical features of our nature, features that neither philosophy nor psychology, while remaining on a natural level, are able to provide. Even if they take some account of the duality, their solutions show that they do not fully face it. Thus they try to give us hope in light of our obvious limitations and mortality by pointing to worthwhile and attainable goals. Such goals sell us short; we aspire to so much more than anything this world can give. This is clearly evident from our attitude toward our mortality.

We want to live well and forever. The sacrifice we must make to accept lesser prospects, which we would have to accept on any secular explanation, is itself testimony to the greatness of our aspirations. Christianity, however, never loses sight of either aspect of our nature and the way both aspects push us back and forth like a shuttlecock in our self-estimation. So we are never allowed to be lost in pride, sunk in despair, nor reconciled to life confined to earthly dimensions. It knows our greatness, a greatness far greater and more realistic than any greatness based on a prideful estimate of our nature.

Although Christianity is not a philosophical nor a psychological theory about human nature, ignoring as it does many questions that these disciplines rightly and helpfully explore, it does call our attention to their limitations. Because of human duality, no nonreligious account of human nature can be definitive. Our doubleness keeps pressing us to recognize that we live in a vast universe, that we are frail and mortal, and yet we have a stubborn sense of significance, a great-ness that cannot be utterly suppressed by our smallness, frailty, and mortality. Christianity keeps these hard facts ever before us and helps to make us compre-hensible to ourselves.

The second part of Pascal's strategy is to show that Christianity is attractive. This is closely related to the previous part of his argument, for it includes the idea that human beings are incomprehensible to themselves apart from God. It describes how we try to evade an awareness of our condition. We hide from ourselves the wretchedness of our plight. Pascal summarizes our condition when we live apart from God as one of "inconstancy, boredom, anxiety" (F 24). Only one fact is needed to make us aware of our inconstancy or lack of stability. "A trifle consoles us because a trifle upsets us" (F 43). If we were more stable and less shallow and so more in control of ourselves, a trifle could not console us. That it does shows how easily we are upset.

Boredom and anxiety are kept in check by constant activity:

> A given man lives a life free from boredom by gambling a small sum every day. Give him every morning the money he might win that day, but on the condition that he does not gamble, and you will make him unhappy. . . . Make him play for nothing; his interest will not be fired and he will become bored. . . . He must have excitement, he must delude himself into imaging that he would be happy to win what he would not want as a gift if it meant giving up gambling. He must create some target for his passions and then arouse his desire, anger, fear, for this object he has created. (F 136)

Even those who have the finest things in the world, if not distracted by activities, are likely not only to become bored but also to start thinking about all the ways they can lose their possessions, their position, or people they care about; about possible diseases that may strike them; and about death. Deprived of all activities that keep them from thinking about their condition, even well-placed people become anxious.

Pascal has no quarrel with our desire for excitement and possessions. What is erroneous is our assumption that in this way we shall be happy. Instead, it is all too obvious that once we have something, we tire of it or want something else; and if we reflect for a moment, we know only too well that there is no way to achieve complete security. "If our condition were truly happy, we should not need to divert ourselves from thinking about it" (F 70).

So Pascal tries to get people to look at their lives, to see that they know neither where they have come from nor where they are going. Yet this matters, for they are going to die, and their present activity does not give them complete and permanent satisfaction. Only a moment's pause and reflection is needed for them to realize that nothing they pursue can lead to fulfillment. At first glance it seems strange that what we know or can so easily realize about ourselves is kept from our awareness. But it is not really surprising that we keep it hidden from ourselves, since our condition is such a wretched one.

Christianity is attractive because it promises to release us from inconstancy, boredom, anxiety, and ignorance by showing us where to find happiness. Through its doctrine of original sin, it explains why we are miserable, and it points us to Christ, who can remedy our faults and release us from our miserable condition. It leads us toward fullness of life, toward a felicity in the truth and goodness of God.

The great barrier to happiness is our refusal to accept that we are at fault. The doctrine of original sin, the Christian explanation of our wretchedness, says that at the very center of our being we are in the wrong, yet we resist God in whatever way God seeks us.

Even though we do not understand how sin arose in us, the Christian doctrine of sin is illuminating. It tells us that we are unhappy because we do not obey or know God properly, but live without God. Without this reason, our wretchedness remains incomprehensible to us; *for we are unhappy in a peculiar way.* "It is the wretchedness of a great lord, the wretchedness of a deposed king" (F 116). It is not the unhappiness Freud once spoke of when he said that "the aim of psychoanalysis was to replace neurotic unhappiness with normal unhappiness."[2] The unhappiness Pascal speaks of is one that points beyond itself to a supernatural greatness. The unhappiness we suffer is similar to that suffered by those who once were great but now are fallen, of those who have lost what they once had and now are inconsolable. For ordinary people to feel this kind of wretchedness makes no sense from a natural perspective. But from a higher perspective it does: the perspective saying that our happiness is to be found in obedience to God. Through our failure to obey, we have lost our way to our supernatural destiny and are now wretched, subject to inconstancy, boredom, and anxiety, needful of diversions to keep us from thinking about and feeling our wretchedness.

Supernatural truth is revealed to us—the truth that we are created in God's image, fallen, and redeemable. These are revealed to us in the Scriptures by God's inspiration of chosen people. Although they are above reason, they are not contrary to reason and can be held to be reasonable because they illumine the mind. If we expect a response of faith to Christian truths before our reason is led to see the paradoxes about ourselves and to recognize the wretchedness of our condition, we would be subjecting reason to tyranny. The proper response to Christian truth is indeed one of faith, but only after we grasp with our reason the facts of our incomprehensibility and our wretchedness. Only then can we see by our reason the coherence that results from Christian truth, giving us as it does an understanding of the paradoxes that, without Christian truth, utterly baffle our reason and leave us in our wretchedness, without hope of remedy. Even though faith is not produced by reason, yet by God's grace as we become open to faith, our faith is reasonable because Christian truth illumines our intellect on matters that otherwise baffle it. The study of human nature by reason is essential, because without it our intellect would not receive illumination from the Christian truth we hold by faith. Without such study and illumination, submission to Christ (faith) is improper—based on false foundations, such as craven fear or the mistaken idea that Christianity promises earthly rewards.

> The way of God, who disposes all things with gentleness, is to instil religion into our minds with reasoned arguments, and into our hearts with grace, but attempting to instil it into hearts and minds with force and threats is to instil not religion but terror. (F 172)

Faith is thus not blind when it comes *after* reason has examined our nature and condition, and the intellect is illumined by Christian truth.

Pascal's apology was written at the beginning of the scientific revolution and the rise of the Enlightenment. In our day the eminent Polish philosopher Leszek

Kolakowski was expelled from the Communist Party in 1966 and then divided his time between Oxford and the University of Chicago. He gives his estimate of the Enlightenment, which has dominated the secular world and which is now drawing to its end. In a collection of essays, *Modernity on Endless Trial*,[3] Kolakowski writes on "The Revenge of the Sacred" and argues that when a culture loses all sense of limits, it is open to every form of intellectual and political totalitarianism. Having thrown off the limits imposed by Christianity in the name of autonomy and utopian hopes of perfectibility, modern society's repeated failures have led to disillusionment, as seen especially in deconstructionism and other postmodernist creeds. He argues that Christian faith is needed today to restore a tolerable balance between overestimation and underestimation—an echo of Pascal's twin themes of our greatness and our insignificance. Kolakowski points out that intellectuals can analyze the desperate condition of Western society, which is losing confidence in the value of its own heritage. They can even show the value and need of the Christian religion. But what is needed is faith, and moreover, he points out that "to spread faith, faith is needed, and not intellectual assertion of the social utility of faith."[4] In his essay "On the So-Called Crisis of Christianity," he argues that Christianity is intellectually viable, and he looks to those who have faith to reinspire Western culture. He hopes to help us recognize the dependence of the temporal on the eternal, the human on the holy. Pascal and Kolakowski are like two bookends on the rise and demise of the anti-Christian intellectual impulse of the Enlightenment, which was normative for nearly four centuries.

In his apology, Pascal stresses our human nature and condition as the places where Christian truths have illumined the mind. Both he and Kolakowski say little about the natural world and what effects the rise of science had on Christianity. But here too our understanding of the natural world has been greatly illumined by Christian truth. Earlier we talked about the book of nature and the limits of science. Here I want to point out the effects of the Christian understanding of the natural world on the origin of science itself. It will be another example of how Christian truths cast light that illumines our minds and so gives credibility to its claims, even though many of them are beyond the level of the intellect to comprehend.

For many atheists, science stands for rationality, evidence, knowledge, enlightenment. Religion, including Christianity, stands for backwardness, conservatism, superstition, authoritarianism, and it is regarded as the enemy and rival of science. They failed to take note of a series of three seminal articles by Michael B. Foster beginning in 1934,[5] and since then with increasing tempo the study of the history of science, which has radically changed the picture of the relation between Christianity and science. Thanks to this work, we have begun to realize that for its very birth science owes a great deal to Christianity. Rather than being a rival, Christianity is one of the major contributors to science's rise. Yet just the opposite picture has been dominant for more than two centuries. I will summarize some of the main ways in which Christianity has contributed to the rise of science and show the deep harmony between them.

The rise of science is one of the great puzzles of history. We take its existence for granted, yet it is a rather recent phenomenon. There have been several great civilizations, with highly organized cities, impressive achievements in poetry, drama, and politics, yet little that we would call science developed in them. There was technical skill, for example, in metal work, ceramics, and perfume making, but no detailed understanding of the behavior of matter expressed in mathematical terms. There was impressive observation and recording of the stars and planets, but no comprehensive understanding of their motions.

Classical science began to take a clear shape in Europe in the late sixteenth century. The result of the work of many individuals, it is a breathtaking achievement that makes Western civilization unique and has deeply affected every other extant civilization. The vision of the universe and the power it gives us is so startling that historians have been forced to ask, "Why did science not arise in ancient India, Egypt, China, or Greece, especially Greece?" After all, ancient Greece had many of the ideas we have used in our science, and the contribution of the Greeks was essential to the rise of science. Why did we succeed where they failed?

Investigation of this and other questions have changed our estimate of the relation of Christianity and science. The older picture of Christianity as the implacable enemy of science, mostly because of the Inquisition's trial and condemnation of Galileo (1633),[6] has begun to give way because it has been increasingly recognized that Christianity was a major factor and perhaps an essential ingredient in the rise of science. Many civilizations had some of the ingredients that seem to be necessary for the rise of science. For example, they had sufficient technology to make the apparatus needed for elementary experiments; they had sufficient mathematics for measurement and calculation. But what they did not have was a set of attitudes toward the material world, a set of attitudes that are vital for the development of science. Christianity had those attitudes. Some of those attitudes were native to Christianity itself; Christianity found some of the essential attitudes in the ancient Greeks. But Christianity preserved those insights. More and more it seems that it was these attitudes—part of the mental furniture of the people of Christian Europe, including a few geniuses—that enabled Western Europe to create what no other culture has ever created: science.

Christianity was the bearer of fundamental attitudes and convictions that helped people unlock the secrets of nature and develop hitherto unprecedented means to new knowledge. First, it is essential to be interested in the material world. Christians have a strong otherworldly sense: they believe that the entire universe depends for its existence on a perfect being, but they also believe that nature is good, or more specifically, that matter is good. This has not always been the case. There is an ambivalent attitude toward matter in much of ancient Greek thought, and the Gnosticism of the early Christian era considered matter to be evil. But Genesis 1 makes it abundantly clear that the creation is good. However much sin mars our world, the physical universe is innocent. It is the human will, not matter, that is at fault.

Second, Christians believe that nature is orderly; that it behaves in a consistent and rational way. If something measures a certain size one day, it will be the same size the next. If a liquid freezes at a particular temperature, liquid of the same kind will always freeze at that temperature. Nature is orderly because it is created by a good and rational God.

Ancient Greek thought, most of which also stressed that nature is orderly, was significantly modified by Christianity. For Christians, nature's order, though regular, does not have to be the way it is. God could have ordered it differently. Its actual order is just one possible order out of many. This led to the gradual realization that we could not just think up a rational blueprint and then say that because it is rational, nature has to be that way. Because there is more than one possible rational order, we have to examine nature closely to discover what order is actually in operation. Ancient Greek thought assumed that a single rational order could be discovered by sheer thought—or at least mostly by thought. Nature must be that way in spite of the fact that it might appear to be different. The Greeks failed to respect observed fact as having authority. Even Aristotle, who did respect observed fact, especially in biology, did not recognize the hallmark of modern science: quantitative fact. But Christianity has the notion of a personal God as creator, whose wisdom is reflected in the created order but not bounded by it; after much struggle in the Middle Ages to free itself from Greek rationalism, Christianity came to emphasize that the order we observe as rational depends on the choice of an intelligence. We have to experiment, measure, observe to determine as best we can what order our universe actually has and to revise our theories in light of observed facts.

With its conviction of a wise and personal God, Christianity encourages empirical science and is more harmonious with empirical science than is much of Greek rationalism. The operations of nature resemble the work of an artist more than that of an engineer or a craftsman. We cannot predict what a character in a novel will do because the actions of characters are not necessary: they are not deducible from previous actions. But a character's actions will not be arbitrary either. Unexpected actions will occur, but they will "make sense" in terms of the situations and the various other personalities involved in the story. Likewise, the Christian understanding of God as rational encourages a search for order in nature, yet an order that is not logically necessary. Rather, it is contingent, dependent on the action of a wise God who could have created a quite different, yet orderly, universe.

Third, science is only possible if we think that nature can be understood by the human mind. Christians believe that God's creation can be understood to a significant extent. A rational God does not create an irrational universe. So an order is there to be found. In addition, it is part of our God-given vocation to find as much of that order as we can and to praise God for the wonders of creation. Johann Kepler (1571–1630), one of the pioneering giants of classical science, and Francis Bacon (1561–1626) were the most influential proponents of the importance and value of science; both stressed this religious motive for doing science. It is our divinely given vocation to render praise to God by achieving a sounder understanding of God's handiwork. They passionately believed and advocated this view.

Finally, the results of our investigations are to be shared. Science is above all a communal affair. Christians in the seventeenth century were aflame with the idea that we can serve one another with a better knowledge of nature. The church was the bearer of the truth that led to heaven and proclaimed it to all (in contrast to the mystery religions of the ancient world and Gnosticism). A knowledge of nature would enable us to improve human life on earth. For example, Christian laypeople felt that it was their responsibility to study nature and thus improve medicine, thereby reducing pain and saving life. Probably without realizing it, Bacon repeated the motivation of medieval theologians that it was our task to restore creation to its prefallen state by the application of knowledge. The use of our talents in the study of nature and the application of our knowledge are, Bacon said, involved in the process of our redemption and sanctification.

The positive role played by Christianity in the origins of classical science has only quite recently been recognized in the academic community, but even there, eminent scientists can be found who still assert the earlier belief that the effect of Christianity on science was wholly negative.[7] It is still not generally known to most educated people nor to those responsible for educating people nor to many who disseminate ideas. But it is making headway and is increasingly recognized.

PART FIVE
RESPONDING TO GOD

Chapter 16

The Holy Spirit, the Church, and the Sacraments

After Jesus' resurrection from the dead, his exposition of the Old Testament passages indicating that the Messiah must suffer (Luke 24:26–27), and fuller explanations concerning the kingdom of God (Acts 1:3), Jesus ascends to the Father. Just before he ascends, he tells the apostles to wait to receive the power of the Holy Spirit before they begin their mission to be his witnesses to the ends of the earth (Acts 1:8). As we saw in John's Gospel, Jesus has already breathed the Spirit upon the apostles and given them their mission before his ascension. This gives them authority. But now after Jesus' ascension, the apostles receive the Spirit not only with the authority to carry out their mission, but also with the needed power to do so. In both accounts the stress is that it is not the disciples' idea to tell others about Jesus, but as apostles (which means "messengers") they are sent by Jesus. The result of their witness is the church.

The day of Pentecost is when the church begins. According to Jewish tradition, the day of Pentecost is when the law was given, seven weeks after Passover. To be under the law makes one a member of the Jewish community. Here the proclamation of Jesus as Savior and Lord with the power of the Spirit creates a new community, the church. In Acts 2, on the day of Pentecost, there is suddenly a sound like the rush of violent wind, and it fills the house in which the apostles are gathered. Then divided tongues that look like fire appear, and a tongue rests on each one of them. Being filled with the Spirit, they each begin to speak in other languages. (In Greek, as in English, "tongues" means both what we speak with and also languages.) They make such a noise that devout Jews from many different nations gather to find out what this bewildering noise means. To their surprise and bafflement, people of each nationality hear their own language being spoken.

Peter dismisses the cynical remarks that the apostles are drunk by pointing out that it is only nine o'clock in the morning. Then he proceeds to explain that the ancient prophecy of Joel, about God at the end of the present age blessing God's people by the presence of God's Spirit in all of them, is being fulfilled. The gift of the Spirit to all people, and not just to a chosen few, is a mark of the messianic age (Joel 2:28–32). Peter asserts that this gift is given because Jesus is the Messiah. In spite of Jesus' rejection and death, God has raised him from the dead, and he is now at the right hand of the Father. "Being therefore exalted at the right hand of God, and having received from the Father the promise of the Holy Spirit, he has poured out this that you both see and hear. . . . Therefore let the entire house of Israel know with certainty that God has made him both Lord and Messiah, this Jesus whom you crucified" (Acts 2:33, 36).

Peter's witness cuts them to the heart, and they ask him what they should do. Peter replies, "Repent, and be baptized every one of you in the name of Jesus Christ so that your sins may be forgiven; and you will receive the gift of the Holy Spirit. For the promise is for you, for your children, and for all who are far away, everyone whom the Lord our God calls to him" (2:38–39).

The response to Peter's words is enormous and profound. Some three thousand people are baptized, and they devote themselves "to the apostles' teaching and fellowship, to the breaking of bread and the prayers" (2:42). "Day by day the Lord added to their number" (2:47b). The divisions among people into different language groups, as the result of human presumption behind their constructing the Tower of Babel (Gen. 11:1–9), is overcome by the Spirit, who gives the apostles the power to be understood by all their hearers. This breaking down of linguistic barriers is carried over into the life of the newly founded church in another respect. All possessions are held in common and are distributed to all as they have need. In part, this practice is possible because of the expectation that Jesus will soon return and fully establish the kingdom. This does not happen, and even though such a community of common property does not continue, genuine community remains an ideal and it is approximated by the church's care for the needy of the world.

I used to think that the failure of Jesus to return quickly, as the early church expected, would have led to a severe crisis. From a passage on the resurrection of the dead in Paul's First Letter to the Corinthians (15:12–56), apparently the death of some believers before Jesus' return has troubled some of the Christians in Corinth. But in general the delay of Jesus' return did not cause a crisis of faith. This is because the early Christians believed that the kingdom of God had already come with the ministry, death, resurrection, and ascension of Jesus, and the gift of the Holy Spirit. What had already come was in continuity with what was yet to come with Jesus' return: the full establishment of the kingdom of God. The future kingdom of God that was to come was already exercising its reality on them in the present. As Paul put it in his Letter to the Philippians, the local church of which they were a part was a colony of heaven (3:20). This image is quite apt since the city of Philippi was literally a colony of Rome: it was founded as a Roman settlement in Greece for retired legionnaires. Its inhabitants lived as much like Romans as possible, even though they were far from Rome. So too the Christians in Philippi were to live as much as possible in the reality of the kingdom of God. There was not a discontinuity between the life of the church as it awaited the coming of Jesus and the life that would come fully in the kingdom. So Christians could patiently wait for Jesus to return as they lived with the life that Jesus gave them through the Spirit. As Paul put it, "God's love has been poured into our hearts through the Holy Spirit that has been given to us" (Rom. 5:5). Christians believed they were already living "in the last days" (Acts 2:17), or last eon, characterized by the presence of final reality. "If anyone is in Christ, there is a new creation; everything old has passed away; see, everything has become new!" (2 Cor. 5:17). By being united to Christ, one is now part of the body of Christ, and so in a new relationship to God, made a child of God. In theology, what I have been describing falls under the rubric of eschatology, and my interpretation would be classed as an "inaugurated eschatology." Jesus brought the dawning of the kingdom of God, and Jesus' followers live between the inauguration of the kingdom of God and its consummation.[1]

The church as an eschatological community—a community that lives in the light and from the power of the kingdom of God—gives its members a new identity. As part of the church, the body of Christ, a person has now entered into a new pattern of relationship with others in the church. All are to live according to the teachings of Jesus and to be drawn into communion with each other by the power of the Holy Spirit. By following Jesus' teachings and in the life of the Spirit, members of the church become a new people of God, in contrast to the people of the old covenant. Paul expresses this new identity we have as part of the church: "It is no longer I who live, but it is Christ who lives in me." (Gal. 2:20a).

The radical nature of the church, the new people of God, is evident in the breaking down of barriers between peoples. The admission of Gentiles (non-Jews) into the church on equal footing with Jewish Christians was a sociological miracle, as Colin Story, the New Testament scholar, put it. The radical breakdown of the barrier between Jew and Gentile owes more to Paul than to any of the early leaders of the church, but it has their approval (Acts 10; 11:1–18; 15:1–29). In his Letter to the Romans, which is largely devoted to the issue of the relations of Jews and Gentiles, Paul writes, "For there is no distinction between Jew and Greek; the same Lord is Lord of all and is generous to all who call upon him. For, 'Everyone who calls on the name of the Lord shall be saved'"

(10:12–13). Perhaps Paul's most famous declaration of the breaking down of barriers is his statement in the Letter to the Galatians:

> Now before faith came, we were imprisoned and guarded under the law until faith would be revealed. Therefore the law was our disciplinarian until Christ came, so that we might be justified by faith. But now that faith has come, we are no longer subject to a disciplinarian, for in Christ Jesus you are all children of God through faith. As many of you as were baptized into Christ have clothed yourselves with Christ. There is no longer Jew or Greek, there is no longer slave or free, there is no longer male and female; for all of you are one in Christ Jesus. And if you belong to Christ, then you are Abraham's offspring, heirs according to the promise. (3:23–29)

In this passage we see the reason or basis for the removal of barriers between peoples. It is because of our relation to Christ. This is now our primary identity. By our baptism we are united to Christ. This constitutes the death of the old self (our former identity) and the birth of a new self (a new identity). Baptism is the way we become part of the church, the new people of God. This is in sharp contrast to the former people of God, with its largely ethnic basis of being a descendent of Abraham, and an identity that was marked by circumcision. With baptism, which unites us to Christ's death and resurrection, we are free from the vain attempt to establish our own righteousness by obedience to the law. We are now justified or righteous before God, not *according* to the law, but *apart* from the law. We are justified by our faith in Jesus. Being united with Christ, who bears the Spirit and confers the Spirit, we now are increasingly able to live a new life. A major description of the new life is given by Paul (or a disciple of Paul's) in the Letter to the Colossians.

> So if you have been raised with Christ, seek the things that are above, where Christ is, seated at the right hand of God. Set your minds on things that are above, not on things that are on earth, for you have died, and your life is hidden with Christ in God [your new life is secure in God, hidden with Christ and from the world]. When Christ who is your life is revealed, then you also will be revealed with him in glory. (3:1–4)

Through baptism into Christ, we are now related to Jesus' Father as our Father and are privileged to address God as Jesus taught us pray: "Our Father in heaven" (Matt. 6:9). Our relations to each other are as children of the same Father, who takes precedence over our earthly parents and establishes us as brothers and sisters. The passage from Colossians describes our new relations to one another as members of the body of Christ, the church, as follows:

> Put to death, therefore, whatever in you is earthly: fornication, impurity, passion, evil desire, and greed (which is idolatry). (3:5)
> But now you must get rid of all such things—anger, wrath, malice, slander, and abusive language from your mouth. Do not lie to one another, seeing that you have stripped off the old self with its practices and have clothed yourselves with the new self, which is being renewed in knowledge

according to the image of its creator. In that renewal there is no longer Greek and Jew, circumcised and uncircumcised, barbarian, Scythian, slave and free; but Christ is all and in all!

As God's chosen ones, holy and beloved, clothe yourselves with compassion, kindness, humility, meekness, and patience. Bear with one another and, if anyone has a complaint against another, forgive each other; just as the Lord has forgiven you, so you also must forgive. Above all, clothe yourselves with love, which binds everything together in perfect harmony. And let the peace of Christ rule in your hearts, to which indeed you were called in the one body. And be thankful. Let the word of Christ dwell in you richly; teach and admonish one another in all wisdom; and with gratitude in your hearts sing psalms, hymns, and spiritual songs to God. And whatever you do, in word or deed, do everything in the name of the Lord Jesus, giving thanks to God the Father through him. (3:8–17)

Our union with Christ is strengthened and renewed with every celebration of Jesus' death, resurrection, and ascension in the Eucharist ("thanksgiving"), or Holy Communion. Both baptism in the name of the Father, Son, and Holy Spirit and the celebration of Holy Communion were instituted by Jesus. Hence, they constitute the sacraments for the churches of the Reformation. The rites of confirmation, ordination, holy matrimony, confession of sins, and unction (anointing with oil) for the sick and dying are practiced by many churches of the Reformation as means of grace, but in contrast to the Roman Catholic Church, they are not regarded as sacraments.

There is far less controversy over baptism than over Holy Communion. For example, the Roman Catholic Church accepts the validity of baptism received in other churches. This contrasts sharply with the conviction that even though we are all members of the body of Christ, as a member of a particular denomination, we may not be eligible to participate in the celebration of Holy Communion in another denomination. The ecumenical movement of the nineteenth and twentieth centuries regarded this as a scandal, and it has led to a considerable amount of intercommunion among the churches. Several churches of the Reformation welcome all baptized persons, including children, to receive the bread and wine of Holy Communion.

One of the most contentious issues over Holy Communion is the nature of the bread and wine in Communion. In what sense are they the body and blood of Christ? J. N. D. Kelly in his *Early Christian Doctrines* says that in the early church all theologians were "realist": all believed that the consecrated elements of bread and wine were the body and blood of Jesus. But there were two ways that this was understood. The first makes a distinction between the visible elements and what they signify and mediate by God's power. The visible elements are not mere pointers to an absent reality; instead, the bread and wine are signs of a reality that is somehow actually present, though the reality is apprehended only by faith. So although there is a distinction between the consecrated, visible elements and the reality they signify, Christ is present. This was the view of such great theologians of the early church as Athanasius, Tertullian, and Augustine.

The second was a later tendency to explain the identity as being the result of an actual conversion of the bread and wine, so that they become the actual body and blood of Christ. This Kelly calls the materialist view.[2]

Now when the visible signs were interpreted in a materialist way in the high Middle Ages in the Western church, it provoked an opposite reaction in some Reformers such as Ulrich Zwingli (1484–1531). The bread and wine were interpreted in an antimaterialist way, rejecting an actual conversion of the bread and wine into the body and blood of Christ, as well as the earlier view in which the bread and wine are signs that signify the presence of Christ. So these Reformers rejected both realist views identifying the bread and wine with the body and blood of Christ. Holy Communion for such Reformers became only a memorial of Christ's death.

Here I will limit myself to stating the characteristic view of the Anglican Communion, to which I adhere, and which I believe is in harmony with the view of the Presbyterian Church—at least in John Calvin—to which I also adhere.[3] Indeed, it is also in line with some major Roman Catholic theologians.[4] It is the first view of real presence, as held by the early and undivided church, in which there is a distinction between the visible and the invisible. The consecrated bread and wine are the visible signs that enable us to partake in the body and blood of Christ. In Holy Communion, there is a "real partaking of the body and blood of Christ by means of the sacramental signs of bread and wine."[5] As an important part of its nature, Holy Communion includes a remembrance of Christ's death and resurrection—an *anamnēsis*—recalling a past event in such a way as to bring it before us, so that the past becomes a reality in the present. The people of God commune with God through Christ's sacrifice, of which we as his body are a part. This communion is by means of the consecration of the bread and wine into sacramental signs. William R. Crockett explains the relation of the bread and wine to the reality they signify as follows:

> In true Augustinian fashion seventeenth-century Anglican writers distinguish between the *res* of the sacrament, that is, the reality or inward and spiritual grace conveyed by it, and the *sacramentum* or outward and visible sign, by means of which the grace is communicated to the faithful recipient. At the same time, they maintain a "sacramental union" between the elements and the reality signified by them. The union, however, does not abolish the distinction between the *sacramentum* and the *res*; otherwise the sacrament would cease to be a sacrament, since the sacrament always consists of two parts, a visible and invisible, an earthly and a heavenly. . . . Only the faithful recipient receives the *res* of the sacrament along with the outward sign. The outward signs are received by the mouth and enter into the stomach. The inward grace of the sacrament is only eaten by faith.[6]

In spite of some differences on this historically contentious matter, I think that the majority of Christian churches worldwide would agree that by taking part in Holy Communion, we participate in the death and resurrection of Christ, receive the forgiveness of our sins, are renewed and strengthened in our commitment to and union with Christ, receive spiritual nourishment, and have a foretaste of the heavenly banquet in the kingdom of God, which is yet fully to come.

Perhaps it will help us to recall that in baptism God the Holy Spirit is actually present so that remission of sin takes place and union with Christ is enacted. But the water, which is a sacramental sign when consecrated, is not converted into anything else but a sacramental sign. Visibly it is water. But when consecrated, it is a visible sign of divine grace. So why, in order to have a real presence in Holy Communion, must we have a materialist interpretation of the bread and wine whereby they are converted into the physical body and blood of Christ, rather than converted into *consecrated* bread and wine that enable us to receive divine grace by participation in Christ's body and blood?

In the latter half of the twentieth century, there has been less focus on the contentious matter of the relation of the bread and wine to Christ's body and blood. Attention has been increasingly turned to a recognition that the celebration of Holy Communion is a celebration of the community, the body of Christ, the people of God, in contrast to a mere collection of individuals in acts of personal or even isolated communion. This is a restoration of the early and traditional view of Holy Communion that had been eroded by a strong stress in modern times on individualism in Western culture. In Holy Communion we *together* are in communion with Christ and, because of this communion, we are in communion with each other. Thus the kind of life described in Colossians and elsewhere in the New Testament is the kind of life we are being helped to grow into more fully by the grace of God in Holy Communion.

Because of the recovery of this understanding of Holy Communion, our relation to the world is understood eschatologically. As we realize the communal life of the kingdom that is yet fully to come among ourselves in the church, we are to carry that life into the world. The hallmark of Christ's ministry is loving service. The kingdom that Christ brought and is bringing is one of just relations and peace between all peoples. The kingdom that is to come fully with Jesus' return is to guide and inspire us as a people in the world.

> A meal celebrated in prospect of the reign of God gives rise to a new social vision, grounded in the promise of the kingdom. Such a vision challenges the *status quo* in society and the prevailing set of economic and social relationships. Sharing in a community meal anticipates a just sharing of all the gifts of creation in justice and love.[7]

This is why the worship service ends with a challenge, such as "Go in peace to love and serve the Lord." That is the thrust and outcome of our worship of God, of our attending to the story of God's actions in our creation and redemption, our communion with God as a people.

The passage we quoted from Colossians 3 describes our new relations with each other in the church and is quite overwhelming. It and the rest of the New Testament hold before us what we are to become in the fullness of the kingdom. Our destination gives us our new identity. But we are like a people on a journey who have not yet reached our destination. What we are to become is not fully realized now. For example, we more often think of ourselves in terms of our social position as seen by our culture than as Paul described us, with our self-identity in Christ's body, with all barriers between us removed. Among genuine Christians, self-understanding and relations toward others are indeed significantly affected by the goal of life in the kingdom of God. But there are few of us who live in a community such as is described in the passage I quoted from Colossians, or who can honestly claim to fit the description of those whom Jesus called blessed or happy.

> Blessed are the poor in spirit, for theirs is the kingdom of heaven.
>   Blessed are those who mourn, for they will be comforted.
>   Blessed are the meek, for they will inherit the earth.
>   Blessed are those who hunger and thirst for righteousness [justice], for they will be filled.
>   Blessed are the merciful, for they will receive mercy.
>   Blessed are the pure in heart, for they will see God.
>   Blessed are the peacemakers, for they will be called children of God.
>   Blessed are those who are persecuted for righteousness' sake, for theirs is the kingdom of heaven.
>   Blessed are you when people revile you and persecute you and utter all kinds of evil against you falsely on my account. Rejoice and be glad, for your reward is great in heaven, for in the same way they persecuted the prophets who were before you. (Matt. 5:3–12)

These words are supposed to be encouraging. But they are so different from the values of the social world in which we live. Just consider the third beatitude. To be meek or humble is to be gentle and unaggressive. Robert N. Bellah, the noted sociologist, writes:

> The unaggressive are not only happy but they are going to inherit the earth? Whoever heard of such a thing? Everyone knows that it is only the go-getters, the really aggressive, who ever get anything on this earth, certainly if we want global power it is only armed might that will get it.[8]

Bellah makes a similar point with each of the beatitudes. They clash brutally with the attitudes and actions of our society. He writes:

> What Jesus is teaching is an affront to more or less all the cultures of human history, but to none more so than our own. We have, probably more than any culture in history, emphasized competition, survival, and success. Perhaps, only in America could someone say and be respected for saying, "Winning isn't everything, winning is the only thing." But Jesus is saying it does not have to be that way. Life does not have to be lived as a harrowing struggle for survival with the honors going to the foremost. Those who haven't "made it" don't deserve to be despised and neglected and those who have "made it" don't need to be so desperately anxious about constantly achieving more. Instead Jesus holds up to us the poor, the outcast, the rejected, the persecuted as the place where the kingdom of God is, where *he* is (the Last Judgment passage in Matthew 25).[9]

Even though Christian values have strongly affected at least some parts of our society, if we enter at all into the reality of Christ's ways, we are daily and even moment by moment exposed to the clash of ways of life. Our formation by our culture's values and their daily reinforcement constantly overwhelm the identity that Christ confers on us. We can be successful by the conventional measures of wealth, position, power, and achievements, and yet be on the wrong path to a full life.

This is well portrayed in a novel by John P. Marquand, *Women and Thomas Harrow.* In spite of its racy title, it is about the typical rags-to-riches theme of American society. Thomas Harrow is a coming man when he becomes engaged to a daughter of a Harvard professor of geology. One weekend he is invited to visit the family's summer cottage in New Hampshire. Thomas is completely out of his element. He arrives dressed in a suit, with thin leather shoes that do not protect his feet against the sharp stones on the path leading to the cottage. Once there, neither he nor anyone in the family can think of anything to talk about together, even though the family is usually quite lively, with lots of conversation and activity. It proves to be a long weekend. In desperation, at one point the professor asks his prospective son-in-law, "Is it true that you make $100,000 a year?" (The setting is the 1930s, so that is an enormous amount of money.) The young man happily replies, "Yes, I do." The professor shakes his head from side to side and says, "That's a lot of zeros." The implication is the young man will continue to add zeros, and that his life will amount to zero.[10]

How different is this scene from a much more famous novel, *Emma,* by Jane Austen:

> Mrs. Bates, the widow of a former vicar of Highbury, was a very old lady.
> . . . Her daughter enjoyed a most uncommon degree of popularity for a woman neither young, handsome, rich, nor married. Miss Bates stood in the very worst predicament in the world for having much of the public favour; and she had no intellectual superiority to make atonement to herself, or frighten those who might hate her into outward respect. She had never boasted either beauty or cleverness. Her youth had passed without distinction, and her middle of life was devoted to the care of a failing mother, and the endeavour to make a small income go as far as possible. And yet she was a happy woman, and a woman whom no one named without good-will. It was her own universal good-will and contented temper which worked such wonders. She loved everybody, was interested in everybody's happiness, quick-sighted to everybody's merits, thought herself a most fortunate creature, and surrounded with blessings in such an excellent mother, and so many good neighbors and friends, and a home that wanted for nothing. The simplicity and cheerfulness of her nature, her contented and grateful spirit, were a recommendation to everybody, and a mine of felicity to herself.[11]

Miss Bates lacks everything we think necessary to happiness, and yet she is happy. The creator of the character, Jane Austen, knows and can show what the gospel means in everyday life far better than most, if not all, theologians.

Jesus interpreted many passages of the Old Testament, such as the figure of the Suffering Servant in Isaiah, as foreshadowing the Christ. After his ascension, his followers read or interpreted the entire Old Testament in light of Christ and in terms of the activities of the Holy Spirit, whom they had experienced in the founding of the church at Pentecost and in its continuing life. For example, in Genesis 1:2, where it is said that "a wind from God swept over the face of the waters," this was understood as a reference to the Holy Spirit, since the Hebrew word that means "wind" or "breath" also means "spirit." The word of God that gives structure or order to the creation ("And God said . . . ") is understood as the Word of God that became incarnate (John 1:1–18); both the structure that God's word gives and the energy given by God's breath are necessary for the creation and continuation of the universe.

To better understand the Spirit's relation to Christ and to us, let us review the work of the Spirit in the Old Testament. Exceptional strength, as in the case of Samson (Judg. 13–16), or exceptional power of leadership, as in the case of Saul (1 Sam. 10–11; 19) and David (1 Sam. 16:13; Ps. 51:10–12), were attributed to the Spirit of God, as was the ecstatic speech and behavior of the seventy elders (Num. 11:25). These are all *temporary* visitations of the Spirit. Only in Isaiah, in the prophecy of a messianic king, do we have a figure who will be the *permanent* bearer of the Spirit (11:2; 61:1). In the New Testament, in contrast to the temporary presence of the Holy Spirit, Mark (1:8, 10) stresses that Jesus is the permanent bearer of the Spirit, as well as the one who gives the Spirit to others. We saw this gift to the apostles in one of the resurrection appearances of Jesus in John (20:22–23) and at the beginning of Acts (1:8; cf. 2:4), just before Jesus' ascension. This gift is not temporary. The prophet Ezekiel saw his famous vision of the valley of the dry bones, over which he was told to invoke the life-giving breath of God, as a sign that God would renew his people (37:1–14). Closely connected to Ezekiel is the important prophecy of Joel (2:28), in which the distinctive mark of the messianic age is the gift of the Holy Spirit to *all* the people of God. This, as we saw earlier, took place at Pentecost with the founding of the church (Acts 2:16–21).

The gift of the Spirit then is associated with the time of fulfillment. The Messiah will bear the Spirit permanently, and the Spirit will be given to all the people of God. At Jesus' baptism the Spirit descended in the form of a dove; this does not mean that this is when Jesus first received the Spirit, but that at his baptism it first became manifest. His baptism is thus the *start* of the fulfillment of the prophetic hope. Because of the presence and activity of the Holy Spirit, people are moved to respond to Jesus' proclamation of the beginning of the kingdom. The Gospel of John particularly stresses that Jesus' entire ministry is directed by the Spirit, and throughout the book of Acts the entire missionary task is the work of the Spirit, who operates in the missionaries and who opens people to receive Jesus as the Christ and Son of God.

John has the most extensive teachings about the Holy Spirit in the New Testament. He uses the word "Paraclete," which is a term from the lawcourts. A paraclete is a defending attorney rather than the prosecutor. So the Spirit will be like Jesus: as Paraclete the Spirit will be our intercessor before the Father. The Spirit will also be present with the disciples and the church after Jesus ascends to the Father, and so be a presence that comforts, strengthens, and encourages the church and each believer (John 14:18, 26; 15:26; 16:14). As Basil the Great points out, God the Holy Spirit is the way God is present to us individually and personally.

> After the likeness of the sunbeam, whose kindly light falls on him who enjoys it as though it shone for him alone, yet illumines land and sea and mingles with the air. So too, is the Spirit to everyone who receives It, as though given to him alone, and yet It sends forth grace sufficient and full for all [hu]mankind, and is enjoyed by all who share It.[12]

John stresses that the Spirit's activity will also enable Jesus' followers to understand more fully Jesus' teachings, as well as inspire obedience to them. This connects directly to the point I emphasized in the preface. In theology, intellectual inquiry cannot properly be detached. As Simone Weil put it,

> There is a great difference between a truth which is recognized as such and introduced and reviewed in the mind as such, and a truth which is active in the soul [the whole person] and endowed with the power to destroy within the soul those errors that are clearly incompatible with it.
>   The active power of the truth is the *pneuma hagion* [Holy Spirit], the divine energy.[13]

Ultimately, Christian truth is about God. To know God is to know the living God, who is at work in us by his Word, on which we reflect, and by means of the activity of the Spirit in us becomes the life of God at work in us, transforming our hearts, minds, and actions. To be engaged with God is to have our person continually affected and renewed by God's Spirit. In her *Revelations* [*Showing*] *of Divine Love,* Julian of Norwich, the fourteenth-century English mystic, compares knowledge of God to wounds. To be engaged with God through God's Son and Spirit so affects us that it is as though, in our growth in knowledge of God, we suffer wounds. God's Word and Spirit batter our ego because of our self-centeredness, our evil inclinations, our indifference, and our conformity to the ways of the world, and so we are wounded by God. Julian specifies three wounds in particular: the wound of contrition (repentance and continuing repentance for our disobedience); the wound of compassion (love for neighbor, which wrings our heart because love involves our sorrow for human distress); the wound of longing (as love for God increases, we suffer a longing for the fullness of God's presence in the kingdom, as does a lover for the beloved). People can be taught theology and, given intelligence and diligence, even perform well as academic theologians. But this may be no more than a knowledge *about* God, not a knowledge *of* God.

In the spread and growth of the church, Paul expresses the close relation between Christ and the Holy Spirit as two aspects of the same action: Christ is the exterior aspect, and the Spirit is the interior aspect (1 Cor. 2; Gal. 4:4–6). Augustine similarly expresses the relation of Christ and the Spirit in the church as that between the body and the animating spirit or soul. This close relation between the church as Christ's body and the work of the Holy Spirit in animating and building up the body of Christ appears in Paul's description of the variety of the Spirit's gifts bestowed upon the church. In the young and immature church in Corinth, controversies arose between the members over the Spirit. In chapter 12 of 1 Corinthians, Paul describes the variety of gifts, services, and activities distributed to various members of the community, but they have a unity because they are from one and the same Spirit, and they are given for the purpose of building up the community, for the common good, not for private exploitation. The Spirit makes the living Christ, through his words and teaching, effective in our lives. As we saw in the quotation from Simone Weil, by means of the Spirit, Christ and his truth are *active* in the whole person that is open to Christ, lead us into truth by destroying errors, purify, and inspire various activities for the building up of the church and spreading its life. In making Jesus and his words active in our lives, the Holy Spirit brings us closer to the fullness of Christ in our lives. In 1 Corinthians 13, Paul points out that the highest spiritual gift is not highly emotional behavior or ecstatic experiences, as in the pagan cults around the early church, but love. Without love, all other actions and gifts become perverted and lose their value. The love that is given by the Spirit is not love in an ordinary sense, but a divine love for each other. Thus Paul writes:

> Love is patient; love is kind; love is not envious or boastful or arrogant or rude. It does not insist on its own way; it is not irritable or resentful; it does not rejoice in wrongdoing, but rejoices in the truth. It bears all things, believes all things; hopes all things, endures all things.
>
> Love never ends. But as for prophecies, they will come to an end; as for tongues, they will cease; as for knowledge, it will come to an end. For we know only in part, and we prophesy only in part; but when the complete comes, the partial will come to an end. . . . And now faith, hope, and love abide, these three; and the greatest of these is love. (13:4–10, 13)

Chapter 17

Sin, Evil, and Hope
for the Future

The inability of followers of Christ to live up to the ideal described in Colossians is the result of the power of sin and evil still at work in us in spite of our being part of the body of Christ and having the Holy Spirit's presence in our lives. Few have ever been more convinced of the reality of the risen Lord and striven harder to obey him than Paul. Yet in Romans, Paul himself describes an inner conflict that is like a war in which he is taken captive:

> I can will what is right, but I cannot do it. For I do not do the good I want, but the evil I do not want is what I do. Now if I do what I do not want, it is no longer I that do it, but sin that dwells within me. (7:18–20)
>
> For I delight in the law of God in my inmost self, but I see in my members another law at war with the law of my mind, making me captive to the law of sin that dwells within my members. Wretched man that I am! Who will rescue me from this body of death? Thanks be to God through Jesus Christ our Lord! (7:22–25)

Here Paul denies the possibility of freeing oneself from the power of sin, but he makes it clear that because of Christ, we are forgiven and delivered from the threat of death. In the following chapters in Romans, he makes it clear that because of Christ, we can greatly improve in our obedience to God. Nonetheless, Christians know from experience that to become wholly conformed to Christ is a long and difficult process, one that is not fully accomplished in this life. The more we strive to be like Christ, the more we become aware of how far we have to go, how mixed our motives are, how full of self-deception we are, and even how hard it is to repent of some sins.

Consider the experience of Rose Macaulay, once a well-known English novelist. She had a long, happy affair with a married man. After he died, she slowly recovered her lost faith. In one of her many letters to an Anglican priest, she describes her repentance and reorientation:

> I told you once that I couldn't really *regret* the past [her affair]. But now I do regret it, very much. It's as if absolution and communion and prayer let us through into a place where we get a horribly clear view—a new view—so that we see all the waste, and the cost of it, and how its roots struck deep down into the earth, poisoning the springs of our own lives and other people's. Such waste, such cost in human and spiritual values. . . . Not all the long years of happiness together, of love and friendship and almost perfect companionship (in spite of its background) was worth while, it cost too much, to us and to other people. I didn't know that before, but I do now. . . . If only I had refused, and gone on refusing. . . . I see now why belief in God fades away and has to go, while one is leading a life one knows to be wrong. The two can't live together. It does not give even intellectual acceptance a chance. Now it *has* its chance. . . . After what has occurred to me lately, I *know* there is [a personal relationship with God].[1]

But with the rise of the modern mentality, the Christian account of the human journey as one of sin, repentance, and restoration has been increasingly set aside. The rejection of the reality of sin was a major part of the Enlightenment program of many eighteenth-century intellectuals and social reformers. They projected an optimistic picture of human beings and human progress: Human beings were not born with inherited sin and an orientation toward evil. At birth we are neither good nor evil, and some social reformers went so far as to claim that we are born good. But all claimed that we become corrupted by inadequate social institutions and misguided upbringing. Reform of social institutions, introducing better education and enlightened upbringing, and the spread of a more enlightened society—these would lead to a progressive improvement of human beings and the reduction of evil, possibly even its elimination. Many came to believe not only in progress but also in *inevitable* progress. Education, coupled with the progress of science, would free us from destructive social bondage and vulnerability to nature—according to the Enlightenment. Yet this impetus for social reform has deep Christian roots.

Today the optimism of the modern world has been seriously eroded. We are now faced with the failure to eradicate such serious social and economic problems as crime, pollution, global warming, poverty, racism, and the danger of cataclysmic war. We have become uneasy and are beginning to feel that we may not be able to surmount all our difficulties. There is an increasing recognition that evil cannot be fully removed merely by educational and social reform. Our difficulties do not mean that we are not to strive for improvements. Indeed, it is central to the good news of the beginning of God's kingdom in Christ's coming that we are so to strive. But these difficulties do mean that we shall have to strive without the assurance from our social philosophies that we are bound to succeed. Optimism is not the same thing as Christian hope. Throughout history, Christians have continued to work to improve our life on earth in even the most pessimistic times, such as during the destruction and disintegration of the Roman Empire. Christian hope is probably the major source and impetus of reform and progress in Western civilization.[2]

After several centuries of "Enlightenment," a long article in the business section of the *New York Times* titled "The Strange Agony of Success"[3] indicates something of the depths of human need that was ignored by the optimistic Enlightenment. It reports on several recent books on the pursuit of success. It estimates that 40–60 percent of people in Manhattan—those successful in the conventional ways of wealth, position, prestige, and power—are in therapy. Most of them are not neurotic. Rather, they have achieved everything our society teaches us about how to become fulfilled and happy, but they are unhappy, unfulfilled, and often feel like failures and frauds. In a series of more recent studies, the *New York Times* reports on what is sometimes called "the quarter-life crisis."[4] It points out that all the stages of life are being telescoped, so that what used to occur in the 40–50-year-old range, now is occurring in the 20–30-year-old range. This is not an encouraging situation. It testifies to the superficiality of the modern world's understanding of human beings.

For all of the good the Enlightenment project of reform accomplished (and it was considerable), the stubbornness of our problems indicates that rejecting the existence of sin in our understanding of human beings has been too hasty. The erosion of the eighteenth-century optimism that has inspired Western societies for several centuries now strongly indicates that a reexamination of our spiritual condition as found in the Christian understanding of sin and evil is very relevant. Modern people, including many church people, need to learn how to use the categories of sin and evil in order to understand their lives, society, and history.

It has often been said that sin is the only Christian doctrine that is empirical. I think what is meant is that all of us are aware that everyone does evil in various degrees. This much is evident to most people. Although evil is obvious, what it signifies and what sin actually is can be understood only in relation to God as understood in the light of Jesus, the true human being that we fail to be. Sin and evil are to be understood in relation to the kingdom of God, the future that God has in store for us in Christ.[5] People often use sin and evil interchangeably; for example, they may count waste or cruelty as sins. But these are sins because they are understood to be opposed to the will of God. To call them sins, rather than just evils, presumes a belief in God, and presumes that God rejects such actions. In other words, sin is a theological term.

Christians today and for many centuries have assumed that the story of Adam and Eve in Genesis 2–3 is the source of the belief in original sin. Adam and Eve were created good and placed in a garden or paradise, with the responsibility of maintaining the garden. They had only one prohibition: not to eat fruit of the tree of the knowledge of good and evil. They disobeyed and thereby caused the fall of humankind. From their disobedience, we inherit a corrupt will (cf. Gen. 6:5).

According to Norman Powell Williams, a great authority on the history of the fall and original sin, the paradise story *originally contained no idea of original sin, nor of a fall from original righteousness.* The idea of a fall arises only *after* the return of the Jews to Palestine from their exile in Babylon in the sixth century. The Jews' line of reasoning was that since God creates only good, the inherent tendency to sin does not belong to human nature as it was created. So some time after the creation, there must have been a fall. Confirmation for this view was sought in the Scriptures, and some found it in the story of the lustful angels that sexually assaulted mortal women in Genesis 6:1–4. But this interpretation of the origin of sin was largely replaced by finding the fall in the story of Adam and Eve.

According to Williams, the fact that there were two different explanations of the fall in ancient Israel is a confirmation that *neither story is the real source or basis of the doctrine of a fall.* Moreover, the interpretation of the two accounts as stories of a fall belongs to *popular* Jewish religious thought, rather than to the official teachers. According to Williams, the stories are the clothing for the *previous* conviction in the goodness of God and human responsibility for evil. The rabbis did teach that in human beings was a *yetzer hara,* or evil impulse, but this is not a doctrine of a fall or inherited original sin.[6]

Therefore, I believe we are justified, at least *for the moment,* to set aside the biblical story of a paradise in our discussion of original sin and evil. All theologians up to perhaps Friedrich Schleiermacher (d. 1834), the father of modern theology, assumed that the story of Adam and Eve was historical. But at the same time many early theologians, especially in the Eastern part of the church, believed that the reality of original sin could be seen to be operative in all people. This means that even though they believed in a historical Adam and Eve, they did not need the story to be able to argue for the reality of original sin. I argue that the story of Adam and Eve does not need to be historical for us to believe in the reality of original sin, and yet the story can be read with great profit for its understanding of our relation to God.[7]

First let us look at the Eastern church's teaching about original sin. By the fourth century, in all the East (and widely in the West) there was a strong ontological approach to questions of sin and evil. It was based on the contrast between the being of God and creatures. God's being has no contrary as ours does. Thus God's being has no tendency whatsoever to turn toward nonbeing. Another way to say this (as we saw earlier with Anselm) is that God is a necessary being. Everything else that exists is a contingent being. Although a contingent being exists, it might not have existed, and it can cease to exist. Neither is true of God's being. Human beings, like all finite creatures, were created from nothing by God's word. We lack the ability to sustain ourselves. So we are liable to change and revert to nothing. Decay is a perpetual reality, and death is a perpetual threat. Only by communion with God through the good news in Christ is it possible for us to live with these liabilities fruitfully and faithfully, and finally through Christ's resurrection to overcome these natural tendencies.

Finitude itself is not equivalent to evil. It is simply an account of what it is to be in the condition of not being God, and to be always dependent on God for existence. Sin and evil arise because we fail to have proper communion with God and so fail to achieve God's purposes.

Because of our needs as contingent beings, we are easily distracted by the material world, which is closer to us and attractive, and many of its goods meet many of our needs. So we turn our attention and efforts in that direction and so lose an orientation on God and God's purposes for us. As we saw earlier, this is *typified or modeled* in Christ's first temptation in the wilderness; in contrast to us, he overcomes this temptation. Also, as finite and therefore changeable beings (always under the threats of decay and death), we are anxious to establish ourselves, as we saw *typified* in Christ's victory over the second and third temptations in the wilderness. The attempt to establish ourselves in one way or another is pride, the attempt to live without a fundamental and primary relation to God. Our disorientation leads to disorder among our appetites and desires, and this affects our sense of judgment as to what is good, right, true, and honorable. As I observed in presenting Jesus' temptations in the wilderness, we are tempted not by evil as such, but by what is good (material goods) or needful (security and the need to think well of ourselves). Jesus overcomes these temptations and thus lives a life as a human being should: he is properly related to his Father. We fail to withstand these temptations and so are not properly related to our Father, nor open to hear and pursue God's purposes for us, as Jesus was.

This understanding of our human situation and sin, although independent of the story of Adam and Eve, fits comfortably with that story. Our primal sin—to provide for ourselves apart from God—was understood by the Eastern church to have been Adam and Eve's primal sin too. They are our *type*. With knowledge of good and evil, meaning the consequences of their actions, they thought they would be able to control the future and so not need to rely on the care and providence of God to achieve God's purposes. Adam and Eve's disobedience wounded the nature of their progeny so that they are in a weaker condition to deal with their unruly appetites.

The story of Adam and Eve, as used by the Eastern church to account for our inherited weakness to withstand temptation as an effect of Adam and Eve's sin, can fruitfully be understood today without a historical Adam and Eve but instead with an evolutionary and social understanding of human beings. In the course of biological and social evolution, any group of creatures capable of any degree of relationship to God that fails to be properly related to God commensurate with their stage of development—any such group will have some network or other of social relations that are not as God intends. People born into a particular social group inherit that social network and act more or less in accord with it, and so inherit the effects of its sin. By being formed and shaped by the inherited social network, each individual is "weakened" in its ability to wrestle with the temptations to which its ontological nature as finite creature is subject. When a fall occurred, when a prepeople or people did not live up to the intentions of God in their common life commensurate to their stage of development, it was probably not at any one specific time; it may have occurred at different times for different groups until failure to be properly related to God was universal in all societies. But by historic times, human development is at a stage that the story of Adam and Eve is a fitting *type* or model of our situation in relation to God: human beings seeking to provide for themselves apart from God and God's purposes.

This ancient understanding of original sin and evil seems to me both illuminating and, with the evolutionary understanding that I have added to it, thoroughly defensible. I can easily apply it to myself and also use it to understand other people, as I have done in presenting Pascal's analysis of our condition.

Some theologians are willing to grant that the story of an *actual* Adam and Eve is not necessary for Christian theology, but they still hold that there had to have been a historical situation of original righteousness or innocence and an actual fall from this state. Otherwise, God, not human beings, would be responsible for our condition, and the goodness of creation would be fatally compromised.[8] My account does have a temporal dimension.

All of us are born without an awareness of God in our lives. God is near us as our creator, generating us each moment of time; but it is as if God is, so to speak, behind us, and we, by looking only in front of us, do not perceive God in our world at all. So we do not take God into account in our lives. This is when distortion in our hearts, minds, and desires begins to occur. Our de facto personality, with our self at the center of all reality, is innocent when we are an infant but ceases to be innocent as it is reinforced by society's way of life, encouraging us to walk away from God and so into evil. We walk away from God by pursuing earthly goods and in seeking to meet our needs for security and significance.

But God calls us back in many ways. We can become aware of the inability of finding any lasting satisfaction in the things of this world (the first temptation Jesus faced in the wilderness), and of the need and failure to make ourselves secure, and of our futile effort to establish our significance (the second and third temptations Jesus faced in the wilderness). The order of the world moves some of us to think about its source; and other things we have mentioned much earlier in the preface can move us to think of God, so that we are open to the proclamation of the gospel of Christ. If we repent—turn around (the Greek word for "repentance" is *metanoia*, which means turning around in life and reorienting one's entire outlook to God)—we can start to become aware of God. No longer is God behind us, so to speak, but now we face toward God. But even when repentant, we still are not fully oriented on God, since we are distant from God through having walked away from God by our evil thoughts and actions. Our understanding is still clouded, and our motives are not fully ordered on God. Some of us have walked further into evil than others. So although all of us are equally sinners, initially facing away from God, we are clearly not equally evil and equally corrupted. So we have different distances to walk to return to God. Since we are now facing in the direction of God, we are justified, regarded as righteous by God, but we are still not fully conformed to God's will. Some people who have repented and begun their walk toward God are still more evil than some people who have not repented, but who have not walked as far away from God as some repentants had done. So it is not surprising that there are some non-Christians who, for a time at least, lead better lives than some Christians.

According to this account, then, we begin life innocently, without any awareness of God; we become guilty through our own thoughts and actions; we need to turn toward God (whether rapidly with a "born-again" experience or gradually without such a dramatic experience); and finally we need to walk toward God by seeking to conform our life to God's will. There are many accounts of conversion and of the long walk or journey toward God, from Paul's account of his conversion to that of the third- and fourth-century desert fathers and mothers (monastics), to Bonaventure's *The Soul's Journey into God*, to John Bunyan's *Pilgrim's Progress*. These and other accounts make up the large body of writings and practices on Christian spirituality.[9]

A deep difference between the Eastern church (the Greek-speaking part) and the Western (Latin-speaking part) arose because of Augustine's introduction in the late fourth century of a novel interpretation concerning original sin. Augustine claimed that every person is personally guilty of original sin from their very conception and birth. After the fall of the Western Roman Empire (476), the Latin church was largely cut off from the Greek-speaking church, so its influence on the Western church was greatly diminished. During the long Dark Ages that followed the barbarian invasion of Western Europe, Augustine was by far the greatest theologian in the Latin West. So Augustine's view that we are personally guilty of original sin was followed in the West and eventually adopted by Luther, Zwingli, and Calvin; it still predominates in the West to this day. Largely because of Augustine's view that we are from conception personally guilty of original sin, the Eastern church has often been viewed by Western theologians as "soft" on sin and as holding a more "optimistic" view of human nature.[10]

I myself do not agree with Augustine's view of inherited guilt. I do not think that it should be held up as a standard. It reminds me of the theory of Greek tragedy in which the progeny, such as Oedipus, inherit the guilt of an ancestor who committed a grave offense and then are made to suffer for it. It is only by taking Augustine's extreme view as the standard of what original sin is that the Eastern church can be said to be "soft" on sin.

To say the Greek-speaking church does not take sin with sufficient seriousness is specious. Consider the way Athanasius struggled to maintain the full divinity and full humanity of Christ against the Arians, who deposed him five times from his office as bishop of Alexandria. Athanasius insisted, against the Arians, that God and only God could possibly save us from sin and death. No one else could do it. Perhaps more telling at the level of practice are the widespread ascetic practices of clerical and laypeople alike. Such people as the desert fathers and mothers lived in the wilderness, struggling to overcome the power of sin in their lives. According to Evagrius of Pontus, who left his exalted post as archdeacon of Constantinople to become a desert monk, the desert ascetics counted three levels of spirituality. The first level is the active life, in which one struggles against the Eight Deadly Thoughts (the source of the Seven Deadly Sins in the Western church). Next is the passive, or contemplative, life; it divides into indirect contemplation of God through Scripture and nature, the second level of the spiritual life; and the direct contemplation of God, the rarely attained, third spiritual level. Almost all monks spent their entire lives at the active level, the *first* level of the spiritual journey to God, because of the immense power of sin. They knew only too well what Paul had experienced: "I do not understand my own actions. For I do not do what I want, but I do the very thing I hate" (Rom. 7:15). They knew as well as Augustine how the human will (or heart, in the Bible) is divided against itself, and how alienated one is from oneself, so that it is as if at times one feels possessed and driven. Even with the redemptive work of Christ and the gift of the Holy Spirit at work within us, the monks knew all too well how slow the work of mending the heart was. All this hardly suggests that failure to think that we have inherited the guilt of Adam and Eve (or the guilt of anyone else) was to go light on sin.

When discussing original sin, we need to distinguish three questions. What is the definition of sin? How is it personally experienced? How does it affect relations with others? We have defined original sin as the direction in which we are pointed, or our orientation. All of us begin without an explicit awareness of God. We do not have any guilt for being this way. Yet in time we become guilty by our own consent to this orientation. This is approaching original sin in negative terms: *not* being oriented toward God. Put dynamically, the mark of original sin is our resistance to whatever draws us toward God's kingdom, or rule/reign. We seek to remain self-directed and so become guilty or responsible for our condition. Sin is not itself a *motive,* but the *condition* of not being oriented toward God and, because of that orientation, resisting all that would draw us toward God's kingdom, or rule.

One of the most powerful motives, as we have seen, is to retain our de facto person: to perceive and evaluate everything with ourselves at the center, so distorting everything, since we are not truly at the center of reality. We have also seen that Jesus' three temptations in the wilderness each indicate a different motive (the desire for material goods, security, and social standing) that would keep him from full obedience or orientation toward his Father. The very things that tempt Jesus, the true human being, are temptations to which we succumb. We are focused on material goods, seeking security, seeing to establish our worth.

How we personally *experience* sin has been described in many ways. Here is a selection: disorder or lack of self-control; alienation; estrangement; isolation;

fear; suspicion; rivalry; pride (overestimating ourselves), and its counterpart, self-pity and a feeling of unworthiness (thinking too lowly of ourselves); guilt; anxiety (this was a favorite in Augustine and in his revival by neo-orthodox theologians of the twentieth century, such as Paul Tillich and Reinhold Niebuhr); despair, or to be without hope; and remorse. Although they may be operative, many of these are actually only experienced by many people *after* they begin to become drawn toward God or after they begin to have an awareness of God's grace and mercy. In a specific case, it is not always easy to tell whether a person is suffering from a neurotic condition, a healthy experience of separation from God, or even perhaps a mixture of the two.

Finally, and closely connected to how a person individually experiences the effects of sin, are the effects of sin on our relations to one another, in society at large, and in the direction of history. Our sin is not just an isolated, individual matter, as Macaulay made clear by her reference to its high cost "to other people," and not just to herself and her lover.[11]

When we confess our sins together in worship—our corporate confession of sin—it is not only what we have done or failed to do as individuals that is at issue, but also the network of relations that constitutes our life together in the church as a colony of heaven. What we are as a community is flawed, even deeply flawed, and inadequate compared to what we are called to be as a community, and what we are is not fundamentally easily or quickly remedied. Hence, we make our corporate confession of sin at every service in almost every Christian church. How we act in making our decisions, how we treat each other in our procedures, the nature and extent of our service to each other and others—all these are measured against life in the kingdom of God, the kingdom for which Jesus taught us to pray: "Thy kingdom come. Thy will be done in earth, as it is in heaven" (Matt. 6:10 KJV). We use the nature of the kingdom as revealed above all by Jesus as the standard for the way we ought to be related to each other; that kingdom reveals to us the nature and social effects of sin. And our corporate or common life in the social and political order constitutes the inherited history of preceding generations. Our flawed legacy, and our contribution to its continuation, is part of our corporate confession of sin.

Even though the story of Adam and Eve is not the source or basis of the conviction that evil has its source in the primal sin of not being oriented to God, it is written with the conviction that this is the nature of sin. In addition, the story is extremely valuable for its insights into our relation to God. Rather than history, the story is like an extended parable, or even legendary in character, as are the stories of the patriarchs, such as Abraham and Isaac. The name "Adam" means "man" or "human being," so that Adam in the story is our representative or "type," as it is technically put. The story describes human beings as having such an intimacy with God that we became living beings, in contrast to a pile of dust, by having received God's breath. "Eve" or "woman," who is created by God from Adam's rib, indicates that "to be fully human one needs to be in relation to others who correspond to oneself."[12] Human beings occupy a privileged position by being charged with ruling over the animals and caring for God's garden or paradise in a way analogous to God's rule over all creation.

As I have mentioned earlier, although Adam and Eve have responsibilities, they are limited in their knowledge of the effects of their actions for good or evil. Without a knowledge of the effects of their actions, they cannot be sure what they should do. But they are clearly told to leave the fruit of the tree of the knowledge of good and evil alone even though it would give them knowledge that they need. They must therefore act on the garden and the animals without full knowledge of the consequences of their deeds. This implies that they must trust in God's providential care that things will turn out well and, if things do not seem to be working out as they think they should, to continue to have faith in God's providence. This does not mean they may act thoughtlessly and foolishly, relying on God to bail them out. That would be what the Scripture calls "putting God to the test," or tempting God. (We saw that Jesus rejected putting God to the test when he rejected the temptation to jump from the top of the temple.)

Just as Adam and Eve are to be partners, so too they and we are to seek to meet our responsibilities as a partner with God. We must make every effort to act responsibly, which means in our case to seek to learn from experience as much as possible and to make every effort to succeed. But it is a quite delicate matter to balance responsible action with dependence on God's providence. We can go wrong either by an overdependence, so that we neglect our responsibility for the future, or by losing faith in God's providence, and so in effect reject God from our lives, as individuals, as a colony of heaven, and as a society. Our situation is a daunting one.

Because of the need to act, the lack of knowledge and thus a lack of control of the future, Adam and Eve are vulnerable to the temptation from the serpent. The serpent, in effect, suggests that given their responsibility, they must surely have misunderstood God as prohibiting their use of the fruit of the tree of the knowledge of good and evil. He makes it appear that they would not really disobey God by eating its fruit. Surely God would not have given them an important task and at the same time prohibit them from using an important means that is needed to achieve the task. This is such an attractive idea, that there would be no harm whatsoever from eating the fruit of the tree, that it is reinforced by the appearance of the fruit as good for food and a delight to the eye. They eat fruit from the tree in the interest of caring for the garden and thus for the purpose of serving God's will; hence, they can deceive themselves easily about the interpretation of God's prohibition. They can believe that they are not rejecting their partnership and their dependence on God.

The undetermined and uncontrolled future is a source of anxiety for us too. We too have responsibilities; to overcome our anxieties and fulfill our responsibilities, we are tempted to forget that we are in a partnership with God. We often seek either to go it alone, or to become wholly passive and let God sort everything out without us. Partnership is the way God has specified for us, a much more demanding path to follow. We are tempted to reject the situation in which God has put human beings of every generation: learning how to be active partners of God, as individuals and as a society. There is a strong tendency in us as individuals and societies to seek to control the future on our terms, and to rely solely on our own views of what is best for us, regardless of God's commandment, of what we have learned from Jesus about the kingdom of God, and of what we can learn from human action in the past. For ancient Israel, this often meant a failure to be faithful to the covenant. For us, it is a failure to trust in God's providential care as we seek to live in the light of the kingdom of God as revealed by Jesus and to realize it as fully as possible.

Our need to be concerned about the effects of our choices for the future is absolutely proper for responsible action. But as Jesus pointed out, excessive anxiety is not appropriate, since it can be crippling and destructive, and it means a lack of confidence in God's care:

> Therefore I tell you, do not worry about your life, what you will eat or what you will drink, or about your body, what you will wear. Is life not more than food, and the body more than clothing? Look at the birds of the air; they neither sow nor reap nor gather into barns, and yet your heavenly Father feeds them. Are you not of more value than they? And can any of you by worrying add a single hour to your span of life? And why do you worry about clothing? Consider the lilies of the field, how they grow; they neither toil nor spin, yet I tell you, even Solomon in all his glory was not clothed like one of these. But if God so clothes the grass of the field, which is alive today and tomorrow is thrown into the oven, will he not much more clothe you—you of little faith? Therefore do not worry, saying, "What will we eat?" or "What will we drink?" or "What will we wear?" For it is the Gentiles who strive for all these things; and indeed your heavenly Father knows that you need all these things. But strive first for the kingdom of God and his righteousness, and all these things will be given to you as well.
>
> So do not worry about tomorrow, for tomorrow will bring worries of its own. Today's trouble is enough for today. (Matt. 6:25–34).

Yet this teaching is not intended for dire situations of mass starvation. Jesus was addressing the widespread anxiety he witnessed among those in relative affluence. Spiritual discernment is needed for us to have a proper concern for our well-being. But clearly continuous increase of national and international wealth (especially with insufficient care for its distribution) has gotten out of hand. It is not only successful people who suffer from the consequences of an uncontrolled passion for material success. As individuals, as a society, and indeed increasingly worldwide we resemble the early-twentieth-century philosopher George Santayana's definition of a fanatic: "Fanaticism consists in redoubling your efforts when you have forgotten your aim."[13]

The need to make our future secure and the temptation to seek to make ourselves secure apart from God—these also disrupt our relation to others. This is true not only of individual relations, and of individuals related to various groups or organizations, but it is especially true in the relations between nations. All too often the need for security leads a nation to seek mastery of others, not the development of mutual trust. But as we know, such security gained at the expense of others leads to instability and is itself a source of destructive conflicts. Rather than seeking mutual trust, we all too often end up in mutual conflict. Something that is good and needed—security—becomes a source of anxiety and fear and thus leads to more insecurity. Throughout history we find groups and nations calling upon God as an ally against others, as if the welfare of others is not also God's concern. This is a common theme in the Old Testament (though mitigated, for example, in the book of Jonah), and it is repudiated by Jesus, who firmly and repeatedly refused, in the face of great expectations, to be a military Messiah. For example, at Jesus' trial before Pilate, Jesus said, "My kingdom is not from this world. If my kingdom were from this world, my followers would be fighting to keep me from being handed over to the Jews" (John 18:36a).

Our failure to work properly with God and to trust God by seeking to follow God's ways is the primal sin because it is the source of other sins. Without an orientation on God, our desires and appetites lack a source of restraint and order, our minds are directed toward our purposes and ends, and our hearts become centered on false hopes. We fail to heed a most obvious truth: Only in God can we find our bearings and cleanse our minds and hearts sufficiently to seek God's kingdom. Simone Weil put this truth in a form that we can recognize for ourselves:

> We all know that there is no true good here below, that everything which appears to be good in this world is finite, limited, wears out. . . . Every human being has probably had some lucid moments in his life when he has definitely acknowledged to himself that there is no final good here below. But as soon as we have seen this truth we cover it up with lies.[14]

It is the neglect of this simple, accessible, and foundational truth that leads us to look for our true good in a myriad of ways that fail to give fullness of life, and to neglect looking in the one direction in which it is to be found. We are turned the wrong way; we are not properly oriented. To know that our final good is to be found in God leads to a reevaluation of what *this* life is, what it is to make progress in life, how to view success, how to be related to people. Everything can slowly, often painfully, but finally move toward its proper place. We saw this earlier in the case of Rose Macaulay.

The story of Adam and Eve and their mishandling of human responsibility is a theme that is continued in the rest of the Bible's story. The Bible presents, reiterates, extends, and deepens the theme of our limited knowledge and God's guidance; it stresses the need for faith and trust in God, rather than reliance solely on human knowledge, experience, wisdom, and power. Whether it be the rivalry between the first two brothers, Cain and Abel; the indifference of people toward God in the time of Noah; the pride of those building the Tower of Babel; the failure to be faithful to the covenant in the ups and downs of the patriarchs, in the exodus and the wilderness wanderings, in the promised land, in the warnings of the prophets—in all these we find the theme of mishandled human responsibility and the repeated call to attend to God. In different ways we are taught—through covenant, law, prophecy, wisdom, judgment, and restoration—that we are to seek to live according to God's way because God's way leads to our true good.

So even though the story of Adam and Eve is not the source of the idea of original sin, nor the source of the idea that human beings, not God, are the source of evil, its placement at the beginning of the Bible in its finally editing is appropriate. It so graphically states the theme that we may live properly only with faith in God, the theme that runs throughout the entire Bible. We are neither to think and act as if we can fully control our fate and make ourselves secure, nor to despair of trying to improve our situation. We are to have hope for the future, a future lived according to God's way.

Epilogue

As I was writing this book, I discussed it chapter by chapter at weekly meetings with a small group of people who were mostly but not exclusively Christians. Many of their comments led me to make changes and additions. Near the end of our sessions, one person said, "I am having trouble grasping the book as a whole. Could you review the main points?" Perhaps at this point you feel that way too. So here is a summary of its leading ideas.

God is different from the idea of God in philosophical theism, in which God is described only as omnipotent, omniscient, and all good without any consideration of how God is described in the Bible, including how God's power, wisdom, and goodness are to be understood. There is no mention of God's holiness. Yet the Bible reveals that God and only God is holy. That is to say, God is transcendent; in a different dimension; a necessary being; "wholly other," and so beyond our limited powers to know God's essence. Although transcendent in holiness, God is also immanent, and so can be present to humans. God's presence or manifestations are called God's "glory."

God's holiness and glory are exhibited in the call of Moses to lead the Hebrew people out of slavery in Egypt, making them into a nation with a covenant as part of God's purposes for all humanity. In the call to Isaiah God shows his concern for justice, which, unlike justice as understood in ancient Greece, has as its core care of widows, orphans, and the needy.

God's ultimate purpose is to share God's life with us forever, revealed in his incarnate son, Jesus. In such parables as the Lost Sheep, the Lost Coin, the Lost Son (Prodigal Son), Jesus reveals that God's love renders every human being to be of irreplaceable value. The effect on Western civilization of the dignity and value of every human being is evident in every phase of life, from law to morals to care of the needy, and is increasingly affecting all societies.

Following Pascal, human nature is understood as paradoxical: human beings experience themselves as both significant and insignificant; our condition (result of original sin) is one of boredom, instability, and anxiety. This analysis of human beings is combined with an interpretation of Jesus' temptations in the wilderness (Matt. 4:1–11) in which Jesus shows us that

— we do not live by bread alone (by material goods),
— we cannot make ourselves completely secure (anxiety),
— our need to think well of ourselves cannot be secured by our standing relative to others.

Christianity enables us to understand our nature: as creatures, however great our accomplishment, we are limited and will perish; as creatures with a divine destiny, we are irreplaceably significant. God promises us a remedy for our condition: yielding our lives to God's son.

God is one God in three persons: Father, Son, and Holy Spirit. As good, God expresses God's being by begetting a son. As a perfect self-expression of God, the Son is also God. Likewise, the Spirit is God as the perfect expression of the Father's and Son's love. Since the Son is the perfect expression of God's goodness, there is only one Son. Since the Spirit is the perfect expression of the Father and the Son, there is only one Holy Spirit.

The creation is an expression of God's self-limitation. God withholds God's self in order to allow other things to be and express their natures, which in our case includes our will. The act of love in creation is also expressed in the salvation of the world. The Father sends the Son into the world: that is, the Son becomes incarnate. As incarnate, the Son is subject to the laws of nature, and so must eat and sleep as we do. This is a profound act of self-limitation, indeed, degradation. The Son does not impose himself on us, or promise us material goods, earthly security, or social prestige (the three temptations), but exhibits the Father's love for all humans and calls us into his Father's kingdom.

In the crucifixion, Jesus took the sins of the world onto himself. Sin and holiness are separated by an infinite distance. So on the cross Jesus is separated from the Father, but at the same time Jesus and the Father are united in love. Love spans the infinite distance between sin and holiness. In the suffering of the Son, God takes into God's self our disobedience and overcomes the power of sin by his love.

God vindicates Jesus' teachings, life, and death by raising Jesus from the dead. In one of his resurrection appearances Jesus gives the apostles a mission to spread the good news, and by the gift of the Holy Spirit gives them authority and power.

The apostles' proclamation of Jesus establishes the church. It is to be a colony of heaven—of the kingdom of God—until Jesus returns to fully establish the kingdom. We enter the church through the sacrament of baptism in the name of the Father, Son, and Holy Spirit, by which we participate in the benefits of Jesus' death and resurrection. By the sacrament of Holy Communion we participate in the final banquet in God's kingdom that is to come and are strengthened and encouraged in our journey.

A theme throughout this book is suffering. In the Bible the philosophical problem of evil does not arise: How is an omnipotent, omniscient, and all-good God compatible with suffering, both human and animal? In the Old Testament the question is, Why do the righteous or just (both as individuals and as a nation) suffer, while the unrighteous prosper? The issue is one of justice: the distribution of suffering. The book of Job rejects the idea that we obey God in order to receive rewards; Job suffers innocently and yet, in spite his terrible suffering and loss, he continues to affirm that God will vindicate him against the charge that his suffering is the result of his sin. Job confesses that the reason for his and others' suffering is far beyond his comprehension, but he affirms that his relationship with God is so rich as to transcend all other goods and losses. In the New Testament, Jesus explicitly disassociates a direct match between obedience and reward, disobedience and punishment that marks much of the Old Testament when he says, "[Your Father] makes his sun rise on the evil and on the good, and sends rain on the righteous and on the unrighteous" (Matt. 5:45b). Jesus also strongly affirms God's love for the poor and for those who suffer, refusing to identify prosperity as a mark of God's approval.

The promise of life with God forever is at the center of the gospel. So although we do not understand the reasons for the distribution of suffering, we are promised that nothing can separate us from the love of God. This is based above all on Jesus' unjust death and his resurrection from the dead into God's glory.

Suffering is part of our nature and condition as physical beings. To accept this hard fact is at the same time to recognize that we are spiritual beings, more than just part of the natural world, because a piece of matter cannot accept its status, as we can. There are ample examples of this in the Bible, and also in the reflections of the Stoics. The acceptance of our vulnerability enables us not only to praise and thank God for God's glorious creation, but also to receive strength, courage, comfort, and hope in the midst of our suffering and distress as we call upon God. To love righteousness or justice is a mark of a genuine faith; to endure suffering and loss with faith and hope is the mark of a mature faith.

Endnotes

Preface: A Different Approach to Introducing Theology

1. Francis S. Collins, *The Language of God* (New York: Free Press, 2006).
2. See Michael Paffard, *Inglorious Wordsworths: A Study of Some Transcendental Experiences in Childhood and Adolescence* (London: Hodder & Stoughton, 1973).
3. Austin Farrer, *A Celebration of Faith* (London: Hodder & Stoughton, 1970), 59, 60.

Introduction: What Is Theology?

1. Athanasius, *The Incarnation of the Word of God* (New York: Macmillan, 1946), 31–34.
2. Ibid., 56.
3. See Basil Mitchell, *Morality: Religious and Secular* (Oxford: Oxford University Press, 1981). This is also argued by Michael J. Perry in several books, including *The Idea of Human Rights* (Oxford: Oxford University Press, 1998). An important discussion of the sacredness of human beings is presented by Max L. Stackhouse, "Reflections on 'Universal Absolutes,'" *Journal of Law and Religion* 14, no. 1 (1999–2000): 97–112.
4. Blaise Pascal, *Pensées,* trans. A. J. Krailsheimer (New York: Penguin Books, 1966), fragment 978.

Chapter 1: The Holy One of Israel

1. The term "Jew/Jewish," though rarely used before the fall of the northern kingdom, is here used as equivalent to the term "Israel/Israelite."
2. According to Ray E. Brown, "In the tradition, however, the most noticeable covenant was that which God made with Moses and Israel (Exodus 19:5; 34:10, 27), whereby Israel became God's special people." *An Introduction to the New Testament* (New York: Doubleday, 1997), 3.
3. Rudolf Otto, *The Idea of the Holy* (Oxford: Oxford University Press, 1923).
4. Norman H. Snaith, *Distinctive Ideas of the Old Testament* (London: Epworth Press, 1944), 31–32.
5. Geoffrey Wainwright, in *Oxford Companion to the Bible*, ed. Bruce M. Metzger and Michael D. Coogan (New York: Oxford University Press, 1993), 285.
6. Antony Flew, *There Is a God: How the World's Most Notorious Atheist Changed His Mind* (New York: Harper One, 2008), 213.
7. Wainwright, in Metzger and Coogan, *Oxford Companion to the Bible*, 285.

8. See Yehezkel Kaufmann, *The Religion of Israel, from Its Beginnings to the Babylonian Exile*, trans. and abridged by Moshe Greenberg (Chicago: University of Chicago Press, 1960); Michael Fishbane, *Judaism: Revelation and Traditions* (San Francisco: Harper & Row, 1987).

9. Theodore J. Lewis, "Religion of Israel," in Metzger and Coogan, *Oxford Companion to the Bible*, 333.

10. Blaise Pascal, *Pensées*, trans. A. J. Krailsheimer (New York: Penguin Books, 1966), fragment 242.

11. Michael Foster, *Mystery and Philosophy* (London: SCM Press, 1957).

12. Anselm, in *Prayer and Meditations of St. Anselm*, trans. Benedicta Ward (Harmondsworth, UK: Penguin, 1973). Anselm cites Isaiah 7:9, page 87.

13. Augustine, *Sermon 43* 7 and 9: *Crede, ut intelligas*; "Believe in order that you may understand."

14. Bruce M. Metzger and Roland E. Murphy, eds., *The New Oxford Annotated Bible, with the Apocryphal/Deuteronomical Books* (New York: Oxford University Press, 1991), OT-95n, on Exod. 20:4–6.

15. John of Damascus, in *The Oxford Companion to Christian Thought*, ed. Adrian Hastings et al. (New York: Oxford University Press, 2000), 318.

Chapter 2: Holiness for Today

1. R. B. Y. Scott, "The Book of Isaiah, Chapters 1–39," in *The Interpreter's Bible*, ed. George A. Buttrick, vol. 5 (Nashville: Abington Press, 1956), 207.

2. Ibid., 209.

3. Ibid., 207.

4. Ibid.

5. Ibid., 210.

6. Geoffrey Wainwright, in *Oxford Companion to the Bible*, ed. Bruce M. Metzger and Michael D. Coogan (New York: Oxford University Press, 1993), 286.

7. This is carefully argued by Lawrence A. Blum and Victor J. Seidler in *A Truer Liberty: Simone Weil and Marxism* (New York: Routledge, 1989).

8. Austen Ivereigh, "The Tablet Interview," *The Tablet*, March 20, 2004, 8.

9. Arthur Miller, *Death of a Salesman: Certain Private Conversations in Two Acts and a Requiem*, 50th anniversary ed. (New York: Penguin Books, 1999).

Chapter 3: The Maker of Heaven and Earth

1. Gerhard von Rad, *Old Testament Theology*, trans. D. M. G. Stalker, vol. 1 (New York: Harper & Row, 1962).

2. Ibid., 136, with emphasis added.

3. Ibid.

4. Ibid., 137.

5. Ibid., 138–39, with emphasis added.

6. Ibid., 137.

Chapter 4: The Limits of Science

1. C. S. Lewis, *Reflections on the Psalms* (New York: Harcourt, Brace, 1958), 79).

Chapter 5: What Is Meant by "God"

1. John A. T. Robinson, *Honest to God* (Philadelphia: Westminster Press, 1963).

2. Flew later modified his position and has conceded that God might reveal himself and indeed be active, as the Bible claims. See Antony Flew, *There Is a God* (New York: Harper Collins, 2007).

3. The metaphor "book of nature" originated in early Christian theologizing and was famously reused by Galileo in 1623 to defend his astronomy. See http://physicsworld.com/cws/article/print/26529.

4. David Hume, *Dialogues concerning Natural Religion* (1781; Mineola, NY: Dover Publications, 2006); Immanuel Kant, *Critique of Pure Reason* (1781; Mineola, NY: Barnes & Noble, 2004).

5. Besides the atheism I have mentioned, there is the so-called new atheism. It includes Richard Dawkins, *The God Delusion* (New York: Houghton Mifflin, 2006); Sam Harris, *The End of Faith: Religion, Terror, and the Future of Reason* (New York: W. W. Norton, 2004); Christopher Hitchens, *God Is Not Great: How Religion Poisons Everything* (New York: Hachette Book Group, USA, 2007). These works are inferior examples of atheistic criticism of religion. John F. Haught writes that he, and other academics who study the question of God, want their students "to be exposed to the most erudite of the unbelievers. Our rationale was that any mature commitment that intelligent young people might make to a religious faith, if they so chose, should be critically tested by the very best opponents. . . . In my own classes the new books by Dawkins, Harris, and Hitchens would never have made the list of required reading. These tirades would simply reinforce students' ignorance not only of religion, but ironically also of atheism. At best the new atheistic expositions would be useful material for outside reading. . . . It would [show] how well the relatively light fare the new atheists serve up compares with the gravity of an older and much more thoughtful generation of religious critics." See John F. Haught, *God and the New Atheism* (Louisville, KY: Westminster John Knox Press, 2008).

Chapter 6: Nature as a Witness and Innocent Suffering

1. See H. Strathman, "*Martys* . . . ," in *Theological Dictionary of the New Testament*, ed. Gerhard Kitttel, trans. Geoffrey W. Bromiley, vol. 4 (Grand Rapids: Eerdmans, 1967), 474–508, esp. 496–502.

2. William Temple (1881–1944), cited by S. L. Terrien, "The Book of Job: Introduction and Exegesis," in *The Interpreter's Bible*, ed. George A. Buttrick, vol. 3 (Nashville: Abingdon Press, 1954), 902).

3. See http://justus.anglican.org/resources/bcp/1789Selections/Communion.htm.

Chapter 7: Innocent Suffering and Life beyond Death

1. In chapter 3 we argued that on the basis of Jesus' teaching in the parable of the Good Samaritan, it is unjust to allow *anyone* in great distress to suffer. Here Plato's and Kant's moral outrage is focused specifically on the wretchedness of the righteous or just.

2. Peter Geach, *Providence and Evil* (Cambridge: Cambridge University Press, 1977), 9.

Chapter 8: Suffering from Nature and Extreme Human Cruelty

1. David Hume, *Dialogues concerning Natural Religion* (Indianapolis: Bobbs-Merrill, 1947), 211.

2. Epictetus, *The Discourses as Reported by Arrian*, trans. W. A. Oldfather, 2 vols. (New York: G. P. Putnam's Sons, 1926–28), 1:41.

3. Ibid.
4. Ibid., 45; and esp. 113 along with the rest of chap. 16.
5. Ibid., 45–59.
6. Ibid., 49.
7. Ibid.
8. Ibid., 211.
9. Ibid., 43.
10. Ibid.
11. Ibid., 145.
12. Ibid., 133.
13. Ibid., 113.
14. Ray Lindquist, *Common Life* (Austin, TX: Cold Mountain Press, 1973).
15. Soon after World War II, Sister Basilea Schlink founded a Protestant order of nuns, the *Marienschwestern*, with its home base near Darmstadt, Germany. She has a series of such aphorisms printed on individual cards, as well as several books on the spiritual life, including accounts of the benefits of illness.
16. See Simone Weil, *The Need for Roots* (New York: Harper & Row, 1971), 283–302. Also see Edith Barfoot, "The Joyful Vocation to Suffering," reprinted in *The Witness of Edith Barfoot* (Oxford: Basil Blackwell, 1977). Edith Barfoot spent 70 of her 87 years in suffering: rheumatoid arthritis successively deprived her of movement, of eyesight, and ultimately of hearing. To prevent a possible serious misunderstanding, let me explain that those I am citing were not quietists. Schlink and Weil were extremely active in seeking to alleviate and prevent suffering and to improve human life and social institutions.
17. Simone Weil, *Waiting for God* (Glasgow: Collins, 1959), 35–36.
18. I have shown the *philosophical* grounds on which to hold to the validity of the reported experiences in "Manifestations of the Supernatural according to Simone Weil," *Cahiers Simone Weil* 17 (September 1994): 290–307. To repeat it here would take us too far afield into philosophical matters.
19. See E. H. Madden and P. H. Hare, *Evil and the Concept of God* (Springfield, IL: Charles C. Thomas, 1968). My article "Motives, Rationales, and Religious Beliefs," *American Philosophical Quarterly* 3 (April 1966): 111–27, anticipates this argument and answers it.
20. Iulia de Beausobre, *Creative Suffering* (Westminster, London: Dacre Press, 1940).
21. There is an extensive literature of Christian responses to the Holocaust. They are surveyed by William Gravely in "Christian Responses to the Holocaust: Changing Perspectives," *Theology Forum Brief*, October 1980; and by Isabel Louise Wollaston, "Christian Responses to the Holocaust," *Farmington Papers*, ed. Martin Rogers (Oxford: Farmington Institute for Christian Studies, November 1999). A very important document is "Jewish-Christian Relation in Western Europe," *Face to Face: An Interreligious Bulletin* 7 (Summer 1980).
22. The situation seems to be much more complex than this. See Owen Chadwick, *Britain and the Vatican during the Second World War* (Cambridge: Cambridge University Press, 1987).

Chapter 9: The Sacrifice in Creation

1. *National Geographic Atlas of the World*, 5th ed. (Washington, DC: National Geographic, 1981), 6.
2. W. H. Auden, in *Protestant Mystics*, ed. Anne Freemantle (New York: American Library, 1965), 69–70.

3. A similar experience is described in many other places, as in Samuel Taylor Coleridge's poem *The Rime of the Ancient Mariner*, in the writings and experiences of the philosopher Simone Weil, in the writings of the soldier and writer Laurens van der Post, and by the writer G. K. Chesterton—all of whom I treat in my book *The Path of Perfect Love* (Cambridge, MA: Cowley Publications, 1992).
4. The inner life of God is called the immanent Trinity in contrast to God in God's relation to what God creates, which is called the economic Trinity. Our understanding of God's inner life is actually based on God's relation to God's creation, and in particular to the ancient people of Israel and the early church.
5. As found in J. N. D. Kelly, *Early Christian Doctrines*, rev. ed. (San Francisco: Harper, 1978), 264. For more on the eternal giving and receiving that is the life of the Trinity, see Diogenes Allen, *The Path of Perfect Love*, 47–53; and Diogenes Allen and Eric Springsted, *Philosophy for Understanding Theology*, 2nd ed. (Louisville, KY: Westminster John Knox Press, 2007), 65–72.

Chapter 10: Incarnation as a Sacrifice

1. The comments in brackets are from the notes provided by *The New Oxford Annotated Bible, with the Apocryphal/Deuterocanonical Books*, ed. Bruce M. Metzger and Roland E. Murphy (New York: Oxford University Press, 1991), NT-281nn, on Phil. 2:6–11; and NT-292n, on 1 Thess. 1:1.
2. N. T. Wright, in Antony Flew's book *There Is a God: How the World's Most Notorious Atheist Changed His Mind* (New York: Harper One, 2008), 189.
3. Søren Kierkegaard, *Philosophical Fragments* (Princeton, NJ: Princeton University Press, 1936), chap. 2; cf. http://www.religion-online.org/showchapter.asp?title=2512&C=2380.
4. David F. Strauss, *The Life of Jesus Critically Examined* (1835 German original; reprint of 1846 ET, 3 vols., London: Continuum, 2005), introduction.
5. See, for example, Howard Clark Kee's article on miracles in *The Oxford Companion to the Bible*, ed. Bruce M. Metzger and Michael D. Coogan (New York: Oxford University Press, 1993), 519–20.

Chapter 11: The Temptations in the Wilderness

1. Blaise Pascal, *Pensées*, trans. A. J. Krailsheimer (Harmondsworth, UK: Penguin Books, 1966), 124, fragment 308.
2. Ibid.

Chapter 12: The Sacrifice of the Cross

1. John Habgood, in the (London) *Times Literary Supplement*, March 21, 2008, 8.
2. Although not in the world in the sense of not being subject to its forces, the Father is present to all creatures as their continuous creative source. As the continuous creative source, God is omnipresent.
3. My analysis of affliction and its significance is based on Simone Weil's essay "The Love of God and Affliction," in *The Simone Weil Reader*, ed. George A. Panichas (New York: David McKay, 1977), 439–68.
4. Alternative translations are possible. I have used "by the faith of Jesus Christ" since I understand that our salvation is the result of Jesus' trust in his Father's

love and way, even when he is afflicted on the cross. The expression of that faith is his victory on the cross, a victory over sin, evil, and death. The alternative translation of the Greek "through faith in Jesus Christ" does not bring out the feature that we are saved by faith in Jesus who, while on the cross, had faith in his Father and so was victorious. The alternatives in the Greek texts are recognized in the Revised Standard Version, and the translation I have given of the passages is also supported by the well-known New Testament scholar Luke Timothy Johnson. (Luke Timothy Johnson, *The Apostle Paul*, audio CD, The Teaching Co., 2001.)

5. George Herbert, *The Country Parson; The Temple*, ed. John N. Wall Jr. (New York: Paulist Press, 1981), 151.
6. Ibid., 140.
7. Ibid., 142.
8. Ibid., 146.

Chapter 13: The Resurrection of Jesus and Eternal Life

1. The edited conference papers were later published as *The Fountain of Youth: Historical, Scientific, and Ethical Perspectives on a Biomedical Goal*, ed. Stephen Post and Robert Binstock (Oxford: Oxford University Press, 2004).
2. N. T. Wright himself, in his account of the historical grounds for the resurrection of Jesus, often makes points that are very powerful in revealing the meaning and significance of the resurrection for those who follow Jesus.
3. Mark has an abrupt ending, with no appearance of Jesus himself. But when the women enter the empty tomb, an angel ("a young man dressed in a white robe"; Mark 16:5a) tells them that Jesus "has been raised" and that they are to tell the disciples that he has gone on ahead of them to Galilee, where they will see him (16:6–7). So the agreements in the appearance stories we cite are from the Gospels that give an account of Jesus' appearances.
4. Raymond T. Stamm, in *The Interpreter's Bible*, ed. George A. Buttrick, vol. 10 (Nashville: Abington Press, 1953), 509, on Gal. 3:13.
5. Bruce M. Metzger and Roland E. Murphy, eds., *The New Oxford Annotated Bible, with the Apocryphal/Deuteronomical Books* (New York: Oxford University Press, 1991), NT-157n, on John 20:23.
6. Ludwig Wittgenstein, *Culture and Value*, ed. G. H. von Wright, trans. Peter Winch, rev. 2nd ed. (Oxford: Blackwell, 1980), 6e.
7. Maurice O'Connor Drury, *The Danger of Words* (London: Routledge & Kegan Paul, 1973), xiii.

Chapter 14: Jesus as Lord and Jesus as Servant

1. Georg Wilhelm Friedrich Hegel, *Phenomenology of Spirit* (German original, 1807), trans. A. V. Miller (Oxford: Oxford University Press, 1979).
2. See Raymond E. Brown, *An Introduction to New Testament Christology* (New York: Paulist Press, 1994), 79. Brown has many examples of this type of consideration.
3. Raymond E. Brown, *Introduction to the New Testament* (New York: Doubleday, 1997), 820 n. 6.

Chapter 15: Revelation and Faith

1. The numbers I use to cite each fragment are taken from A. J. Krailsheimer's translation from the French: Blaise Pascal, *Pensées* (New York: Penguin Books,

1966). Krailsheimer follows Pascal's classification and the order in which his papers were left. All in-text references to the *Pensées* are cited as F (for Fragment) plus Krailsheimer's number.

2. Cited by Maurice O'Connor Drury, *The Danger of Words* (London: Routledge & Kegan Paul, 1973), 22.

3. Leszek Kolakowski, *Modernity on Endless Trial* (Chicago: University of Chicago Press, 1990).

4. Ibid., 9.

5. Michael B. Foster, "The Christian Doctrine of Creation and the Rise of Modern Science," *Mind* 43 (1934): 446–68; idem, "Christian Theology and the Modern Science of Nature I," *Mind* 44 (1935): 439–56; idem, "Christian Theology and the Modern Science of Nature II," *Mind* 45 (1936): 1–27.

6. For a fuller treatment of the relation of science and Christianity in the seventeenth century, and especially for the trial of Galileo, much misrepresented by atheists, see my *Christian Belief in a Postmodern World* (Louisville, KY: Westminster/John Knox Press, 1989), chaps. 1–2. Here I want to put to rest one widely and frequently repeated reason why Christianity was said to resist the rise of science: the claim that the new Copernican hypothesis, putting the sun at the center of the universe, reduced people's importance by removing them from the physical center of the universe. As Sir James Jeans, a major physicist, put it in his *Physics and Philosophy* (Cambridge: Cambridge University Press, 1942), "his home was not the majestic fixed center of the universe round which all else had to revolve" (1). This has become part of the atheist litany. But they ignore the fact that in Aristotle's cosmology, which was generally held, the center of the physical universe is the place of decay and death, in contrast to the heavens. See E. M. W. Tillyard, *The Elizabethan World Picture* (New York: Macmillan Co., 1944).

7. For example, see James L. Gould's review of Ernst Mayr's *The Growth of Biological Thought* (Cambridge, MA: Belknap Press/Harvard University Press, 1982), in *New York Times Book Review*, May 23, 1982, 7.

Chapter 16: The Holy Spirit, the Church, and the Sacraments

1. William B. Nelson Jr., "Eschatology," in *The Oxford Companion to the Bible*, ed. Bruce M. Metzger and Michael D. Coogan (New York: Oxford University Press, 1993), 192–94.

2. J. N. D. Kelly, *Early Christian Doctrines*, 5th rev. ed. (London: A. C. Black, 1977), 440–49.

3. See Howard G. Hageman, "Reformed Spirituality," in *Protestant Spiritual Traditions*, ed. Frank C. Senn (New York: Paulist Press, 1986), 55–79. Hageman argues that the prime mover of what was to become the Reformed tradition was Ulrich Zwingli, and he plus other developments in the eighteenth century took it in quite a different direction from Calvin's understanding.

4. For example, see Stephen W. Sykes in *Christian Theology: An Introduction to Its Traditions and Tasks*, ed. Peter C. Hodgson and Robert H. King, updated ed. (Minneapolis: Fortress Press, 1994), 292–94, briefly presenting the views of John Henry Newman, Edward Schillebeeckx, and Karl Rahner.

5. Stephen Sykes, John Booty, and Jonathan Knight, eds., *The Study of Anglicanism*, rev. ed. (Minneapolis: Fortress Press, 1998), 312.

6. Ibid., 311.

7. Ibid., 318.

8. Robert N. Bellah, in *Postmodern Theology: Christian Faith in a Pluralist World*, ed. Frederic B. Burnham (San Francisco: Harper & Row, 1989), 82.

9. Ibid., 84.
10. John P. Marquand, *Women and Thomas Harrow* (Boston: Little, Brown, 1958).
11. Jane Austen, *Emma* (Edinburgh: Thomas Nelson & Sons, n.d.), 17–18.
12. Basil the Great, *On the Holy Spirit* in *Nicene and Post-Nicene Fathers*, 2nd series (Grand Rapids: Eerdmans, 1983), 15.
13. Simone Weil, *First and Last Notebooks*, trans. Richard Rees (London: Oxford University Press, 1970), 352.

Chapter 17: Sin, Evil, and Hope for the Future

1. Rose Macaulay, *Letters to a Friend, 1950–52*, ed. Constance Babington Smith (London: Collins, 1961), 61–62.
2. For a full treatment of the origins of the idea of reform in Jesus' teachings and throughout Western history, see Gerhart Ladner, *The Idea of Reform* (New York: Harper & Row, 1967).
3. Daniel Goleman, "The Strange Agony of Success," *New York Times*, August 24, 1986, http://www.nytimes.com/1986/08/24/business/the-strange-agony-of-success.html.
4. Rick Marin, "Is This the Face of a Mid-life Crisis?" *New York Times*, June 24, 2001, http://www.selfknowledge.org/resources/press/nyt_quarterlife.htm.
5. In the Old Testament, sin and evil certainly are not understood in relation to Jesus, and so there is a different—even if overlapping—understanding of sin and evil in Judaism. In Judaism, sin is understood above all in relation to the failure of the people of Israel to live properly as the holy people of God, as a community formed and based on God's law. The Jewish people are to live before God, and their failure as individuals and as a people to do so is sin. It is a failure to be oriented on God, an orientation largely specified by obedience to the law.
6. Norman Powell Williams, *The Ideas of the Fall and Original Sin* (London: Longmans, Green & Co., 1927), 3–36.
7. For a full, careful, and subtle treatment of the issues raised in this paragraph, see James William McClendon Jr., *Systematic Theology*, vol. 2, *Doctrine* (Nashville: Abingdon Press, 1994), 122–29. He is good in showing that Augustine's interpretation of Paul in Rom. 5:12—as saying that in Adam's action of disobedience all human beings have sinned—is incorrect for two reasons. First, scholars generally agree that Augustine's Latin Vulgate Bible says that in Adam all have sinned, but that the Greek text of Rom. 5:12 does not. Second, the passage on Adam should be read as a type or model. "The relation of believers to Adam is not said here to be one of sin inherited; it is rather the relation of a model (*typos*) of failure to those whose lives are governed not by it but by the 'one man, Jesus Christ,' who by his grace has become *our* type (v. 19)" (125–26).
8. See "Fall," in the *Oxford Companion to Christian Thought*, ed. Adrian Hastings, Alistair Mason, and Hugh Pyper (Oxford: Oxford University Press, 2000), 234.
9   A treatment of the main teachings of the Eastern and Western churches on the goal, path to the goal, motivation for the Christian life, hindrances, aids, and criteria of progress in the Christian journey can be found in my book *Spiritual Theology: The Theology of Yesterday for Spiritual Help Today* (Cambridge, MA: Cowley Publications, 1997). Also see my article "The Role of Technology and Commerce in Spiritual Growth," *Bulletin of Science, Technology and Society* 18 (December 1998): 441–45.

10. See Williams, *Ideas of the Fall*, and J. N. D. Kelly, *Early Christian Doctrines* (London: A. C. Black, 1977), chaps. 7 and 14.
11. See note 1 for this chapter.
12. Bruce M. Metzger and Roland E. Murphy, eds., *The New Oxford Annotated Bible, with the Apocryphal/Deuteronomical Books* (New York: Oxford University Press, 1991), OT-4n, on Gen. 2:18–21.
13. George Santayana, *The Life of Reason; or, The Phases of Human Progress*, vol. 1, *Introduction; and, Reason in Common Sense* (New York: Charles Scribner's Sons, 1905), 13.
14. Simone Weil, *Waiting for God* (London: Collins, 1950), 162.

Index

CPSIA information can be obtained at www.ICGtesting.com
Printed in the USA
LVOW12s0427070813

346598LV00002B/80/P